P9-CFY-960

COUNSEL AND CONSENT

Counsel and Consent

Aspects of the Government of the Church as exemplified in the history of the English Provincial Synods

by

ERIC WALDRAM KEMP, D.D.

Fellow of Exeter College, Oxford;
Canon and Prebendary of Caistor in Lincoln Cathedral;
Hon. Provincial Canon of the Church of the Province of South Africa;
Proctor in Convocation for the Clergy of the University of Oxford.

The Bampton Lectures for 1960

LONDON

S·P·C·K

1961

First published in 1961 by
S.P.C.K.
Holy Trinity Church
Marylebone Road
London N.W.1
Made and printed in Great Britain by
Billing and Sons Ltd., Guildford and London

TO MY WIFE

EXTRACT FROM
THE LAST WILL AND TESTAMENT

of the late

REVEREND JOHN BAMPTON

Canon of Salisbury

". . . I give and bequeath my Lands and Estates to the Chancellor, Masters and Scholars of the University of Oxford for ever, to have and to hold all and singular the said Lands or Estates upon trust, and to the intents and purposes hereinafter mentioned; that is to say, I will and appoint that the Vice-Chancellor of the University of Oxford for the time being shall take and receive all the rents, issues, and profits thereof, and (after all taxes, reparations, and necessary deductions made) that he pay all the remainder to the endowment of eight Divinity Lecture Sermons, to be established for ever in the said University, and to be performed in the manner following:

"I direct and appoint, that, upon the first Tuesday in Easter Term, a Lecturer may be yearly chosen by the Heads of Colleges only, and by no others, in the room adjoining to the Printing-House, between the hours of ten in the morning and two in the afternoon, to preach eight Divinity Lecture Sermons, the year following, at St. Mary's in Oxford, between the commencement of the last month in Lent Term, and the end of the third week in Act Term.

"Also I direct and appoint, that the eight Divinity Lecture Sermons shall be preached upon either of the following Subjects—to confirm and establish the Christian Faith, and to confute all heretics and schismatics—upon the divine authority of the holy Scriptures—upon the authority of the writings of the primitive Fathers, as to the faith and practice of the primitive Church—upon the Divinity of our Lord and Saviour Jesus Christ—upon the Divinity of the Holy Ghost—upon the Articles of the Christian Faith, as comprehended in the Apostles' and Nicene Creed.

"Also I direct, that thirty copies of the eight Divinity Lecture Sermons shall be always printed, within two months after they are preached; and one copy shall be given to the Chancellor of the University, and one copy to the Head of every College, and one copy to the Mayor of the City of Oxford, and one copy to be put into the Bodleian Library; and the expense of printing them shall be paid out of the revenue of the Land or Estates given for establishing the Divinity Lecture Sermons; and the Preacher shall not be paid, nor be entitled to the revenue, before they are printed.

"Also I direct and appoint, that no person shall be qualified to preach the Divinity Lecture Sermons, unless he hath taken the degree of Master of Arts at least, in one of the two Universities of Oxford or Cambridge; and that the same person shall never preach the Divinity Lecture Sermons twice."

CONTENTS

PREFACE

ON AN OCCASION in the year 1833 an elderly country clergyman in Northamptonshire by name the Reverend T. Sikes was in conversation with a group of younger friends. He said to them:

> I seem to think I can tell you something which you who are young may probably live to see, but which I, who shall soon be called away off the stage, shall not. Wherever I go all about the country I see amongst the clergy a number of very amiable and estimable men, many of them much in earnest, and wishing to do good. But I have observed one universal want in their teaching: the uniform suppression of one great truth. There is no account given anywhere, so far as I see, of the one Holy Catholic Church. . . . Now this great truth is an article of the Creed; and if so, to teach the rest of the Creed to its exclusion must be to destroy "the analogy or proportion of the faith" . . . This cannot be done without the most serious consequences. The doctrine is of the last importance, and the principles it involves of immense power; and some day, not far distant, it will judicially have its reprisals. And whereas the other articles of the Creed seem now to have thrown it into the shade, it will seem, when it is brought forward, to swallow up the rest . . . And woe betide those, whoever they are, who shall, in the course of Providence, have to bring it forward . . . They will be endlessly misunderstood and misinterpreted. There will be one great outcry of Popery from one end of the country to the other. It will be thrust upon minds unprepared . . . Some will take it up and admire it as a beautiful picture, others will be frightened and run away and reject it; and all will want a guidance which one hardly knows where they shall find.[1]

On 14 July that same year the Reverend John Keble preached from the pulpit of the church in which the Bampton Lectures are delivered his sermon on "National Apostasy",

[1] Quoted in H. P. Liddon, *Life of Edward Bouverie Pusey* (London, 1893), i. 257f.

and on 9 September were published the first three of the *Tracts for the Times*, of which the second was entitled "The Catholic Church". Seldom can any prophecy have been so quickly and exactly fulfilled.

The leaders of the Oxford Movement were the immediate instruments by which the doctrine of the Church was brought again to the forefront of theological discussion and were also the victims of the attacks which old Mr Sikes had foretold. But the doctrine, once revived, was taken up by theologians of very diverse traditions, in this country and abroad, and has been one of the dominant themes of theological study in the past hundred years. The present happier and closer relations between Christians of differing ecclesiastical allegiance are in large part a result of the controversies which its revival caused, and to these controversies several previous holders of the Bampton lectureship have contributed. In 1840, for example, the Reverend James Garbett addressed the University on the subject of *Christ, as Prophet, Priest, and King: being a vindication of the Church of England from Theological Novelties*. Mr Garbett dealt at length with various aspects of the doctrine of the Church, in criticism of the views of the Tractarians. In 1871 the Reverend George Herbert Curteis, Fellow and Sub-Rector of Exeter College, delivered the lectures on *Dissent in its relation to the Church of England*, and his book contains much that is still of interest. In 1901 Dr Archibald Robertson, in a masterly work of undiminished value,[1] surveyed the idea of the Kingdom of God in the history of Christian thought. In 1920 Dr A. C. Headlam, lecturing with his accustomed vigour on *The Doctrine of the Church and Christian Reunion*, provided the Lambeth Conference of that year with its marching orders. More recently there have been Dr Jalland's lectures on *The Church and the Papacy* in 1942.

The course which came closest to the theme of the present lectures was that given in 1880 on *The Organization of the Early*

[1] A. Robertson, *Regnum Dei* (London, 1901).

Christian Churches, by the Reverend Edwin Hatch. In the very first of the Tracts Mr Newman, by his appeal to the doctrine of Apostolic Succession, had put the nature of the Christian ministry in the forefront of discussion about the Church, and much of the subsequent argument has necessarily concerned itself with the origins of the episcopate and its place in God's design, as well as with the concept of priesthood. It has never been possible to make the neat distinction which some would like, between matters of Faith and matters of Order. Dr Hatch was one of those who attempted to draw this distinction in a way which would diminish the importance of some controversies respecting ecclesiastical organization. He pointed out with clarity and learning that there was not a fixed but a developing organization in early times, and so loosened the rigidity which has so often introduced anachronism into the study of ecclesiastical institutions. Where perhaps he was deficient was in failing to draw attention to those elements and ideas which persisted throughout the changes of outward form.

The aim of the present course of lectures is to study the mutations of certain principles of Church government as they are seen in the history of the provincial synod, more usually known to the modern Church of England as Convocation, and there are special reasons for this choice. When we survey the history and constitution of that overwhelmingly major part of Christendom which has retained the episcopal ministry of early times we become aware of its organization into a hierarchy of three principal members, the diocese, the province, and some larger grouping. The third of these raises the whole question of the Papacy, about which Dr Jalland spoke from this pulpit, a question which the Ecumenical Movement will some day have to face more seriously than it has done hitherto; and it raises also the problems of patriarchates, and of national Churches. The first has also been the subject of much discussion, entering, to some degree at least, into most examinations of the early history of the ministry, and the diocese is perhaps the unit of which the clergy of the Church of England, if not the laity, are most acutely aware.

It is, however, the second of the three members which forms the special subject of these lectures and it may seem strange that it has been so little studied in Anglican writing. An effect of the Reformation in these islands was to isolate six provinces[1] with no other organizational link between them than was provided by the Royal Supremacy and a common form of worship. As Anglicanism has spread overseas it has developed on the assumption that the proper form of growth is first the establishment of dioceses, and then the grouping of dioceses into provinces. The Anglican Communion is itself a federation of provinces together with a few dioceses which, for practical reasons, have not yet become part of any province but are under the jurisdiction of the Archbishop of Canterbury.

This assumption is made abundantly plain by a passage in Dr C. A. H. Green's book, *The Setting of the Constitution of the Church in Wales*. Archbishop Green writes:

> In A.D. 1920, when the State declared by the Welsh Church Act, 1914, that the Diocese of Wales should no longer be represented in the Convocation of Canterbury, a situation of extreme delicacy was created. The Church in England and in Wales repudiated the right of the State to do this without the consent of the Church. The difficulty was resolved by the act of the Archbishop of Canterbury, proclaiming in full Synod of the Province of Canterbury that he had released the Welsh Bishops from their allegiance to the See of Canterbury, and that he counselled them to form a separate Province for Wales. At the instigation, and with the goodwill of the Archbishop of Canterbury, the Province of Wales was formed, and the first Metropolitan elected in 1920.[2]

An examination of the origins of provincial synods and of

[1] Canterbury, York, Armagh, Dublin, Cashel, and Tuam.

[2] C. A. H. Green, *The Setting of the Constitution of the Church in Wales* (London, 1937), p. 210. This book earned for its author the degree of D.C.L. at Oxford.

their history among us may not, therefore, seem wholly irrelevant to the present problems of the Church of England, and may perhaps help towards an understanding of the nature of the Christian Church.

I have spoken of two other units besides the province, and it will not be possible to tell the story wholly without reference to them. The relation of the province to the whole Church is a big and important subject of which I can do no more than touch the fringe, but it will be necessary to spend rather more time in considering the province and the diocese. Necessary because the English provincial synods are historically unusual in their large representation of the diocesan clergy, and because the Church of England is at present considering proposals that representatives of the laity be added also. It is not possible to consider these matters adequately as regards the provincial synod without referring also, however briefly, to the relationship of bishop, clergy, and laity in the diocese.

In the first two lectures I am concerned to provide a study of the origin of the provincial system and the way in which it worked in the Primitive Church, and then such an account of the Medieval Church as is necessary for an understanding of the early development of the convocations. The third and fourth lectures deal with this development and show how and why the provincial synod was changed into the much larger body that we find on the eve of the Reformation. The fifth lecture analyses and discusses certain aspects of the convocations in the fifteenth century which are important for an understanding of the relations of Church and State in the years immediately preceding the Reformation, and this is continued in the first part of the sixth lecture which, however, deals in the main with the great religious upheaval of the sixteenth century in so far as it affects the theme of this study. The seventh lecture begins with an account of the factors which brought about the decline and eventual suppression of the convocations, and then goes on to outline the story of their revival in the nineteenth century. The problems of the relations with parliament and of the admission of the laity to church synods, which arose directly out of the revival, are reserved for special treatment in the last lecture, and there, too, my conclusions are drawn, and certain suggestions are made.

My original intention was to combine the publication of these lectures with the history of the convocations upon which, at the request of the Archbishop of Canterbury (Dr. Fisher) and the S.P.C.K., I have been working since 1948, but Sir Maurice Powicke, who has very kindly read the first four chapters of the present book and also two chapters of the larger work, has convinced me that such a combination would obscure the theme of these lectures. With the agreement of the Director of the S.P.C.K., therefore, I hope in due course to follow the publication of this book by producing a more strictly historical work dealing in greater detail with the constitutional development and internal history of the convocations. For that reason I have thought it right to indicate at several points in the present work that fuller evidence will be published later in support of statements made rather summarily here.

Here I must express my deep gratitude to Sir Maurice for his advice on this, as on many previous occasions. My special thanks are also due to Professors C. R. Cheney and V. H. Galbraith, the Dean of York who by his hospitality increased the pleasure of my visits to the York Archives, Drs Emden, Chaplais, Kay, and Storey, the Reverend A. H. Couratin, Principal of St Stephen's House, Oxford, Mr F. S. Ferguson, my colleague Mr G. D. G. Hall, and many others who have answered my questions and given me the benefit of their advice on particular points that have arisen in the course of the preparation of this book.

My thanks are also due to those who have made available to me the archives under their control, to the Registrars of York, London, Winchester, Carlisle, Exeter, Hereford,

Lichfield, and Salisbury, the Archivists at Canterbury Cathedral, St Anthony's Hall York, Durham, Ely, Lincoln, Norwich, and Worcester, and to the staffs of Lambeth Palace Library, the British Museum manuscript department, the Public Record Office, the Institute of Historical Research, and the Bodleian Library.

I have to thank the following for permission to quote from copyright works: The Syndics of the Cambridge University Press (Norman Sykes, *From Sheldon to Secker* and *William Wake*); the Central Board of Finance of the Church of England (*Church and State*, 1936, and *Church and State*, 1952); Constable and Co., Ltd (T. S. R. Boase, *Boniface VIII*); Longmans, Green and Co., Ltd (T. F. T. Plucknett's chapter in *Tudor Studies*, ed. H. Seton-Watson); The Oxford University Press (F. Iremonger, *William Temple*); Sweet and Maxwell, Ltd (C. A. H. Green, *The Setting of the Constitution of the Church in Wales*). The text of the Church of Scotland Act 1921 is Crown Copyright, and the extract from it included here is reproduced by permission.

Needless to say, no one but myself has any responsibility for the views expressed here. My conclusions are based in part upon my twelve years' historical study of the subject, and in part upon a similar length of time as a member of the Canterbury Convocation and of the Church Assembly which in turn have involved me in membership of a number of committees and commissions concerned with the revision of the canon law and the problems of synodical government that have arisen therefrom. I am acutely conscious of my lack of practical experience in some other relevant fields, and my suggestions are submitted tentatively for the consideration and criticism of those who are of wider knowledge in these matters.

E.W.K.

Oxford
Christmas Eve, 1960

MAPS

Thanks are due to Professor E. W. Gilbert and the Royal Geographical Society for permission to reproduce the map illustrating Professor Gilbert's suggestions for divisions for England and Wales, which originally appeared in the *Geographical Journal*, Vol. 99 (1942), and was reprinted in Vol. 111 (1948); also to Mrs Margaret Cole for the map illustrating the proposals put forward by the late Professor G. D. H. Cole in 1921 and representing his views at that time.

PRINCIPAL ABBREVIATIONS

BIHR	*Bulletin of the Institute of Historical Research.*
CCR	Calendar of Close Rolls.
CFR	Calendar of Fine Rolls.
CPR	Calendar of Patent Rolls.
CS	Camden Society.
CY	Canterbury and York Society.
EHR	*English Historical Review.*
HMC	Historical Manuscripts Commission.
JEH	*Journal of Ecclesiastical History.*
JTS	*Journal of Theological Studies.*
MGH	*Monumenta Germaniae Historica.*
PL	Migne, *Patrologia Latina.*
PRO	Public Record Office.
RDP	*Reports from the Lords Committees touching the dignity of a peer of the realm etc. etc. with Appendices* (London, 1829), Vol. iii.
RHE	*Revue d'Histoire ecclésiastique.*
RS	*Chronicles and Memorials of Great Britain and Ireland during the Middle Ages, published under the direction of the Master of Rolls* (Rolls Series).
SS	Surtees Society.
ZSSR. Kan. Abt.	*Zeitschrift der Savigny Stiftung für Rechtsgeschichte, Kanonistische Abteilung.*

LECTURE 1

31 January 1960

COUNCILS AND PROVINCES IN THE EARLY CHURCH

Where no wise guidance is, the people falleth: But in the multitude of counsellors there is safety.

Proverbs 11. 14.

THE CHIEF ministers of the Church have from early times had a double relationship. On the one hand they are chosen by, and for the most part exercise their ministry in, a particular local church. On the other, they share in a ministry which is that of the whole Church, and periodically they exercise what is, potentially at least, an universal jurisdiction in council, judgement, and consecration.

It seems that in the earliest days there were types of ministers in whom one or the other aspect of this double relationship was uppermost. The apostles, of course, had a special relationship to the Jerusalem Church, but very quickly their horizon widened and we find them moving out into the pagan world and founding churches over which they continued to exercise supervision. Others were gradually associated with them in this itinerant, evangelistic, and supervisory ministry. Barnabas, Silas, Timothy, and Titus all became, as it were, supplementary apostles, but after this second generation the superintendent who was bishop of no diocese, to use a convenient anachronism, seems to have died out. We shall see later how the principle was preserved in other ways.

The type of minister in whom the local relationship was uppermost is represented by the bishops, presbyters, and deacons of the earliest documents. Here we tread on difficult ground, and it is not possible to proceed without making some assumptions. In the opinion of the present writer it is highly probable that the development of the ministry was somewhat different in different churches. In some the three orders of bishops, presbyters, and deacons existed from the time of the apostles much as they are found in the fourth century. In others it is more probable that for a period there were only two orders, the diaconate and a governing order which itself came to be differentiated into two degrees and so assimilated to the threefold ministry prevailing elsewhere. Whether these differences were geographical, as between East and West for example, or whether they were differences between small churches and the churches of great cities such as Rome and Alexandria cannot be stated with any certainty.[1]

The selection of these ministers, or at least of the bishops and presbyters, seems to have been the responsibility of the whole local church. Undoubtedly there were variations of practice in different places at various times, but the practice which prevailed to such an extent that it may be called that of the Early Church was as stated at the end of the first century by Clement of Rome, "Those who were appointed . . . with the consent of the whole Church",[2] and in the fourth by Leo the Great in language worthy of Justinian: "Qui praefuturus est omnibus ab omnibus eligatur."[3] Two passages from the letters of St Cyprian may be set beside these. One is the famous description of the election of Pope Cornelius:

> Cornelius became bishop by the judgement of God and his Christ, by the testimony of almost all the clergy, by the suffrage of the people who were present, by the college of old and good bishops, when no-one was ordained before him; when the see of Fabian, that is the see of Peter and the episcopal chair was vacant.[4]

The other is a sentence from a letter written from his hiding-place during persecution to the presbyters, deacons, and the whole people of Carthage: "In clerical ordinations, dearest brethren, my custom is to consult you beforehand, and by common advice to weigh the character and merits of each."[5]

[1] Cf. J. Wordsworth, *The Ministry of Grace* (London, 1901), ch. 1; E. W. Kemp, "Bishops and Presbyters and Alexandria", *J.E.H.*, vi. (1955), 125–42.

[2] 1 Clement 44.3. [3] Leo I, *Ep.* 89.6. [4] Cyprian, *Ep.* 55.8.

[5] Id., *Ep.* 38.1; cf. *Ep.* 67. On the whole subject of the appointment of bishops see the evidence conveniently collected in the *Report of the Joint Committee on Crown Nominations to Ecclesiastical Offices* (1920).

Here we see the close unity of clergy and people in the local churches of the early centuries. As a rule no man entered the ranks of the clergy unless he was already well known in character and manner of life to the community in which he was to serve. The first Christians believed strongly in what a later age has called "in-breeding". They also regarded their judgement as declaring the voice of God.

No Christian community, however, lives to itself. The early churches shared a common faith which was menaced by common errors. They shared a common pattern of life in which, like members of a family, they communicated their news and their problems to one another, and wrote letters of encouragement and exhortation. Much of the earliest surviving Christian literature is of this kind, many of the New Testament Epistles, the so-called First Epistle of Clement, the letters of Ignatius of Antioch, the Martyrdom of Polycarp of Smyrna, the letter of the Churches of Lyons and Vienne. But speech is an easier method of discussion than letter writing, and when a half-crazed enthusiast attracted a following by his claim to inaugurate the new era of the Paraclete "the faithful throughout Asia met frequently and at many places in Asia" for discussion "and on examination of the new-fangled teachings pronounced them profane, and rejected the heresy, and these persons were thus expelled from the Church and shut off from its communion."[1] Thus an anonymous writer, quoted by Eusebius, describes what many would regard as the earliest reference outside the New Testament to Christian councils. The date is somewhere in the third quarter of the second century. About thirty or forty years later Tertullian writes of councils as a regular thing among the Greek-speaking Christians:

> Besides, throughout the provinces of Greece there are held in definite localities those councils gathered out of all the churches,

---

Canterbury Convocation Report No. 516, and the *Interim Report of the Appointment of Bishops Committee* (1929), Church Assembly Report No. 282,

[1] Eusebius, *Hist. Eccl.*, V. 16.10.

> by whose means not only the deeper questions are handled in common, but the actual representation of the whole Christian name is celebrated with great veneration.[1]

Half a century later still Firmilian, Bishop of Caesarea in Cappadocia, writes to Cyprian of Carthage:

> For which cause it is of necessity arranged among us, that we, elders and prelates, meet every year to set in order the things entrusted to our charge.[2]

Going back a little in time, the notice, given in Eusebius, of the Paschal controversy in the eighties of the second century, speaks of councils in several parts of the Christian world.[3] Polycrates, Bishop of Ephesus, wrote on behalf of the churches of the Province of Asia. Theophilus, Bishop of Caesarea, and Narcissus, Bishop of Jerusalem, jointly presided over an assembly of the churches of Palestine. Palmas of Amastris presided over the bishops in Pontus. Letters were also written on behalf of the communities in Gaul, over which Irenaeus was bishop, and of the bishops in Osrhoene and the cities in that part, and there was a personal letter from Bacchyllus, Bishop of the Church of the Corinthians.

This list is important as suggesting that at that early date the organization of the Christian churches was conceived in terms of the civil divisions of the Roman Empire. The suggestion is strengthened by the list of the correspondence of Dionysius, Bishop of Corinth, who died some time before the Paschal controversy.[4] Corinth has acquired a civil predominance as the seat of the pro-consul,[5] and its Bishop

[1] Tertullian *De ieiunio adv. psychicos*, 13: "Aguntur praeterea per Graecias illa certis in locis concilia ex universis ecclesiis, per quae et altiora quaeque in commune tractantur, et ipsa repraesentatio totius nominis Christiani magna veneratione celebratur."

[2] Cyprian, *Ep.* 75.4: "Qua ex causa necessario apud nos fit ut per singulos annos seniores et praepositi in unum conveniamus ad disponenda ea quae curae nostrae commissa sunt.

[3] Eusebius, op. cit., V. 23–5.

[4] Id., IV. 23.

[5] Acts 18. 12; cf. T. Mommsen, *The Provinces of the Roman Empire* (London, 1886), i. 260f.

seems to have assumed also some position of leadership. Eight of his letters are listed by Eusebius. One is addressed to an individual Christian, three are to the churches of Sparta, Athens, and Nicomedia, one is to Gortyna and the other Cretan dioceses (παροικίαι) one to the church in Amastris and the other churches in Pontus, one to Pinytos, Bishop of Cnossus and one to Soter, Bishop of Rome. Here it is to be observed that the two letters which are intended for all the churches of a province, namely Crete and Pontus, are in each case addressed to the church of the civil metropolis, Gortyna and Amastris. In the middle of the following century we find Dionysius of Alexandria similarly coupling the name of one principal bishop with the churches of a whole province in the cases of Cilicia and Cappadocia.[1]

The fragmentary nature of the early Christian literature and uncertainty about some of the civil divisions make it impossible to present a tidy picture in the ante-Nicene period,[2] but the indications are clear enough to show that the full provincial and metropolitical system which is assumed in the Nicene canons was well developed in the eastern half of the empire by the end of the second century. In some provinces at least, councils were meeting regularly by that time. It is to the Nicene decrees that we must now turn.

Canons four to seven of the Council of Nicea (A.D. 325) presuppose a system of ecclesiastical provinces each presided over by a bishop who is known as the metropolitan. The Council is concerned to safeguard the regular appointment and consecration of bishops and to provide that appeals against sentences passed by bishops may be settled in an assembly of the province. The consecration of bishops is not to take place without the consent of the metropolitan and

[1] Eusebius, op. cit., VII. 5.

[2] For a fuller discussion of this subject see K. Lübeck, *Reichseinteilung und kirchliche Hierarchie des Orients bis zum Ausgange des vierten jahrhunderts* (Munster, 1901); J. Gaudemet, *L'Église dans l'Empire romain* (Paris, 1958), 377–407, is mainly concerned with the fourth and fifth centuries but has some bearing on the earlier period.

preferably should be performed by all the bishops of the province, though three will suffice if the absent give their assent by letter. Synods of the province, when all the bishops come together, are to be held twice a year, one before Lent and the other in the autumn, and appeals are to be heard in them.

A few years after Nicea the Council of Antioch[1] speaks more fully about the position of the metropolitan. He has to take thought for the whole province because all who have business to do come to the metropolis. He is therefore to have precedence in rank and the other bishops are to do nothing extraordinary (περιττὸν) without him. They have authority over their own dioceses and should not undertake anything more without the metropolitan, nor he without the consent of the rest.[2] The presence of the metropolitan is the test of a proper synod.[3] The council is especially concerned to see that disputes are settled within the province, and lays great stress upon the provincial synod as the proper body to deal with such matters, even though in some cases it may be necessary to reinforce it by bringing in bishops from a neighbouring province.[4] The metropolitan is to summon the synod twice a year, the first meeting to be held between the third week after Easter and the fourth week after Pentecost, and the second to begin on the Ides of October.[5]

The general tenor of these provisions is repeated by other Greek councils, notably by the two great assemblies of Constantinople[6] (A.D. 381) and Chalcedon[7] (A.D. 451). These two councils, indeed, carry things a stage further and fit the provinces and their synods into a hierarchy which is plainly modelled on the civil reorganization of the Empire begun by Diocletian and developed by his Christian

[1] On the problems connected with this Council and its canons see H. Hess, *The Canons of the Council of Sardica* (Oxford, 1958), 145–50.

[2] Antioch, canon 9; cf. canon 19.

[3] Ibid., canon 16.

[4] Ibid., canons 6, 12, 13, 14, 15, 18, 22, 23.

[5] Ibid., canon 20.

[6] Constantinople, canons 2, 6.

[7] Chalcedon, canons 9, 12, 17, 19.

successors. Above the province there is now the larger unit of the διοίκησις, the civil diocese, one of the fifteen great areas into which the provinces were grouped. Appeals may go from the provincial synod to a council of the bishops of the διοίκησις, and by 451 there has appeared a new official, the exarch, the chief bishop of the diocese. Above him, for we are dealing with the East, stands the see of Constantinople.[1] But this elaboration did not mean greater activity in the province, for the Council of Chalcedon complains that provincial synods are not being held,[2] a complaint echoed by many later councils.

The bishops who made the decrees which we have summarized had in mind the Church in the Eastern Empire where was the great bulk of the Christian population, and where bishoprics abounded. The development of a provincial system in the West was, with the possible exception of Africa, later than in the East. We must look at this in a moment, but let us hasten to observe that the Greek character of the development we have examined does not make it irrelevant to a study of Western institutions. The Greek canons were quickly translated into Latin.[3] The canons of Nicea seem to have appeared first, and in more than one version. To one such translation were added the decrees of Ancyra, Neocaesarea, and Gangra, and later came Antioch, Laodicea, and Constantinople. The Latin version used at the Council of Chalcedon did not apparently contain the canons of Constantinople. The earliest complete version passes under the name of Isidore, and the first half of it can be dated before 451, the second half being between that year and 500. Another version, the Prisca, also falls into two parts, the first being before 451, and the second, which contains Constantinople and Chalcedon, being after. The importance

[1] Ibid., canons 9, 17. [2] Ibid., canon 19.

[3] For what follows see F. Maassen, *Geschichte der Quellen und der Literatur des canonischen Rechts im Abendlande* (Graz, 1870, reissued 1956), 71–130; C. H. Turner, *Chapters in the history of Latin MSS. of Canons* (*J.T.S.*, i (1900), 435; ii (1901), 266; iv. (1903), 426; xxx (1929), 225 and 337).

of this translation from East to West is perhaps most quickly indicated by observing that of the seventeen canons which compose the section which deals with provincial synods in the *Decretum* of Gratian, the great eleventh century text-book of canon law, five are canons of Greek councils, and they include Nicea, Antioch, and Chalcedon.

While Greek was passing into Latin in this way, however, the West was beginning to form its own corpus of canon law. One of the earliest Western lands to be evangelized was the Roman province of Africa, and there, by the middle of the third century we find a flourishing and well-developed church presided over by the Bishop of Carthage whose primatial position seems almost to equal that of Alexandria and Antioch in the East, and who had under his care not only Africa Proconsularis, but also Tripoli, Numidia, and Mauretania. During the episcopate of St Cyprian (A.D. 248–258) Carthage stands out as one of the great sees of Christendom, and the African Church, then and for long afterwards, manifested a self-consciousness and independence which are unique in the West. Under Cyprian important councils were held, to which we shall have to return in another connection, but they have left little trace in the texts of the canon law. More enduring was the influence of the later councils of the fourth and fifth centuries. By this time a provincial organization had developed, Numidia and the two Mauretanias had their own synods and chief bishops, although they were distinguished from what we have seen elsewhere by the fact that the title primate was used, instead of metropolitan, and this for the good reason that the primacy went according to seniority, and was not attached to the church of the civil metropolis. The surviving records of African councils are, almost without exception, the proceedings of assemblies representing the whole African Church. There was a rule that such a council, generally called universal, should be held every year and that two or more bishops should be sent to it from the council of each province.[1] It seems likely that the provincial councils met only once a year and even then provision had to be made for attendance by representation.[2] The great distances and the frequent public disorder made the holding of full and regular councils difficult. It was, however, considered that the primate of each province was the proper person before whom accusations against bishops should be laid, and it seems probable that he would deal with them in the provincial synod if possible, or else in an assembly of such bishops of the province as he could collect. The accused had a right of appeal to the annual universal council.[3] Two of the African canons have passed into Gratian's *Decretum*, where they are clearly applied to provincial councils.[4]

In Italy and Gaul, too, provincial organization becomes apparent in the course of the fourth century, as the Church increased in numbers and extent. In the time of St Ambrose and for a short while after, the Bishop of Milan presided over the area which fell under the jurisdiction of the *vicarius Italiae*. In the fifth century the sees of Aquileia and Ravenna became the centres of separate provinces.[5] Gaul consisted of seventeen civil provinces and gradually an ecclesiastical organization corresponding in the main to the civil, developed. The southern provinces, where the population was larger, and where Christianity first took root, were much smaller than those of the north, which answered more to ancient tribal divisions, and which also suffered more disorganization from the barbarian invasions than did the provinces of the south.[6] In Spain it is probable that provincial development was a little slower, but it becomes apparent in the fifth century.[7]

[1] III Carthage, canons 2, 7.
[2] *Codex can. Afric.* c. 76.
[3] III Carthage, canon 7; for other business of the provincial councils see *Cod. can. Afric.* canon 26, and for the relations between bishops and primates II Carthage, canon 12, II Carthage, canon 28.
[4] D. xviii, cc. 9 and 10.
[5] J. Gaudemet, op. cit., 384f.
[6] E. Loening, *Geschichte des deutschen Kirchenrechts* (Strassburg, 1878) i. 367–76; E. Griffe, *La Gaule chrétienne à l'époque romaine* (Paris, 1947–57) i. 249–55, ii. 107–33.
[7] J. Gaudemet, op. cit., 387f.

Although provincial councils were held from time to time in these areas it seems likely that the principle of once or twice a year was an ideal rather than a rule strictly observed, and even when councils were summoned there seems to have been constant difficulty in securing a full attendance. The second Council of Arles, in the mid-fifth century, and the Council of Agde (A.D. 536) both issued decrees against absentees, decrees which are to be found in Gratian.[1] The Councils of Epaon, in 517, and Orleans in 549, made similar canons.[2] The Third Council of Orleans, in 538, imposed penalties on metropolitans who neglected to summon a provincial council for two years, and the Councils of Riez (439), V Orleans (549), and II Tours (567) repeated the requirement of annual or twice yearly councils.[3] In Spain the Council of Tarragona (A.D. 516) decreed the excommunication of bishops who neglected to attend the provincial synod, and this canon too has passed into Gratian.[4] The influential *Capitula* of Martin of Braga repeated the Antiochene decrees on the holding of such synods, and the Fourth Council of Toledo (A.D. 633) is notable for having provided what appears to be the oldest known *Ordo* for the holding of a provincial synod.[5]

Before going on to procedure something must be said about the membership of the early councils. The close association of clergy and laity in the life of the local churches in earliest times has already been emphasized together with the part played by the laity in the election of bishops and other ministers. Letters were written in the name of one whole local church to another, and there are indications that in the first and early second centuries the whole community co-operated in the exercise of discipline.[6] There can be little doubt that

[1] D. xviii, cc. 12 and 13; II Arles, canon 19, Agde, canon 35.
[2] Epaon, canon 1; V Orleans, canon 18.
[3] Riez, canon 10; V Orleans, canon 33; II Tours, canon 1.
[4] D. xviii, c. 14; Tarragona, canon 6.
[5] IV Toledo, canon 3. See below, pp. 75–8.
[6] 1 Corinthians 5. 1–5; 2 Corinthians 2. 4–8; 7. 12; *Epistle of Polycarp to the Philippians* 11.

the early councils were predominantly councils of bishops but each bishop present was, in a much fuller sense than any modern English or Roman Catholic bishop, the representative of his church. What is less clear is the position of presbyters and others of the clergy, and of the laity in relation to the councils. The expression used by the Anonymous who wrote about the anti-Montanist councils is ambiguous.[1] It could imply the attendance of the lower clergy and the laity, but is not definite enough to be used as evidence. Tertullian's remarks about the Greek councils provide no clue to membership. The councils held in connection with the Paschal controversy are described only as councils of bishops. If others were present and contributed to the discussions it nevertheless seems plain that the decisions ran in the name of the bishops alone.[2]

More detail is available for the middle of the third century. Firmilian's use of two words *seniores* and *praepositi* seems to imply that at the Greek councils others besides bishops were present.[3] That this was so in Africa the letters of Cyprian make plain. In the very first of them he writes of a *concilium episcoporum*, whose decrees he regards as binding, but there are other passages which show that presbyters, deacons and members of the laity were present and participated in the councils. At the Council of Carthage held by Cyprian in April 251, after the persecution had slackened, the bishops assembled in the presence of a company of the clergy and people,[4] and that the latter were not there simply as an audience is shown by a passage in a letter written to Bishop Antonian immediately after the council, in which Cyprian refers to the advice he himself had given to the Roman Church about dealing with those who had lapsed in the persecution:

> that the peace of the Church must be awaited, and then, in a full conference of the bishops, presbyters, deacons and con-

[1] Eusebius, *Hist. Eccl.* V. 16.10: τωυ γὰρ κατὰ τὴν 'Αοίαν Πῖστῶυ.
[2] Id., V. 23–5. [3] Cyprian, *Ep.* 75.4. [4] Id. *Ep.* 45.2.

fessors, with those of the laymen also who have stood fast, account be taken of the lapsed.[1]

In the letter to Quintus after the council of 255 Cyprian says that he has sent a copy of their decisions on the rebaptism of heretics, decisions taken by himself and his fellow-bishops with their fellow-presbyters who were there.

> Whereon that you may know what very many of ourselves, the bishops, with our fellow-presbyters, decreed lately in council, I send you a copy of our Epistle.[2]

The letters which convey the decision of the council of the following year on the same subject speak only of bishops,[3] but the *acta* of the second council held that year (256) say: "Cum in unum Cartaginem Convenissent kalendis Septembribus episcopi plurimi . . . cum presbyteris et diaconibus, praesentibus etiam plebis maxima parte."[4] We can be sure that the African *plebs* did not stand dumb throughout the proceedings.

The evidence of Cyprian's correspondence seems to show that the conciliar decisions were in the name of the bishops, but that in arriving at these decisions great weight was attached to the views of the clergy and laity. His principle seems to have been that stated by the Roman presbyters and deacons who wrote to him in 250:

> It seems to us both very invidious and oppressive, to examine without the advice of many, what many have committed, and for one to pass sentence when so great a crime is known to have spread and extended itself among great numbers; neither indeed can a decree be firm, which shall not appear to have the consent of numbers.[5]

[1] Id. *Ep.* 55.5: "prius esse ecclesiae pacem sustinendam, deinde sic conlatione consiliorum cum episcopis presbyteris diaconis confessoribus pariter et stantibus laicis facta lapsorum tractare rationem."

[2] Id. *Ep.* 71.1: "De qua re quid nuper in concilio plurimi coepiscopi cum conpresbyteris qui aderant censuerimus ut scires, eiusdem epistulae exemplum tibi misi."

[3] Id. *Ep.* 72, 73.

[4] *Sententiae Episcoporum*, in *S. Cypriani Opera*, ed. G. Härtel (Vienna, 1868), 435–61.

[5] Cyprian, *Ep.* 30.5.

The context shows that the laity were included. It is possible, however, that a distinction ought to be drawn between councils which were concerned with discipline and those which were defining doctrine. There is, as we have seen, evidence that the laity were taken into close consultation in the matter of the treatment of the lapsed. It is much less clear that they had any decisive, or indeed consultative voice on the doctrinal issues involved in the question of re-baptism.

A further question arises about the nature of lay participation in the councils which discussed the treatment of the lapsed. The bishops obviously assembled from all parts of Africa, Numidia, and Mauretania, and the evidence of other councils makes it at least possible that some of them brought presbyters and deacons with them, or sent such to represent them. It must, however, remain obscure whether lay representatives of the other churches assembled at Carthage. There seem to have been in the North African Church certain lay officials known as the *seniores laici*. The evidence concerning them is almost entirely of the fourth century but is such as to suggest that they existed in the third. They appear as having charge of the fabric and property of churches, but also as connected with ecclesiastical discipline, and they had the right to present complaints to the councils of the African Church.[1] The evidence is fragmentary and the Italian scholar P. G. Caron seems to build on it more than it will bear, but it is nevertheless evidence for the existence of a class of lay officials associated with the councils and administration of the Church. It is improbable, however, that they had any voice in the definition of doctrine.

It is also doubtful whether the presbytery had at this

[1] P. G. Caron, *I poteri giuridici del Laicato nella Chiesa Primitiva* (Milan, 1948), 55f, 152f, 208–12; Id., "Les premiers 'seniores laici' de l'Église africaine" (*Rev. internat. des Droits de l'Antiquité*, vi (1951), 7–22); Y. M-J. Congar, *Jalons pour une Théologie du Laicat* (Paris, 1954), 350–2. P. Monceaux, "Les seniores laici des Églises africaines", *Bull. de la Soc. nat. des antiq. de France*, 1903, 283–5, gives the earliest review of the evidence.

period any such voice, though individual presbyters were called in as experts, as indeed were deacons and laymen on occasion. Origen was more than once asked to assist episcopal synods in dealing with doctrinal cases.[1] The presbyter Malchion played a similar rôle in the examination of the teaching of Paul of Samosata.[2] Presbyters, deacons, and lay philosophers attended and disputed in connection with the Council of Nicea, and an influential part in the proceedings of the council was taken by the deacon Athanasius.[3] None of this however suggests that the final decision resided anywhere but with the bishops. Nevertheless we must remember that the views of other persons were ascertained, and that the bishops were fully representative of their churches.

It has been demonstrated beyond question by Pierre Batiffol that the procedure of these early councils followed closely what is known to have been the procedure of the Roman senate in the later Empire.[4] Similar conclusions had also been reached independently by H. Gelzer, and have been supported by A. Steinwenter, and more recently by Dr Hess in his examination of the Council of Sardica.[5] The surviving formal *acta* of councils of the third and fourth centuries suffice to make the procedure plain. The president delivered a *relatio* or statement of the question to be settled, the bishops were asked in order of seniority to give their views and each stated his *sententia*. After this the prevailing opinion had usually become apparent. In many cases the *sententiae* were unanimous but otherwise the decision seems to have been reached by the will of a substantial majority. The conclusion was embodied in a *libellus* usually composed

[1] Eusebius, op. cit., VI. 33, 37.
[2] Id., VII. 29.
[3] Socrates, *Hist. Eccl.*, I.8.
[4] P. Batiffol, *Etudes de Liturgie et d'archéologie chrétienne* (Paris, 1919), 84–153.
[5] H. Gelzer, "Die Konzilien als Reichsparlamente" in *Ausgewählte kleine Schriften* (Leipzig, 1907), 142–56; H. Hess, op. cit., 24–41; A. Steinwenter, "Der antike kirchliche Rechtsgang und seine Quellen", *ZSSR*, kan. Abt. xxiii (1934), 48–9.

by the president and communicated to the heads of the principal churches of Christendom. This somewhat formal procedure was, however, frequently accompanied by other methods of action. In the case of accusations of heresy the accused was interrogated in the council, and sometimes, as we have seen, the bishops, like a Roman magistrate, were assisted by experts. The Council of Aquileia in 381, at which two bishops were condemned for Arianism, affords a good example of this kind of procedure.[1] On other occasions when the business was more to make canons the formal sessions seem to have been preceded by less formal general discussion. This was clearly so at Sardica and at the first Council of Carthage (348). At the Council of Carthage in August 403, Bishop Aurelius opened the proceedings by saying:

> Although when we were in session yesterday, besides our ecclesiastical proceedings we discussed carefully what should be done, to-day, however, yesterday's discussion must be confirmed by formal ecclesiastical acts.[2]

The provincial organization of the Church and the provincial synods appear to have grown out of the need for consultation about common problems and an awareness of the importance of providing some degree of oversight over the local churches. In the first century these needs were supplied in the main by the work of the apostles and their assistants, but as that generation died out there were no obvious successors. When problems arose, therefore, representatives of the local churches began to meet in particular regions and its was natural and convenient to use both the civil geography and the accustomed procedure of civil assemblies. So, by the end of the third century the Church in the East found itself in possession of an instrument that

[1] Ambrose, Letters, between Epp. 8 and 9; cf. F. Homes Dudden, *Saint Ambrose, his Life and Times* (Oxford, 1935), i. 199–206.

[2] *Codex can. Afric.*, between canons 90 and 91: "Licet hesterno die de hac re considentibus nobis praeter gesta ecclesiastica diligentius quae gesserint tractaremus, hodie tamen oportet tractatum hesterni diei actis ecclesiasticis confirmari."

was capable of dealing with most of the ordinary routine problems as they occurred, though not equal to settling important doctrinal issues. The great councils were occasional assemblies summoned for particular business, the provincial councils were the regular routine assemblies of the Church. In the course of the fourth and fifth centuries provincial organization developed almost as fully in the West as it had done in the East, but was from time to time checked and disrupted by the barbarian invasions.

These councils were essentially councils of bishops, though others, both clerical and lay, might from time to time be present and share in the discussions. The representative character of the episcopate has been emphasized, but two further points need to be made. The first concerns the metropolitan. As regards the consecration of bishops in the province he may be said to have had a veto, but it does not appear that his powers in the provincial synod were nearly so great. There he was *primus inter pares* and nothing more. Without him the council was not perfect, it should not be held apart from him, but he does not seem to have been more than its convener and president. He was not yet an *arch*bishop.

The second point concerns the limitations upon the provincial councils. We have seen the hierarchy above the province which came to be provided in the East for disciplinary matters. The West has no close parallel at this early time, though bishops were already writing to Rome for advice and direction. But in most countries of the West, in Africa, Gaul, and Spain, there were from time to time regional councils whose authority was greater than that of the province and which occasionally laid down rules for the provincial councils. It is easier to draw up a hierarchy of councils on paper than to show it working in practice, but it is plain that the provincial councils were subordinate to the larger assemblies.

It must, however, be observed that the authority of any council however large was limited by the subsequent acceptance or rejection of its decisions by the Church as a whole. Nobody could have foreseen in A.D. 325 the veneration with which the Council of Nicea would later be regarded or have felt sure that its doctrinal decisions would stand. Councils met under the invocation of the Holy Spirit, and bishops claimed to give the judgement of God, but it was through the *consensus fidelium*, given or withheld in subsequent years, that the Holy Spirit showed whether the judgement was human or divine. *Vox populi vox dei* was a maxim in which the Early Church believed firmly, as applied to ecclesiastical appointments. The historian can see that it operated also in the discerning of authority.

LECTURE 2

7 February 1960

LAW AND PRACTICE IN THE MIDDLE AGES

At the laste let be renewed those lawes and constitutions of fathers of the celebration of councels, that commaunde prouinciall councels to be oftener vsed for the reformation of the churche. For there neuer hapneth nothyng more hurtefull to the church of Christe, than the lacke both of councell generall and prouinciall.

John Colet, *Convocation Sermon*, 1512.

1

WHEN IN the subject that we are considering, one turns from the practice of the early Church to the classical canon law of the Middle Ages no change is more apparent than that in the position of the metropolitan. He has become exalted above the other bishops of the province who take an oath of obedience to him and are now spoken of as his suffragans. He has also become strictly subordinated to the authority of the pope from whom he receives the pallium which is now the symbol of metropolitical jurisdiction. In bringing about this change Anglo-Saxon influence was powerful and we must, therefore, take a brief view of it.[1]

The title of archbishop is of eastern origin and is thought to appear first in St Athanasius's *Apology against the Arians* (A.D. 348) where it is applied to the saint's predecessor, Alexander of Alexandria. A little later there seems to be a tendency for it to be applied to the bishop of the city which stood at the head of a civil diocese, who is sometimes also called "exarch", and a long list of such use in the fifth century can be compiled.[2] It is possible that the Third Council of Carthage in 393, had this development in mind when it forbade the use of titles such as *princeps sacerdotum* and *summus sacerdos* for the metropolitans who were to be called simply *primae sedis episcopus*.[3] However this may be, the title is scarcely found in the West before the sixth century. Isidore of Seville, no doubt inspired by eastern sources,

[1] This development is described in considerable detail by E. Lesne, *La hiérarchie épiscopale, provinces, métropolitains, primats, en Gaule et Germanie depuis la réforme de saint Boniface jusqu'à la mort d'Hincmar. 742–882* (Lille, 1905).

[2] Article "Archevêque" by A. Amanieu, in *Dict. de Droit canonique,* ed. R. Naz (Paris, 1935ff) i. col. 927–34.

[3] *Codex can. Afric.* canon 39.

lists archbishops between patriarchs and metropolitans in a four membered hierarchy of bishops,[1] but the word is used by Gregory the Great more as a courtesy title, and appears to bear little relation to function.[2]

It seems to be with the episcopate of Theodore at Canterbury from 668 to 690 that the title "archbishop" comes to imply a definite jurisdiction, and, if the *acta* of the Councils of Hertford and Hatfield, as given by Bede are to be trusted, the change may be placed somewhere between 673 and 680. At Hertford, in 673, Theodore describes himself as *Doruvernensis ecclesiae episcopus*,[3] and seven years later the *acta* of the Council of Hatfield, 17 September 680, refer to *praesidente Theodoro, gratia Dei archiepiscopo Brittaniae insulae et civitatis Doruvernensis*.[4] It seems highly probable that the change is connected with the troubles which arose from 678 onwards in connection with Theodore's attempt to divide and reorganize the huge dioceses of the north and the resulting conflict with Wilfrid. In the *acta* of the Roman Council of October 679, which met about this business, he is repeatedly spoken of as *archiepiscopus*,[5] but these *acta* have been interpolated in connection with the later conflict between Canterbury and York, making it difficult to rely very precisely upon their wording.[6]

Berhtwald, who succeeded Theodore after an interval, and held the see from 693 to 731, appears on the evidence of a variety of sources to have been known throughout as "archbishop". The Laws of Wihtred, King of Kent, in 695, refer to him by the vernacular title of *Bretone heahbiscop*,[7] which seems to be the equivalent of *Brittaniae archiepiscopus*.

[1] Isidore, *Etymologies*, VII, ch.12, n4 and 6.

[2] Amanieu, op. cit.

[3] Bede, *Historica Ecclesiastica*, iv. 5.

[4] Id., iv. 15.

[5] A. W. Haddan and W. Stubbs, *Councils and Ecclesiastical Documents relating to Great Britain and Ireland* (Oxford, 1869–78), iii, 131ff.

[6] W. Levison, "Die Akten der römischen Synode von 679" in *Aus rheinischer und fränkischer Frühzeit*, ed. W. Holtzmann (Düsseldorf, 1948), 267–94, reprinted from *ZSSR*. kan. Abt. ii (1912), 249–82, and xix (1930), 672–4.

[7] Haddan and Stubbs, op. cit., iii, 233.

In 704 Pope John IV, in a letter to the kings of Mercia and Northumbria, speaks of having confirmed Berhtwald as Archbishop of Canterbury.[1] In 706 and 716 Berhtwald subscribes charters as *archiepiscopus*,[2] and he is so named repeatedly in Eddius's Life of Wilfrid.[3] By the beginning of the eighth century *archiepiscopus* was in England so usual a title that Bede automatically applies it to the Bishops of Arles and Lyons[4] who certainly did not use it at that date, and to the Bishops of Canterbury from Augustine to Theodore's predecessor Wighard.[5]

In the thought of the Anglo-Saxons of this period the position occupied by the archbishop and his duties as metropolitan seem to have been bound up with the conferring of the pallium,[6] the scarf of white wool which had originally been used by emperors and bishops as mark of honour, but came to be a symbol of jurisdiction. In 601 Gregory the Great had sent to Augustine a pallium with a letter in which he directed him to organize the English Church in two provinces with the metropolitical centres at London and York, each province consisting of twelve bishops. When the organization was sufficiently far advanced the pope would send a pallium also to the Bishop of York.[7] There seems to be no record of any grant of the pallium to Augustine's two immediate successors Laurentius and Mellitus, but Justus who succeeded in 624, received it from Boniface V together with a letter which seems to associate with it the right to consecrate bishops.[8] Justus died in 627, but it was not until 634 that the pallium was sent to his successor, Honorius, and also, at the same time to Paulinus of York.[9] He, however, was driven out of Northumbria shortly afterwards and the

[1] Id., 26. [2] Id., 279, 300.

[3] B. Colgrave, *The Life of Bishop Wilfrid by Eddius Stephanus* (Cambridge, 1927), 92, 102, 106, 108, 110, 124, 128.

[4] Bede, op. cit., i. 27; iii. 25. [5] Id., ii. 3, 4, 7, 18, 20, 29.

[6] Article "Pallium" by R. Naz, in *Dict. de Droit canonique*, vi, cols. 1192–4; W. Levison, *England and the continent in the eighth century* (Oxford, 1946), 19–22.

[7] Bede, op. cit., i. 29. [8] Id., ii. 8. [9] Id., ii. 17.

metropolitan status of York lapsed for a century. Deusdedit, who presided at Canterbury from 655 to 664, is not known to have received the pallium, but after his death the Kings of Northumbria and Kent despatched one of his clerks, Wighard, to receive consecration from the pope. Wighard, however, died at Rome, and in 668 Theodore was chosen by Pope Vitalian and consecrated by him before being sent to England. It seems highly probable that he received the pallium at that time, but there is no record of it. The evidence for Berhtwald's reception of the pallium is late and unreliable.[1] After him the practice of the mid-seventh century was unquestionably observed again. The pallium was sent to Tatwin of Canterbury in 733,[2] and in the following year Bede, in a letter to Egbert, the new Bishop of York, definitely connects its reception with the metropolitan office.[3] In 735 Egbert succeeded in obtaining the pallium for himself,[4] and with it the re-establishment of the separate province of York in which he was metropolitan and, in the language of St Boniface who wrote to him ten or twelve years later, archbishop.[5]

This narrative derives much of its importance in providing the background against which grew up two English missionaries, Willibrord, apostle of the Frisians and the young Wynfrith who, under the name of Boniface, became the apostle of the Germans. The English Church of the seventh century was essentially the child of the papacy. It had been founded by papal missionaries and had grown under papal direction. In Theodore of Tarsus a new papal envoy came to develop the organization which Augustine had begun. Few features of ecclesiastical history are more striking and commendable than the way in which the English Church, almost before it was itself established, began to send out missionaries to preach the Gospel to the related peoples of the Frankish dominions. The Frisian mission was

[1] Haddan and Stubbs, op. cit.. iii. 229. [2] Id., 311.
[3] Id., 319. [4] Id., 335. [5] Id., 358.

begun by Wilfrid in 678–9, but may have lapsed until, in 690, the thirty-eight year old Northumbrian priest Willibrord was sent to Friesland with a group of companions. Very shortly afterwards he went to Rome to ask for papal sanction and advice, and on a second visit in 695 he was, at the request of Pippin II, consecrated Archbishop of the Frisians, by Pope Sergius. He was given the castle of Traiectum, the modern Utrecht, as his cathedral site and the centre from which he was to organize a new ecclesiastical province which should be, like the English Church, in close dependence on Rome.[1]

Some twenty years later this precedent was followed by Wynfrith who, having begun missionary work in Friesland in 716 and received a set-back, sailed again for the continent in 718 and went to Rome to ask for the sanction and help of the pope. This Gregory II gave, changing his name to Boniface and authorizing him to preach the Gospel among the Teutonic peoples. In 722 he went again to Rome and was consecrated bishop taking an oath to the pope similar to that taken by Italian bishops at their consecration. About ten years later, another pope, Gregory III, sent him the pallium and made him archbishop, the intended head of a new German Church.[2]

The area in which Boniface, and the growing band of missionaries who joined him, worked was vast in its extent, a broad band of territory stretching eastwards from the coastline of the modern Holland, Belgium, and Normandy to the modern Austria. The northern parts had never been Christian, but in many of the other districts there were the remains of the ecclesiastical organization of the fourth and fifth centuries which the barbarian invasions had disrupted and which badly needed reform. By the time of the death of Charles Martel in 741, Boniface's work had reached a point at which large scale reorganization had become desirable

[1] Bede, op. cit., v. 11; Levison, *England and the Continent*, 53–60.
[2] Levison, op. cit., 71–3.

and possible, and the means chosen was the traditional one of a series of councils. In the years 742 to 747 Carloman, and his brother Pippin III who had divided the kingdom between them after their father's death, authorized and assisted in the holding of a great series of synods in which lay magnates took part with bishops and priests, and whose decrees were published in name of the secular ruler and made laws of the realm.[1] As part of the general aim of reform was the particular one of establishing ecclesiastical provinces under an archbishop closely dependent upon Rome, and in Gaul this was seen in terms of the restoration of the old provinces. By 744 Boniface was in a position to ask the pope to grant the pallium to the Archbishops of Rheims, Sens, and Rouen, though he had almost immediately to write again asking that it be sent only to Rouen.[2]

Boniface's ideas are set out very clearly in a letter which he wrote at about this time to Archbishop Cuthbert of Canterbury.[3] He speaks of what they have in common: "Our responsibility toward churches and peoples is greater than that of other bishops on account of the pallium entrusted to us and accepted by us, while they have the care of their own dioceses only." He goes on to list a number of decrees passed at a recent synod. They begin with a series of declarations of obedience to the Roman Church: "We shall willingly submit to St Peter and his vicar . . . we shall hold a synod every year . . . our metropolitans shall seek their palliums from that see." Then:

> we have decreed that the metropolitan who has been exalted by the pallium, shall exhort and admonish the other bishops, and he shall investigate who among them is watchful of the salvation of the people, and who is negligent. . . . We have decreed that it is proper for the metropolitan according to the canons to investigate the conduct of the bishops subject to him, and their care for the people, and he shall direct that the bishops on their return from the synod shall each hold a

[1] Id., 84ff. [2] Boniface, *Epp.* 45, 46; cf. Levison, op. cit., 87f.
[3] Boniface, Ep. 62; Haddan and Stubbs, op.cit., 376f.

meeting in his own diocese with the presbyters and abbots and shall order them to observe the decrees of the synod. And every bishop, if he is unable to correct or amend anything in his diocese shall bring it to the synod before the archbishop and openly to all to be corrected, in the same manner as the Roman Church bound us with an oath at our consecration that if I should see priests or people wandering from the law of God and be unable to correct them I would always faithfully report it to the apostolic see and the vicar of St Peter for correction. For thus, if I am not mistaken, should all bishops make it known to the metropolitan and he to the Roman Pontiff if they find anything impossible in the correction of their people.

This letter makes obvious the contrast between the status the metropolitan in the fourth and fifth centuries, and the position which he had come to occupy in the eyes of the reforming missionaries of the seventh and eighth. On the one hand his dependence upon Rome is asserted unequivocally. On the other the subjection of the bishops of the province to him is made equally clear. This subjection was still further emphasized in the first of Charlemagne's capitularies, that resulting from the council of Héristal in March 779 where for the first time in Frankish legislation we find the word *suffraganeus* applied to diocesan bishops of the province.

De metropolitanis, ut suffraganii episcopi eis secundum canones subjecti sint.[1]

At the same period the suffragans begin to combine with their profession of faith at consecration an oath of obedience to the metropolitan.[2] The oldest known example of such an oath in the province of Canterbury is that taken by Bishop Eadulf in 796.[3]

Influential as were his theories Boniface was only partially

[1] A. Boretius, *Capitulare regum Francorum* (*MGH*, 1883) i. 47; cf. P. Hinschius, *Das Kirchenrecht der Katholiken und Protestanten in Deutschland* (Berlin, 1869–97), ii. 9.

[2] Cf. E. Lesne, op. cit., 122.

[3] Haddan and Stubbs, op. cit., 506.

successful in re-establishing the provincial system in northern France, but what he left undone was very largely completed by Charlemagne. In 774 Pope Hadrian sent to the king an enlarged edition of the canonical collection of Dionysius Exiguus, which contained the decrees of the principal councils of the early Church with their references to the metropolitans and the provincial synods. For the next twenty years Charlemagne's task in the ecclesiastical field was to make known the contents of this collection and see that the primitive discipline was observed.[1] This, however, was done in no merely antiquarian spirit. The primitive titles were understood in the contemporary form, so that although the contents of the Dionysio-Hadriana inspired the re-establishment of the provincial system the position of the metropolitan-archbishop and his relationship to his suffragans in the Carolingian Empire were those of Bonifacian theory.

It is unnecessary to repeat the work of the scholars who have traced in detail the ecclesiastical reforms of Charlemagne and his immediate successors, but we must refer briefly to two prominent figures of the ninth century, the anonymous compiler or compilers of the False Decretals and their related forgeries, and Hincmar, the celebrated Archbishop of Rheims. The False Decretals are now usually assigned to the years 846 to 852, a time when the lay control of the church and of ecclesiastical offices which had been so marked a feature of the previous hundred years had become a source of corruption rather than of reform. The first aim of the forger was to secure the independence of the bishops and others of the clergy from lay control. He saw that the royal authority which, fifty years earlier, had seemed so great a support for the Church was in fact of very uncertain value, and he desired above all to find an unimpeachable spiritual authority to support the bishops. To this end great emphasis is laid on the ultimate dependence of each bishop

[1] See C. De Clercq, *La législation religieuse franque de Clovis à Charlemagne* (Louvain, 1936), 156–312; E. Lesne, op. cit., 57–79.

upon the papacy. The pope is the supreme judge by whom alone bishops may be deposed, and to whom belongs the cognizance of all major causes. An effect of this emphasis upon papal authority is that the ranks of the hierarchy intermediate between the pope and individual bishops assume very much less importance, and this is particularly so with the metropolitan against whom the forger shows a certain animosity. The prescriptions of the old law are emphasized and the metropolitan is once again represented as *primus inter pares* having no immediate and personal jurisdiction elsewhere than in his own diocese.[1]

In the matter of the power of metropolitans the views of the forger ran directly contrary to those of the most prominent and energetic ecclesiastic of the ninth century, Hincmar, who held the archbishopric of Rheims from 845 to 882.[2] In regard to the relationship of metropolitan and suffragans Hincmar represents the Bonifacian theory carried to the extreme. When a see becomes vacant the metropolitan sends one of the other bishops to supervise the election of the new bishop and to bring the record of it to him. The new bishop is regarded as the son of the metropolitical church and takes an oath of obedience to the metropolitan. The latter can visit the dioceses of the province at will and give directions to the suffragans for the correction of errors. In the provincial synod he can hear charges against the suffragans and can pronounce their deposition. Hincmar acknowledges the papal authority but opposes any appeal from the provincial synod to the pope. In the synod the metropolitan's position is somewhat confused. The synod is incomplete and cannot act without him, but often its decisions run in his name alone as if he were the sole judge. He has complete control over the business and usually prepares it in advance.

It should be noted that at this period the provincial synod

[1] E. Lesne, op. cit., 185–97.

[2] Id. Parts II and III, particularly 171–84 and 210–24; cf. *Dict. de droit canonique*, v, cols. 1144–9.

was still regarded as competent to deal with matters of doctrine. Pope Nicholas I, for example, submitted to Frankish metropolitans the various charges, some doctrinal and some disciplinary, levelled by the Greeks against the Roman Church, and Hincmar sent an account of them to his suffragans so that they might consider the matters before meeting for discussion of them in the provincial synod.[1] The controversies which surrounded the predestinarian teachings of Gottschalk seem to have been discussed in provincial synods as well as in councils which included bishops from several provinces.[2]

Hincmar's wide learning and powerful personality were important in making his views prevail during the ninth century, but there is no reason to think that the theory on which he acted was peculiar to him. Abundant evidence shows that his views were shared by other archbishops and by most of his own suffragans.[3] In the long run, however, the False Decretals were to modify the position. True, the metropolitan did not return to the limits assigned to him in the organization of the early Church. He remained superior to his suffragans. He confirmed their election, consecrated them and received their oath of obedience to him and his church, controlled the proceedings of the provincial synod, and had the right of visitation of their dioceses; but in other aspects his powers over them were diminished. The Pseudo-Isidorian view of the papal control of the trial of bishops and jurisdiction over other major causes prevailed, and the centuries after Hincmar, therefore, see a certain diminution of metropolitical rights in favour of more direct papal intervention.

The tenth century was for the papacy a period of decline. In the absence of an active central authority there was a marked tendency for the various national churches to go their own ways. Movements of reform were not lacking, but

[1] *PL* cxxvi, cols. 93f.

[2] C. J. Hefele, *Histoire des Conciles*, ed. H. Leclercq (Paris, 1907ff.) IV. i. 137–235.

[3] Lesne, op. cit., 174–84.

it was not until the middle of the eleventh century with the election to the papal throne of the Lorrainer, Bruno, Bishop of Toul, under the name of Leo IX, that they acquired the influence to affect the life of the whole of Western Christendom. The reformers of the eleventh century had a definite programme, and part of it was the assertion of immediate papal sovereignty over all parts of the Church. Like the compilers of the False Decretals they had little use for any rank intermediate between pope and bishop, save for the legates commissioned by the pope to undertake the work of reform in particular lands. Gregory VII tried to bind the metropolitans more strictly to the papacy by requiring that they should come to Rome in person to be examined and to receive the pallium, but he did not envisage them as being a very valuable instrument of reform. The institution was too deeply rooted in Christian history to be suppressed, but its importance could be minimized, and repeated papal interventions could reduce the metropolitan's influence in his province. Provincial synods accomplished little of importance unless a papal legate attended and presided over them, and there was an almost complete withdrawal of the cases of bishops from the competence of metropolitans.[1] The Gregorian plan led to vigorous protests from German archbishops such as Siegfried of Mainz who asserted that he and his colleagues were ready to refer to the apostolic see cases which were too difficult for them to settle but objected strongly to being by-passed altogether as had happened when two bishops of the province were suspended by the papal legate without any hearing before the metropolitan in the provincial synod. In the opposition to the Gregorian Reform there was a powerful element of conservatism, and many bishops considered that the pope was undermining the constitution of the church.[2] The more radical of the oppo-

[1] A. Fliche, *La Réforme grégorienne,* (Louvain, 1924–37) ii. 114–16; 233f.

[2] Id., 142–6; G. Tellenbach, *Church, State and Christian Society at the time of the Investiture Contest* (Oxford, 1940), 142–5.

nents, however, attacked papal power with arguments which asserted the absolute equality of all bishops and would have provided little support for the claims of metropolitans.

Although some of the more extreme positions of Gregory VII and his immediate successors were not able to be maintained in the following century, the whole reforming movement did, nevertheless, result in a great increase in the administrative control over the local churches exercised by the papacy, and this was consolidated by the development of the system of judges delegate, by the use of papal provisions, and in many other ways, which left comparatively little scope for the activity of provincial synods and metropolitans in spiritual matters. Under control, however, the synods were regarded as a normal piece of ecclesiastical machinery.

2

The subject of provincial councils finds its appropriate place in the first part of the *Corpus Juris Canonici*, the great eleventh century compilation of the Bolognese monk Gratian.[1] In Distinctions I to XIV of his *Decretum*, he discusses natural law, constitutions and customs, ecclesiastical constitutions and the bodies which make them. In Distinctions XV and XVI various historical sources in this category are set out, and then in Distinctions XVII and XVIII the subject of councils is discussed more generally. Gratian is most anxious to make plain the papal control of councils and this he does by a series of texts which assert that councils cannot be assembled without papal authority. This leads him into the subject of provincial councils which naturally fall under this limitation, and he also argues that they have no power of defining the faith and making general decrees. Their function is that of correcting error in the provinces. Distinction XVIII is entirely composed of canons about provincial

[1] P. G. Caron, "I poteri del metropolita secondo Graziano" in *Studia Gratiana*, ed. I. Forchielli and A. M. Stickler (Bologna, 1953ff) ii. 253–77.

councils. There are many of the early decrees which were discussed in the previous lecture. The chief points which emerge are the duty of metropolitans to hold such councils once or twice a year, and the duty of the bishops to attend when summoned. It is envisaged that other clerks will be there, and even laymen, for an extract from the *Capitula* of Martin of Braga is given which provides that presbyters and deacons and all who consider themselves aggrieved shall have the right to bring their cases to be judged by the council. Another canon is an extract from a letter of Pope Leo IV who said that presbyters ought not to be required to bring gifts to the councils though they were free to do so if they wished. This is one of the points in the Distinction which is picked out by most of the early commentators on the *Decretum*. The other point which they generally select for particular comment is a parenthesis in Canon XIII, a decree of the Council of Agde, which allows the royal command as a sufficient excuse for absence from the council. Stephen of Tournai says that this applies if the royal summons precedes that of the metropolitan.[1] Rufinus seems to go further than this in distinguishing between a summons by the pope and by the metropolitan. The latter, he says, is subject to the prince in secular matters, whereas the pope is subject in nothing. He adds, however, that the canon does not apply to any bishop but only to one who is in the imperial service.[2] Apart from these two points the early commentators do little but repeat the substance of Gratian's texts.

3

In the matter of provincial councils as in other respects the *Decretum* of Gratian summed up the old law of the Church as it had been modified and interpreted by the

[1] J. F. von Schulte, *Die Summa des Stephanus Tornacensis über das Decretum Gratiani* (Giessen, 1891), 27.

[2] H. Singer, *Die Summa Decretorum des Magister Rufinus* (Paderborn, 1902), 40f.

Gregorian reform. Before going on to the thirteenth century and the papal decretals which are of special importance in this connection, it will be advisable to compare law and practice in a selected example, and for this purpose we may take the councils of the province of Narbonne which, thanks to the work of Baluze, Devic, and Vaissette, are particularly well documented.

For the three centuries between the Council of Port in 896 and the Council of Montpellier in 1195 some thirty-six ecclesiastical assemblies are known. When all allowance has been made for those of which no record survives the number does not suggest that the rule of annual provincial councils was very strictly observed, and the frequent complaints about the negligence of metropolitans which we find in councils and canonists both before and after this period seems to be related to fact. It is clear from the surviving records that the archbishop and bishops of the province formed the core of the provincial council, but the occasions on which they alone are mentioned are chiefly occasions when specifically episcopal functions such as blessing, absolving or excommunicating were in question, as for example at the Tenth Council of Narbonne in October 1055, when excommunication was pronounced against those who attacked the property of the Church of Ausona.[1] In some cases too, when a council is known only because of a grant confirmed in it, we have mention of the bishops only. In the great majority of cases the presence of other clerics, and sometimes of laymen, is noted.

An absent bishop might be represented by one of his clergy, as, for example, at the Council of Fontcouverte in 911, the Bishop of Ausona was represented by a legate, and

[1] C. Devic and J. Vaissette, *Histoire générale de Languedoc* (new edn. Toulouse, 1872–1905), iii. 326; P. de Marca, *Marca hispanica* (Paris, 1688), 451ff; The Council of St Thibéry, 1050, E. Martène and U. Durand, *Thesaurus novus anecdotorum* (Paris, 1717ff), iv. cols. 87ff, shows that such excommunications were sometimes pronounced at a council in which abbots and others took part.

Savaric, Abbot of St Paul's, signed the decrees on behalf of the Bishop of Toulouse.[1] Legates of the absent bishops are mentioned at the Council of St Thibéry, 1050,[2] and at the Council of Narbonne in 1054, the Bishops of Urgel and Uzès were thus represented.[3] These legates are always listed after the bishops who were present in person, but they seem to have deliberated with them, and they signed the decrees on their principal's behalf.

Most councils, if not all, were attended by abbots who might themselves also be represented by legates, as at the Council of Port in 896. On that occasion the archbishop is described as *resedente* with the bishops, the abbots as *sistentibus*, and the other clerks and layfolk simply as *presentibus*. The signatures indicate the presence of four archdeacons and an archpriest.[4] At the Councils of Narbonne in 1091 and 1130 members of the chapter of Narbonne were present, and it is possible that this was a regular thing, although their attendance seems to be noted on this occasion because matters touching the property of the Church of Narbonne were in question.[5] The Council of Lombers, 1165, which was summoned for conversations with the Albigenisans and ended in the condemnation of the heretics, was attended by the Provosts of the cathedrals of Toulouse and Agde, and the Archdeacons of Narbonne and Agde. This, like most councils, took place in the presence of other clergy of the lower ranks, and of certain important laymen and women.[6] Usually the laity are mentioned by name only when a council is dealing with property with which they are

[1] Devic and Vaissette, op. cit., iii. 78; *Marca hispanica*, cols. 379ff.

[2] Devic and Vaissette, op. cit., iii. 311; Martène and Durand, *Thesaurus*, iv. cols. 87ff.

[3] Devic and Vaissette, op. cit., iii. 323; P. de Marca, *De concordia Sacerdotii et Imperii*, ed. I. H. Boehmer (Bamberg, 1788), ii. 282.

[4] Devic and Vaissette, op. cit., iii. 56; S. Baluze, *Concilia Galliae Narbonensis* (Paris, 1668), 1ff.

[5] Devic and Vaissette, op. cit., iii. 461, 670; v. col. 959; Baluze, op. cit., 18ff.

[6] Devic and Vaissette, op. cit., vi. 3–5; vii. No. 1, p. 1; *Chronica Rogeri de Houeden*, ed. W. Stubbs, RS 1868–71.

concerned,[1] or when some subject such as the enforcement of the truce of God arises,[2] and only in such cases do they appear as signatories.[3]

The majority of records of these councils have survived because of their connection with grants of land or the privileges of churches, but two or three councils are of special interest for the light which they throw on procedure. The main business at the Council of Port, 896, was a complaint brought by a certain priest, Adalfredus, and the patron of his church, that the Bishop of Maguelonne had wrongly assigned part of his parish and its revenues to another church. After discussion in the council the bishop acknowledged that the complaint was well founded, and judgement was given in favour of Adalfredus. The wording of the sentence is important as it suggests that the whole assembly took part in the judgement: *omnes pariter, Episcopis quidem primum judicantibus, decreverunt.*[4] At the Council of Barcelona in 906 the Bishop of Ausona complained that the Archbishop of Narbonne had unjustly exacted a tribute from him and his predecessors. After discussion the archbishop said that he thought the complaint well founded, but as only six bishops were present in addition to himself suggested that the matter be postponed to a full council, *ad plenam synodum et perfectum duodenarium numerum confratrum nostrorum.* This was accepted, and at the council of St Thibéry in the following year, when all the bishops were present the case was settled in favour of the Bishop of Ausona.[5] The Council of Narbonne in March, 1091, also dealt with a case in which the Archbishop was both president and defendant.[6]

[1] E.g. Narbonne, 990, Devic and Vaissette, op. cit., iii. 210; Capestang, 1166, id., vi. 5f.

[2] E.g. Tuluges, c. 1045, id., v. chartes no. 186, col. 442; Narbonne, 1054, id., iii. 323.

[3] In the case of Narbonne, 1091, although the archbishop is said to have noted their signatures, in fact no names appear after those of the canons of Narbonne and the notary, Baluze, op. cit., 18ff.

[4] Baluze, op. cit., 4.

[5] Devic and Vaissette, v. col. 118.

[6] Baluze, op. cit., 18ff.

It seems then, that we are to think of the provincial synod of Narbonne during this period as composed of the archbishop and his suffragans, with the attendance of the more important of the clergy, abbots, and cathedral dignitaries, the proceedings taking place in the presence of a considerable congregation of the clergy and laity. The business of the council is the miscellaneous business of the province and includes the hearing of disputes between the bishops as well as of the complaints of clergy and laity.

This evidence accords not only with the law as found in Gratian and elsewhere, but also with the liturgical forms for the holding of provincial synods. In the absence of a thorough study of these forms by a competent scholar they must be used with some caution,[1] but it will not be amiss to take the two *Ordines* which are found in the geniune *Hispana* collection and in its enlarged forms as the False Decretals. The older of the two texts, that which belongs to the *Hispana*, has been mentioned already, and appears to belong to the Fourth Council of Toledo, 633.[2] The other is an expanded version of the same text and is found among the prefatory material of the Pseudo-Isidorian collection.[3] In the Toledan version the *Ordo* is preceded by some general regulations about councils, and it is said that circumstances make it impossible for the provincial synod to meet twice a year as the old decrees required. The place of meeting is to be chosen by the metropolitan, and is assumed to be a church. At the first hour of the day the building is to be emptied and all doors except one closed. Then the bishops are to enter in order of

[1] Dr Richard Kay of the University of Wisconsin is making a study of these *Ordines*. In addition to the two discussed in the text others may be found in E. Martène, *De antiquis Ecclesiae ritibus* (ed. novissima, Venice, 1783), ii. (1788), 306–17, Lib. iii, cap. 1; Andrieu, *Le Pontifical romain* (Vatican City, 1938–41), i. 255; ii. 479; iii. 596; Cf. G. Durandus, *De modo celebrandi consilii generalis*, Rubrica xi (in *Tractatus illustrium . . . jurisconsultorum*, Venice 1584, xiii, pars i, fol. 159v.).

[2] P. Hinschius, *Decretales Pseudo-Isidorianae et Capitula Angilramni* (Leipzig, 1863), 364f.

[3] Id., 22–4.

seniority of consecration, after them the presbyters *quos causa probaverit*, then the *diacones probabiles quos ordo poposcerit interesse*. The seats of the bishops are to be arranged in a *corona*, which probably means a semi-circle. The presbyters are to sit behind them and the deacons to stand in front. A small change here in the Pseudo-Isidorian version is significant of the heightened position of the metropolitan. The presbyters are said to have been chosen by him and to sit with him to judge and define. When these arrangements have been completed then the laity whom the council has chosen to be present shall enter and with them the notaries who are to record the acts, and then the doors are to be closed. After a pause for recollection the archdeacon is to say "Let us pray", and all are to prostrate themselves and remain for some time in silent prayer after which one of the senior bishops is to stand and pray aloud. In the Pseudo-Isidorian version the prayer which he is to say is provided from the *Ordo Romanus*. At the end of the prayer the bishops and presbyters resume their seats and a deacon, wearing an alb, comes forward with the book of the canons and reads the chapters concerning the holding of councils. These are listed in the Pseudo-Isidorian text. Then the metropolitan addresses the assembly. In the Toledan *Ordo* he invites the bishops to bring forward any matter that the reading of canons may have suggested or any cause of transgression of the canons. If any presbyter, deacon, clerk or layman of those who stand outside the assembly have any matter on which they wish to appeal to the council they are to tell it to the archdeacon of the metropolitical church who will report it to the council and they will then be given permission to enter and present their case. No bishop is to leave early and no one is to attempt to dissolve the council until all the business has been settled and the decisions have been subscribed by all the bishops, for God can be believed to be present if all is finished quietly and carefully and without disturbance.

The Pseudo-Isidorian *Ordo* diverges at this point. The metropolitan, who is apparently assumed to have delivered a homily on the canons, first asks any bishop who differs from what has been said to speak openly so that he may either be taught or teach, and then he exhorts the bishops to judge impartially without any respect of persons. Afterwards the clergy in general are admitted to the assembly and three days are spent in a kind of retreat during which instruction is given in the doctrines of the Trinity, and the Incarnation, and in the duties of the various clerical offices. On the fourth day the council passes to other business, and as in the Toledan *Ordo* the archdeacon reports appeals which have been made to the council and they are heard. There are the same prohibitions against early departure and against disturbance. Two or three days before the end of the council the bishops are to revise carefully all the constitutions which they have issued lest they offend in anything, and on the last day the canons made by the council are to be read publicly and at the end all are to say Amen. Then, returning to the place of meeting they (it is not clear whether this means the bishops only) are to subscribe the canons. The metropolitan is to give notice of the date of Easter and of the next year's council, and certain bishops are to be chosen to celebrate Christmas and Easter with the metropolitan. After further prayers the archdeacon says, "In the Name of our Lord Jesus Christ, let us go with peace", the kiss of peace is exchanged, beginning with the metropolitan, and the council is dissolved.

4

The Lateran Council held by Pope Innocent III in 1215 is one of the great climaxes, if not indeed the climax in the history of the medieval Church. In respect of penance and the eucharist, those two great practical centres of medieval religion, it brought a long development to completion. It inaugurated what was intended to be, and in many respects was, a century of ecclesiastical reform. It demonstrated the position of high authority over all Western Christendom which the papacy under Innocent had attained, and which it was still using for religious rather than political ends. It was probably the last great council of the Middle Ages in which political forces were not dominant.

One part of Innocent's scheme of reform was the re-establishment of annual provincial councils, and two of the seventy surviving canons of the council are concerned with this. Canon six, beginning with the words *Sicut olim a sanctis patribus noscitur institutum*, reminds metropolitans of the obligations to hold a council every year with their suffragans, in which matters needing reform are to be discussed and the decrees of the General Council read and applied. That these objects may be more effectively attained suitable persons are to be appointed in each diocese who are to take note throughout the year of what is amiss and report it to the next council. Decrees made in the provincial council are to be promulgated by each bishop in his diocesan synod which is also held every year. Canon thirty, beginning with the words *Grave nimis est et absurdum*, deals with a particular matter for the attention of provincial councils, namely the abuse by which bishops and chapters often appointed unworthy clerks to ecclesiastical benefices. The provincial council is to be vigilant in this matter and to suspend those who persist in wrong-doing after two admonitions. It is also to appoint suitable persons to act in place of those who are suspended. If the metropolitan himself is found guilty the council is to report him to his superior. Persons suspended on this count are only to be restored by the authority of the pope or of their patriarch.

These two canons were taken into the collection of the later legislation of Innocent III which is known as the *Compilatio, IV*, where they appear, the first under the title *De accusationibus* in Book V,[1] and the other under the title *De prebendis* in Book

[1] E. Friedberg, *Quinque Compilationes Antiquae* (Leipzig, 1882), 146.

III.[1] From there they were taken by Raimond of Peñaforte into the Decretal collection which he made by order of Gregory IX and which was published in 1234, and where they appear under the same titles.[2] The *Compilatio V* published by order of Honorius III in 1226 or 1227, contains a decretal of that pope which bears on the subject of provincial synods and may be one of the first outcomes of the Lateran legislation.[3] The cathedral chapters of the province of Sens had complained to Pope Honorius that although their proctors had been summoned to the provincial council the archbishop and his suffragans had refused to admit them to the deliberations, although it was known that matters affecting the chapters were often discussed in such councils. The pope regarded this complaint as well founded and, in the decretal, of which the extract in the Corpus begins *Etsi membra*, laid down that cathedral chapters ought to be invited to such councils, and their representatives admitted to the deliberations, particularly of matters which concerned them. In the *Compilatio* and in the Decretals of Gregory IX this letter exists as a mutilated fragment without date, and in some MSS. is attributed to Innocent III. In the early seventeenth century a copy of the original still survived in the *Trésor* of the Cathedral of Troyes, and happily part of it, including the address and date was printed by a learned advocate, Jean Rochette, in a treatise on beneficiary procedure.[4] This makes it possible to establish the date of issue as 25 February

[1] Id., 142.
[2] c. 25. X. v. 1; c. 29. X. iii. 5.
[3] Friedberg, op. cit., 171.
[4] J. Rochette, *Décisions de plusieurs questions et différens qui se presentent journellement, tant ès Cours Ecclésiastiques que Séculières sur Matières bénéficialdes de Mariages, Preuve, Appellations, circonstances et dépendances* (3rd edn. Troyes, 1614) f. 134. The text which he prints is as follows: Honorius III. &c. *Venerabilibus fratribus Archiepiscopo Seno. & suffraganeis, &c. Vtique nobis & eisdem fratribus nostris Concorditer visum est, vt ipsa capitula ad huiusmodi Concilia inuitari debeant, & eorum nuncij ad tractatus admitti, maxime super illis quae capitula ipsa contingere dignoscuntur. Ideoque volumus & praesentium vobis auctoritate mandamus, quatenus id de caetero sine disceptatione seruetis, &c.*
Datum Laterani, 5. Kal. Martij. Pontif. nostri an. primo 1216.

1217, in the first year of Honorius III. This decretal also passed in to the Gregorian collection where it appears, as in *Compilatio I*, under the title *De his que fiunt vel conceduntur a prelatis sine consensu capituli.*[1]

These three decretals *Sicut olim*, *Grave nimis* and *Etsi membra* provided later canonists with their principal points of comment on provincial councils, though one must supplement them occasionally by other references. This does not appear to be one of the canonical subjects in which a marked development of doctrine can be traced. One of the earliest commentators was Pope Innocent IV who wrote in the middle of the thirteenth century.[2] Because of his position his remarks were much quoted, although some of them did not win general acceptance, particularly his interpretation of *Etsi membra*, which is that the chapters need only be invited when matters concerning them are under discussion. On the whole, however, the amount of verbal repetition of one another in which lawyers always indulge, and comparative absence of development in the comments makes it possible to formulate shortly the canonical doctrine of provincial councils.

First there is the requirement of annual councils which is accepted as being the law, but far from observed in practice. Hostiensis [3] says that few metropolitans keep it, for some never celebrate such a council, some once only and the best only do it every other year.[4] The bishops of the province alone are of necessity bound to attend, and they, with the metropolitan, are the constituent element of the council. The cathedral chapters must be invited, especially, when

[1] c. 10. X. iii. 10.

[2] *Apparatus super V. lib. Decretalium.* I have used the edition published at Lyons in 1535.

[3] Henricus de Bartholomaeis (*al.* Henricus de Segusio), *In I-V Decretalium libros commentaria.* I have used the edition published at Venice in 1581.

[4] Id., comment on *Sicut olim;* cf. F. de Zabarella, *Super V Libros Decretalium Commentaria* (Venice, 1602), comment on the same canon: *Alique n. nunquam faciunt, aliqui semel tantum, aliqui raro.*

business concerning them is before the council. They attend by proctors who, having been invited, must be admitted to the deliberations unless the bishops are dealing with some matter put before them by their superior (pope, patriarch, or primate) which they have been forbidden to disclose, or are treating of some other thing which, for a just cause, should not be made public. Other persons have the right to be present and to be heard if their affairs are before the council, and they may be summoned before the council for trial and sentence.[1]

This appears to be as far as the obligations of attendance go, but there are further discussions of the desirability of persons other than the bishops and the chapters being present. It is said that heads of religious houses are not in general bound to attend, nor are the ordinary clergy, but Hostiensis thinks that it is in their own interests that they should. He points out that they are all bound by the decrees of the council and that if they have not attended they have missed the chance of raising objection to any of them.[2] On this he is quoted by Joannes Andreae [3] and others.[4]

The question is also raised as to whether the laity should attend. The canonists were familiar with a letter of Pope Celestine I, found in the *Decretum*, which opened with the words *Docendus est populus non sequendus*,[5] and the principle thus stated caused them to say firmly that the laity had no right to teach or judge in ecclesiastical matters. On the question of their presence at councils, however, there seems to have been some variety of opinion. There was, of course,

[1] Op. cit., comment on *Grave nimis*; Zabarella, op. cit., commenting on *Etsi membra*, says: "Not. quod citra capitula cathedralium ecclesiarum alia capitula collegiatarum non vocantur ad concilium provinciale, de illis enim disponitur per episcopum et capitulum."

[2] Op. cit., comment on c. 9 *Quod super*, X. i. 33.

[3] *Novella Commentaria.* I have used the edition published at Venice in 1581.

[4] E.g. Antonius a Butrio, *In Quinque libros Decretalium commentaria* (Venice, 1578), and F. de Zabarella, op. cit., in their comments on c. *Quod super*.

[5] c. 2. D. LXII.

no objection to their attendance as spectators and hearers, and the holding of a council was sometimes looked upon as an opportunity for instructing the laity, but the question of their participation in the proceedings was rather more difficult. Hostiensis allows that a layman may speak in a council in order to seek justice or defend himself against any charge, and he quotes from Gratian a letter of Pope Nicholas I (*c.* 865) in support of the presence of the laity in councils in which matters of the faith are being discussed because it concerns them. The like is true, he says, when marriage is the subject, but, he adds, the laity must be excluded when ecclesiastical business and the misdoings of the clergy are being treated.[1] Two lay canonists, Joannes Andreae and Petrus de Ancharano,[2] omit the reference to lay participation in the discussion of doctrine and marriage. Panormitanus [3] on the other hand, in the fifteenth century, somewhat strengthens the case. He notes that the gloss lists three circumstances in which laymen might be present at general councils. First, when they have been specially invited, second, if a matter of the faith is being discussed, and third, if marriage is being discussed *quia matrimonium tangit eos*. And from this last, he says, we may deduce the general rule that laymen can be present at a council whenever it is discussing business which concerns them. He goes on to note that Joannes Andreae much restricts the attendance of the laity saying first that in these cases the laymen attend only to hear, not to judge or teach, and secondly that their attendance is unnecessary as they can be informed in sermons of the decrees of the council. Panormitanus gives his own view on

[1] Op. cit., comment on *Etsi membra*.

[2] Joannes Andreae, op. cit., comment on *Etsi membra*; Petrus de Ancharano, *In quinque Decretalium libros commentaria* (Bologna, 1581), comment on *Etsi membra*.

[3] Nicholas de Tudeschis, *In Quinque libros Decretalium commentaria* (Lyons, 1555), comment on *Etsi membra*; cf. his fuller discussion of the participation of the laity in the work of councils in his *Quaestiones seu disputationes subtilissimae et utilissimae*, qu. 1 no. 27 (in *Quaestiones Iuris variae ac selectae*, Lyons, 1572).

the contrary that the laity are admitted to councils *ut consulant et ut materiam tractent* especially if they are *periti*, and he supports his opinion by quoting two instances of papal use of lay advisers. These examples are given in relation to general councils, but they are introduced into the comments on the decretal *Etsi membra* which concerns provincial councils, and the principles stated would appear to be applicable to them in their more restricted field of business.[1]

The commentators seem to envisage two sorts of meeting of the provincial councils. One is that expected by most of the canons, a regular routine session concerned with the general affairs of the province. The other is one summoned for a specific cause named in the citation. No one, whether bishop or lower cleric, is required to answer in council to a criminal charge unless he has been cited to appear for this purpose, but disciplinary matters of other kinds can be dealt with as part of the routine business. Charges against bishops can be heard and investigated, but the council has no power to depose, nor can it hear charges against the metropolitan. They must be forwarded to the pope. It is also understood by some of the commentators that a provincial council cannot deal with any complicated and lengthy case as its session is rarely prolonged for more than a few days.[2]

Hostiensis raises the question whether anyone who infringes statutes made by the provincial council can be absolved by the archbishop alone, and he says that this depends upon the form in which the statute is promulgated. He gives three variations all of which make the suffragans

[1] There was more medieval argument about the attendance of the laity at councils than can be adequately surveyed here. Reference may be made to R. E. H. J. Hashagen, *Staat und Kirche vor der Reformation. Eine untersuchung der vorreformatorischen Bedeutung des Laieneinflusses in der Kirche* (Essen, 1931); Y. M.-J. Congar, *Jalons pour une Théologie du Laicat* (2nd Edn. Paris, 1954); W. Ullmann, *Medieval Papalism* (London, 1949), 21; B. Tierney, *Foundations of the Conciliar Theory* (Cambridge, 1955), 49.

[2] E.g. Hostiensis on *Grave nimis*; cf. Joannes de Imola, *Commentaria in I, II, III Libros Decretalium* (Lyons, 1525), on the same canon.

legislators with the archbishop so that he cannot absolve alone unless he has been given or acquired by custom special power to do so. These formulae are: *nos concilium*, *nos archiepiscopus et episcopi in concilio suffraganeorum nostrorum in concilio congregatorum*. If however the statute runs in the archbishop's name, as *nos archiepiscopus de consilio fratrum nostrorum* (and he points out that counsel need not necessarily be followed), then the archbishop can absolve by himself.[1] This question of the relation of the suffragans to the metropolitan in respect of conciliar decisions was a difficult one. Most commentators stated that there was a difference of opinion as to whether the suffragans were assessors or judges, and most evaded the issue by saying that whichever they were what was done in council was invalid without them. The surviving provincial statutes of the Middle Ages vary a good deal as to which formula is used, though it seems to be the case that most of them were known as the statutes of particular archbishops.

5

This leads us to a second checking of theory by practice and we will again look at the councils of the province of Narbonne. Here, as elsewhere, there seems to have been some increase in synodical activity during the thirteenth century. Records of thirteen councils in the period 1212–79 survive. Two of these councils were assemblies of more than one province. The first, a legatine council held at Montpellier on 8 January 1215, concerted measures against the Albigensian heretics, elected Simon de Montfort as leader of the Catholic forces, and made a number of statutes concerning the reform of the clergy. It was attended by the Archbishops of Narbonne, Ausch, Embrun, Arles, and Aix, and twenty-eight of their suffragans. The legate, Peter of Benevento, had written to the Archbishop of Narbonne in the previous

[1] Comment on *Grave nimis*.

December, telling him of his intention to hold the council, and ordering him to summon the bishops, abbots, and archdeacons of his province, and any other persons whom he thought suitable. No record has been preserved of any discussion before the promulgation of the canons, but when the legate asked who should be given charge of the suppression of the heretics each bishop discussed the matter with the abbots of his diocese and his own clerks, and then gave his vote in writing. The legate's letter of summons made plain that his decision to hold the council had been taken after consultation with influential laymen, and it is evident that many of the laity attended the opening, but they do not seem to have taken any part in the discussions which the legate had with the bishops and others of the clergy.[1]

The other joint council was held at Béziers in April 1243, and was one of many assemblies which tried to deal with Raymond of Toulouse and the troubles caused by the Dominican inquisitors. It was attended by the Archbishops of Narbonne and Arles, and eight of their suffragans, together with a number of abbots, archdeacons and cathedral dignitaries. Many clerks, knights and other laymen are said to have been present.[2] Legatine councils of the province were held at Le Puy in 1222, and Béziers in 1234. The first of these is known only from a summons addressed to the canons of Narbonne;[3] the second was presided over by the Bishop of Tournai and made statutes concerning heretics, ordination, clerical behaviour, and similar subjects.[4]

Of the provincial councils proper we may note first the Council of Béziers in May 1279, for which a letter of summons has survived. It is addressed by the Archbishop of Narbonne to the bishops of the province, and requires them to put aside all other business and attend him in person at Béziers to discuss certain important and difficult matters which concern

[1] Baluze, op. cit., 38–58.
[2] *Gallia Christiana* (Paris, 1728–85), vi., Instrumenta col. 155.
[3] Id., Instrumenta col. 110.
[4] J. D. Mansi, *Concilia* (Venice, 1769–98), xxiii, col. 270ff.

the common condition of the churches of the province. It is not certain whether any other persons attended the council, but that the various colleges and religious communities of the province were concerned in the summons and in the business discussed is made plain by a letter addressed to them by the Archbishop in the course of which he refers to the council *ad cujus convocationem vestris credimus non modicum pepercisse laboribus et expensis*. He tells them of the decision that he and the Bishop of Toulouse should attend the next Parliament at Paris, to carry there the complaints of the province, and asks that they should seal the procuration which he sends them. The business appears to have concerned the liberties and immunities of the churches of the province, and the feudal dues owed by them.[1] Devic and Vaissette think that the same business was the subject of the provincial council summoned to meet at Béziers in Mid-Lent Sunday 1280 or 1281, and on this occasion the letters of the Bishop and chapter of Elne appointing proctors show that the summons to it had been addressed not only to the suffragans but also to the lesser prelates of the province.[2]

Such records as we have show that the presence of abbots and of representatives of chapters was normal. At Narbonne in April 1212 there were five abbots, an archdeacon, a sacrist, a precentor, a dean, and a canon, all from various churches of the province.[3] At Béziers in May 1255 there were ten abbots, proctors of three absent abbots, many archdeacons, precentors, and other ecclesiastical persons.[4] We may ask what part they took in the proceedings. Some indication is to be found in the terms in which proctors were appointed. In 1272 Peter, Abbot of Villemagne in the diocese of Béziers, constituted one of his monks as his proctor:

[1] Baluze, op. cit., 81–4.

[2] Baluze, op. cit., 84–7; Devic and Vaissette, op. cit., ix, 66; the year should probably be 1280; the two letters are dated 20 and 21 March, 1280, Mid-Lent Sunday fell in 1280 on 31 March, and in 1281 on 23 March, and Elne is a considerable distance from Béziers.

[3] Devic and Vaissette, op. cit., viii. cols. 619f.

[4] Baluze, op. cit., 66.

> to fulfil, ratify and approve what shall have been settled and ordained by you (i.e. the bishops) in the said provincial council, promising that we will ever hold good whatever shall have been done, ratified or approved in the said council by our reverend father in God the Bishop of Béziers or by the said proctor in our name.[1]

In 1280 the proctor of the chapter of Elne was commissioned to appear before the Archbishop in the provincial council, to hear the discussion of business concerning the general state of the whole province *et ad faciendum super praedictis prout memorato Concilio expedire visum fuerit et Deus ministrabit.*[2]

The formulae of legislation show some of the variation that Hostiensis noted. The Councils of Narbonne, 1227, Béziers, 1246, and Montpellier, 1258, all made statutes concerned mainly with reform, and in each case the Archbishop legislated with the counsel of his suffragans and the approval of the whole council. In 1227 a legatine decree was set out and there was added to it the words:

> which constitution we, Peter, Archbishop of Narbonne, with the counsel of our brothers and suffragans, and the approval of the whole provincial council, command, decree and order to be observed inviolably henceforth by all in the province of Narbonne.[3]

In other canons of this council we find the formula shortened to *duxit praesens concilium statuendum,*[4] *item statuit praesens synodus,*[5] and *fuit in praesenti concilio constitutum.*[6] In 1246 the

[1] Devic and Vaissette, op. cit., x, preuves, cols. 121f: "pro complendo ratificando et approbando que per vos (sc. the bishops) fuerint in dicto provinciali concilio constituta seu etiam ordinata promittentes nos perpetuo ratum habituros quidquid per reverendum in Christo patrem nostrum Biterrensem episcopum aut per dictum procuratorem nostrorum nomine in dicto concilio factum fuerit, ratificatum seu etiam approbatum."

[2] Baluze, op. cit., 87.

[3] J. Hardouin, *Conciliorum collectio regia maxima* (Paris, 1714–15), vii. col. 145: "Quam constitutionem nos Petrus archiepiscopus Narbonensis de consilio fratrum et suffraganeorum nostrorum et approbatione totius provincialis concilii, mandamus et statuimus, atque praecipimus, de cetero in provincia Narbonensi ab omnibus inviolabiliter observari."

[4] Id., col. 146. [5] Ibid. [6] Id., col. 147.

Archbishop legislated *de consilio suffraganeorum ecclesiae Narbonensis et totius approbatione concilii*,[1] and in 1258 we have the formula:

> Therefore we, James, by the divine mercy Archbishop of the holy Church of Narbonne . . . with the consent of our venerable brethren and the approval of the present council, have been led to decree the things which are set out below for the good estate of our province.[2]

At the Council of Béziers in 1255 a different form was used. The occasion of the Council was a request from the Seneschal of Carcassone and Béziers for help in the siege of the castle of Querbus which was held by the Albigensians, and the council decided that although its members were not bound by law and feudal obligation to do so they would nevertheless give *ex gratia* assistance. The decisive formula comes at the end of a long list of those present, including abbots, archdeacons, and other ecclesiastical persons, and reads *unanimiter deliberato consilio habita inter se deliberatione diligenti, convenerunt et repperierunt.*[3]

As regards the presence of the bishops at the councils it should be noted that lack of consecration did not preclude them from attendance. The Council of Narbonne in April 1212, met among other purposes for the consecration of a new archbishop. This ceremony, which also included the consecration of a new Bishop of Carcassone, took place on 2 May, but earlier than that the Archbishop-elect had presided over the council which was also attended by the Bishop-elect.[4] The Council of 1272 took place during the vacancy of the archbishopric. The Bishop of Béziers heads the list of those present, and probably presided. The proxy of the Abbot of Villemagne, quoted above, is addressed to the five bishops

[1] Mansi, op. cit., xxiii, col. 691.

[2] Id., col. 989: "Inde est quod nos Jacobus miseratione divina sanctae Narbonensis ecclesiae archiepiscopus . . . de consensu venerabilium fratrum nostrorum, praesenti concilio approbante, ad bonum statum nostrae provinciae duximus statuenda, quae inferius declarantur."

[3] Baluze, op. cit., 66.

[4] Devic and Vaissette, op. cit., vi, 380; viii, cols. 619f.

who were there, the Bishop-elect of Carcassonne, and the chapter of Narbonne or its proctors.[1] This suggests that the chapter ranked with the episcopal college, presumably as guardians of the spiritualities, during the vacancy of the archbishopric.

The Council of Narbonne, 1227, in its last canon required that the provincial council should be assembled each year on mid-Lent Sunday.[2] For the most part, however, the councils of which we have record seem to have been held in the Spring or Autumn. It is most unlikely that the annual rule was observed.

In the fourteenth and fifteenth centuries provincial councils seem to have been noticeably less frequent. We can scarcely count twelve in the period 1299 to 1430, and of these three are known only because the compilers of the *Gallia Christiana* had records of the attendance or absence of Bertrand, Bishop of Nîmes, records which seem to have now vanished.[3] It is some compensation that Baluze has preserved and published unusually full records of the citations and statutes. Two points in respect of composition call for comment. In Narbonne as in other French provinces in 1294 representatives of the parochial clergy were summoned to discuss a grant to the king. We shall have to look at this again in another connection, but it may be emphasized here that their attendance at this council appears to be an isolated phenomenon unless the term *clerus universus* at the Council of Lavaur in 1368 is to be understood to include representatives of the lower clergy.[4]

The presence of the religious, however, assumes greater prominence. To the Council of Béziers in 1299 came abbots, *aliique praelati*, and proctors of chapters.[5] In 1302 the citation contains the formula: *vos prefatum capitulum nostrum necnon abbates, conventus, et ceteros viros ecclesiasticos, qui ad nostrum*

[1] Id., x, preuves, cols. 121f.
[2] Hardouin, op. cit., vii, col. 148.
[3] *Gallia Christiana*, vi, col. 449.
[4] Baluze, op. cit., 117.
[5] Id., 88.

provinciale concilium citari consueverunt seu debent de usu consuetudine vel de jure.[1] In 1351 the bishops were directed to summon *omnes et singulos Abbates, Praepositos, Decanos et Priores Ecclesiarum collegiatarum et alias personas ecclesiasticas regulares et saeculares non exemptas, quae debent et consueverunt in dictis Conciliis interesse de usu, consuetudine, vel de jure.*[2] The council of 1368 was held in pursuance of a letter from Pope Urban V which required all the French archbishops to assemble provincial councils. At their own request the Archbishops of Narbonne, Toulouse and Ausch were allowed to hold their councils together. On this occasion, by papal authority, those religious orders which were normally exempt from diocesan and provincial jurisdiction were required to be present.[3] This was also the case in 1374 when again the Narbonne provincial council was held under papal direction.[4] At the councils of 1302 and 1351 the exempt religious had been exhorted but not required to attend, as were the non-exempt.

The very full records which have been preserved of citations to the councils of 1351, 1368, and 1374 [5] allow us to see something of the procedure involved. The council was always summoned by the archbishop himself or, if he was absent, by the vicar-general at his direction, and the citation was transmitted directly to the other bishops of the province and to the cathedral chapters. Each person who received a summons was required to affix his seal and return the document by the same bearer in token of his acceptance. Generally a formal note expressing obedience was added. The bishops were expected each to summon the representatives of the religious communities in his diocese, and in the diocese of Narbonne the archbishop summoned the abbots through the archpriests to each of whom he addressed a special mandate.

If the archbishop did not attend in person his vicar-general

[1] Devic and Vaissette, op. cit., x, preuves col. 398.
[2] Baluze, op. cit., 93.
[3] Id., 118.
[4] Id., 309.
[5] Id., 91–9; 115–23; 301–6.

presided over the council. This was so at Narbonne in May 1430, when the Bishop of Castres, who was vicar-general at the time, presided over a council attended by five bishops and the proctors of five other absent bishops.[1] The Council of Saint-Thibéry in July 1389, was attended by no bishop in person, but composed entirely of proctors, presided over by John Picorlati, licentiate in decrees, the archbishop's vicar-general and locum tenens. It made arrangements for the reception of the king in the province, drew up a list of gravamina, some to be presented to the king and some to the pope, and agreed upon a tax to be levied in each diocese to defray the expenses of these proceedings. The archbishop was to be asked to confirm what had been done and to summon a provincial council every year.[2]

In 1351 [3] and 1374 [4] the bishops were told to summon diocesan synods before the provincial council met, and to give notice in them of the forthcoming council and its business, so that no one who ought to attend might plead ignorance. In 1368, however, they were told merely to exhibit the summons frequently and in the most public way possible in their cathedral and elsewhere,[5] possibly because the interval between the issue of the citation and the date of meeting was short,[6] and the place of meeting, Lavaur, was some distance outside the province.

In the matter of attendance at provincial councils the evidence for Narbonne may be supplemented by that for the province of Sens. Here we can count twenty councils in the thirteenth century, eleven in the fourteenth, and seven in the fifteenth.[7] In the twelfth and thirteenth centuries those

[1] Martène, *Thesaurus novus*, iv. col. 351. [2] Id., col. 341ff.
[3] Baluze, op. cit., 93. [4] Id., 304. [5] Id., 119.
[6] In 1351 the summons was dated 28 September, and the council fixed for 7 November; in 1368 the summons was dated 28 April, and the council fixed for 27 May; in 1374 the summons was dated 1 February and the council 15 April.
[7] These figures are derived by putting together information found in E. Martène and U. Durand, *Veterum scriptorum et monumentorum amplissima collectio* (Paris, 1724–33); Hardouin, *Concilia*, vii; *Gallia Christiana*; and

summoned seem always to have been the non-exempt abbots and priors and the cathedral chapters, though sometimes the chapters of collegiate churches are mentioned also, and on one occasion, 1257, in a somewhat obscurely worded document the chapters of rural deaneries seem to have been summoned.[1] In the fifteenth century, however, the exempt were cited also, and to the Council of Paris in 1429, representatives of the University of Paris were summoned.[2] In 1461, at the Council of Sens, the abbots, priors and chapters protested against being cited under penalty and secured a declaration from the archbishop that no prejudice to anybody's rights was intended by the citation and that the chapters and others appeared without threat of being punished.[3] In the main the evidence for Sens and Narbonne agrees with that for Bourges,[4] Rheims,[5] and Rouen.[6]

6

Before this introductory section is brought to a close, one further subject must be outlined, namely the taxation of clerical property in the later Middle Ages. By the middle of

---

documents transcribed in Bibl. Nat. MSS. Baluze Nos. 5, 12, and 13. I hope eventually to be able to make a fuller study of the councils of this province.

[1] Martène and Durand, *Vet. Script. Coll.*, vii, col. 147.

[2] MSS. Baluze, Nos. 5, f 139; No. 13, ff 276 and 281 v.; cf. Hardouin, op. cit., viii, col. 1039.

[3] Printed by J. Rochette, op. cit., fols. 134 v.–6; copies still exist at Troyes, Archives de l'Aube, G. 2550, and at Auxerre, Archives de l'Yonne, G. 1818. The relation of cathedral chapters to provincial councils seems to have been a repeated source of trouble in France, see H. Nélis, "La 'Congrégation' des chapitres cathédraux de la province ecclésiastique de Reims à Saint-Quentin (1331–1428)" in *RHE*, xxv (1929), 447–70; J. Filleau, *Traicté des Droicts, Prérogatives, et Preéminences des Églises Cathédrales dans les Conciles Prouinciaux* (Paris, 1628).

[4] L. de Lacger, "La primatie et le pouvoir métropolitain de l'archevêque de Bourges au xiii siècle" in *RHE*, xxvi (1930), 283–94.

[5] Th. Gousset, *Les actes de la province ecclésiastique de Reims* (Reims, 1842–4); H. Nélis, op. cit.

[6] F. Pommeraye, *S. Rothomagensis Ecclesiae concilia ac synodalia decreta* (Rouen, 1677); T. Bonnin, *Registrum visitationum Archiepiscopi Rothomagenesis* (Rouen, 1852).

the twelfth century the property and revenues of the Church had in many countries increased to such an extent that the desirability of subjecting them to forms of taxation similar to those that were being worked out in regard to secular income forced itself upon men's minds. At the Third Lateran Council in 1179 the subject was discussed as being a serious menace to the Church, and a canon was made which strictly forbade lay rulers to exact subsidies from clerks and churches, but allowed the exception that a bishop and his clergy might make a grant if they thought the need sufficiently great and the support to be derived from the laity not adequate.[1] This canon, beginning with the words *Non minus*, passed into the *Compilatio I*[2] and thence into the Decretals of Gregory IX.[3] It was found, however, not to be a sufficient safeguard, and so, at the Fourth Lateran Council, 1215, it was strengthened by the requirement that the pope should be consulted before any such subsidy was granted.[4] This canon also passed into the Decretals of Gregory IX, and will be referred to by its first word *Adversus*.[5]

As will appear later in this book, these prohibitions were occasionally quoted in England in the period 1215–90 to justify clerical resistance to royal requests for a subsidy, and their existence may have been one of the causes for the repeated applications made by Henry III to successive popes for the imposition of a subisdy on the English clergy. It seems probable that in the reigns of Louis IX and Philip III something similar happened in France. Towards the end of the century, however, in both countries papal assistance was not so easily to be had, and in 1294, in contemplation of war

[1] Quocirca sub anathematis districtione severius prohibemus, ne de cetero talia praesumant attentare, nisi episcopus et clerus tantam necessitatem vel utilitatem aspexerint, ut absque ulla coactione, ad relevandas communes necessitates, ubi laicorum non suppetunt facultates, subsidia per ecclesias existiment conferenda.

[2] Friedberg, op. cit., 43.

[3] c. 4. X. iii. 49.

[4] Propter imprudentiam tamen quorumdam romanum prius consulant pontificem, cujus interest communibus utilitatibus providere.

[5] c. 7. X. iii. 49.

with England the government of Philip IV of France decided to raise money by direct dealings with the clergy. In the summer and autumn of that year provincial councils were summoned at the King's request and a subsidy of a tenth for two years was granted.[1] Unfortunately hardly any of the citations to these councils seem to have survived, but that for the province of Bourges, which has, is of exceptional interest as it shows that on this occasion representatives of the lower clergy were summoned in addition to those whom we have seen as the usual attendants at provincial councils.[2] Early in 1296 another council was held in this province, apparently also about the matter of a subsidy, and to it also representatives of the lower clergy were summoned. This time, however, they were told that if they chose to stay away they would not be held contumacious provided that they gave their consent to the decisions of the council in so far as they were affected by them.[3] In view of this provision it is particularly interesting to find among the Baluze manuscripts copies taken from originals in the archives of the Bishop of Albi, of legal agreements made by forty-six rectors, vicars, and chaplains that they will hold themselves bound by whatever the Bishop of Albi shall agree to in the council.[4] It is difficult not to suppose that this unusual attendance of the lower clergy was dictated by the need to obtain their consent to taxation.

On 24 February 1296, however, Pope Boniface VIII issued the bull *Clericis laicos*, which strictly forbade clerical grants without the papal consent and imposed automatic penalties of excommunication.[5] The bull seems to have been inspired

[1] G. Digard, *Philippe le Bel et le Saint-Siège de 1285 à 1304* (Paris, 1936), i. 253–7; J. R. Strayer and C. H. Taylor, *Studies in Early French Taxation* (Harvard, 1939), 25–9; cf. F. Lot and R. Fawtier, *Histoire des Institutions françaises au Moyen Age* (Paris, 1951 ff), ii. *Institutions royales*, 207f.

[2] E. Martène and U. Durand, *Thesaurus novus*, iv. col. 214; MSS. Baluze, No. 6, fols. 5–7.

[3] Martène and Durand, op. cit., cols. 217–20.

[4] MSS. Baluze, No. 6, fols. 19–23.

[5] c. 3. In VI°. iii. 23; cf. *Registrum Roberti Winchelsey*, ed. R. Graham (*CY*, 1952–6), 159–62.

by a concern for Italy as much as by the problems of France and England, but it was in France that the lay reactions were most immediate.[1] Boniface was forced to make a gradual retreat until, on 31 July 1297, in the bull *Etsi de statu regni*, he declared that the French prelates and clergy could make a grant to the king whenever they judged themselves conscientiously able to do it, and as they had been able to do before the publication of *Clericis laicos*.[2] After his death, his successor, Clement V annulled *Clericis laicos* altogether and restored the situation as it had existed before 1296.[3]

The two canons *Non minus* and *Adversus* were the subject of much comment by writers of the fourteenth and fifteenth centuries, and there were divergences of interpretation.[4] Petrus de Ancharano who, it must be remembered, was a layman, thought that the clergy ought to share in the common burden of taxation for the defence of a town or a country, for the upkeep of fortifications and other public works such as breakwaters. It was only reasonable, he argued, that as clerks and laymen enjoyed the same benefits they should both contribute to the expenses. He added that he had heard from a trustworthy person that in England the churches were required to bear a fourth part of the burdens which were imposed generally for the necessities of the realm, but, he observed, this agreement could not be based on law if the Roman pontiff has not been consulted, and he propounded his general view with some hesitation.[5] Panormitanus did not altogether agree with him. He was disposed to hold rather strictly to the wording of *Non minus*. A grant might be made by the bishop and clergy (in this matter the consent of the chapter alone would not suffice) only for the

[1] Digard, op. cit., 261–97; 341f.
[2] *Régistres de Boniface VIII*, ed. Digard et al. (Paris, 1884–1939), no. 2354; see below pp. 69–80.
[3] c. un. in Clem. iii. 17.
[4] G. Le Bras, "L'évolution générale de la théorie canonique de l'immunité réelle depuis la publication des Clémentines jusqu'au concile de Trente", in *Rev. des sciences religieuses*, ii. (1922), 411–27.
[5] Petrus de Ancharano, op. cit. comment on *Non minus*.

common needs and profit of both clergy and laity, and to meet which the means of the laity were insufficient. He added that the canon *Adversus* required that the pope be consulted first. In another paragraph, however, he appears to think that where so great a necessity threatens that recourse to the pope cannot be had without great scandal or danger then the consent of the bishop and clergy alone will suffice.[1] There can be little doubt that arguments such as these were responsible for the wording of some of the writs and citations by which the English clergy were assembled to consider royal requests for subsidies. As will be seen in a later chapter, emphasis was often laid upon the imminent danger to the realm, upon the common peril to all both clergy and laity, and upon the inability of the king to defend the realm without financial assistance from the clergy.

7

The purpose of this lengthy introduction has been to sketch the background against which the development of the English Convocations must be seen and without which it cannot be properly understood. There is still a tendency to regard them as a peculiarly English institution, a tendency illustrated by a sentence in the current (eighth) edition of one of the principal textbooks of Ecclesiastical Law: "The Convocation, in its origin, was for the purpose of taxation and no other; it was altogether unlike the Convocation of the foreign synods, collected to declare what was the doctrine, or what should be the discipline, of the Church."[2] This sentence appears to be divided ultimately, by unintelligent abridgement, from the eighteenth century treatise on Ecclesiastical Law by Dr Richard Burn. There, however,

[1] Nicholas de Tudeschis, op. cit., comment on *Non minus*.

[2] H. W. Cripps, *A Practical Treatise on the Law relating to the Church and Clergy*, 8th edn. by K. M. Macmorran (London, 1937), 5; cf. 4th edn. (1863), 24, and R. Burn, *Ecclesiastical Law*, 5th edn. (London, 1788), ii. 20.

something like it stands in a much fuller and more historical treatment of the subject. Both historically and theologically the origin of the Convocations must be sought in the provincial synod as known both to the primitive Canon Law and to the developed law of the Middle Ages. It has been important to glance at the subject of taxation because, as we shall see, it was the necessity for obtaining consent to taxation which enlarged the membership of the provincial synods and drew them into a close relationship with Parliament.

As we look back over the long development outlined in the preceding pages our first impression may well be one of institutional conservatism, and certainly the persistence of what is recognizably the same institution through thirteen or fourteen hundred years of changing society is very remarkable. But this conservatism should not be allowed to obscure the theme of reform, which is also constant. In the history of the Church there have always been great gaps between theory and practice, between ideals and their fulfilment, but it was never entirely forgotten, before the eighteenth century, that the purpose of the Church's existence is radical and revolutionary. The law and its machinery were not seen as ends in themselves, but as means to teach and enable the people of God to worship and serve God better, and whether it was the Council of Nicea organizing the Church in the new Christian Empire, or St Boniface rebuilding upon the ruins of Roman Christianity in the Rhineland, or Innocent III with his broad vision of the moral and spiritual renewal of Europe, or the prelates of France and England faced with a divided and decadent papacy, the call of those who summoned provincial councils was always *pro excessibus corrigendis et moribus reformandis*.

LECTURE 3

14 February 1960

ENGLISH COUNCILS AND TAXATION IN THE THIRTEENTH CENTURY

Let the lawes be rehersed of the good bestowyng of the patrimony of Christe: the lawes that commande that the goodes of the churche be spent, nat in costly byldyng, nat in sumptuous apparell and pompis, nat in feastyng and bankettynge, nat in excesse and wantonnes, nat in enrichinge of kynsfolke, nat in kepynge of dogges, but in thinges profitable and necessary to the churche.

John Colet, *Convocation Sermon*, 1512.

1

THE PREVIOUS lecture has already touched upon important features of the organization of the pre-Conquest English Church. It is not proposed to discuss the councils of that period in any detail, partly because they are of only limited importance for the development of the medieval Convocations, and partly because any full account of this period would require qualifications as a student of Old English which the present lecturer does not possess.

There is, however, no reason to think that the ecclesiastical assemblies of the period were substantially different from their continental contemporaries and much to suggest that they were similar. There is often the same difficulty as we find in the Carolingian domains in distinguishing clearly between secular and ecclesiastical councils. Close co-operation between crown and episcopate was a characteristic of the English reformation of the tenth century as of the Carolingian of the eighth and ninth. But we must be careful to avoid the suggestion that no distinction is possible. Liebermann has put forward the following criteria:

> To an ecclesiastical synod we ought to assign those documents which were given in an assembly characterized as pontifical or sacerdotal, secondly those which mention churchmen only in the middle of the text as the enacting power, and at the bottom as consenting witnesses, and thirdly those which concern clerical affairs only. Among the latter is to be included the synodal confirmation of an act of the secular power, such as the abolishment of the archbishopric of Lichfield, or the amicable arbitration between ecclesiastics, though their quarrel turns on land or landrent. The assembly may be convened and even presided over by the King; lay nobles may be passively present,

and the secular power may even confirm the decrees: all this would not militate against the character of a synod.[1]

Although for much of the period provincial divisions were not sharply defined it is plain that, as political conditions allowed, regional assemblies of the north or of the south were held from time to time. The bishops seem to have been the enacting parties but abbots, presbyters, and occasionally other clerks, appear frequently among the signatories to the decrees of the councils.

The reorganization of the English Church after the Norman Conquest necessitated the holding of councils, and for some of these it is as difficult as before the Conquest to distinguish between secular and ecclesiastical assemblies. However, sharper distinction between the two jurisdictions was to be introduced gradually under the influence of the ideas of the continental reformers, and a first indication of this is seen in the famous ordinance of the Conqueror which separated the secular and ecclesiastical courts at the diocesan and shire level.[2] But even during the time of the investiture controversy there was still a conjunction of the two authorities, as we can see in the councils of 1102 and 1108 in which ecclesiastical decrees were supported by the king and magnates.[3] Nor did the Becket controversy altogether disturb this harmony. The council of Westminster held by Archbishop Richard of Dover in May 1175, opened in the presence of the two Kings Henry II and his son the young Henry, and its canons were promulgated *assensu domini regis et primorum omnium regni.*[4] This, incidentally appears to be the first council to which in contemporary writing the term *provinciale concilium* is applied.[5]

[1] F. Liebermann, *The National Assembly in the Anglo-Saxon period* (Halle, 1913), 15. Cf. R. R. Darlington, "Ecclesiastical Reform in the late Old English period", *EHR*, LI. (1936).

[2] W. Stubbs, *Select Charters and other illustrations of English constitutional history*, ed. H. W. C. Davis (9th edn. Oxford, 1929), 99f.

[3] Eadmer, *Historia Novorum in Anglia*, ed. M. Rule (*RS*, 1884), 141, 193.

[4] *The historical works of Gervase of Canterbury*, ed. W. Stubbs (*RS*, 1879), i. 251–5.

[5] By William of Newburgh in *Chronicles of Stephen, Henry II and Richard I*, ed. R. Howlett (*RS*, 1884), i. 203.

Nevertheless from the time of Becket, at least, the English clergy were very sensitive on the matter of secular encroachments upon ecclesiastical jurisdiction, and the theme of the liberties of the English Church, which means, shortly, freedom to obey the canon law, and is embodied in the first clause of *Magna Carta*, became dominant in the meetings of Church councils.

The first indication is perhaps to be seen in *generale concilium* of the province of Canterbury held by Hubert Walter in September 1200. In all the references to it there is no mention of any royal participation or secular confirmation of its decrees, and some significance therefore, must be attached to Roger of Howden's statement that the council was held "against the prohibition of Geoffrey Fitzpeter, earl of Essex, at that time chief justiciar of England".[1]

In the thirteenth and fourteenth centuries conflict between Church and State over the limits of their respective jurisdictions was intermittent, and influenced both the development of a system of national taxation and the growth of an ecclesiastical representative assembly. By the year 1200 the needs of the English government were greater than could be adequately met by the recognized sources of taxation. A marked rise in the standard of living, greater complexity in administration and more elaborate methods of warfare had been the chief causes of this development. The country was exceedingly prosperous and the problem how to tap the wealth that was there. Ironically, as it turned out, it was the Church which showed the way in which income and chattels could be taxed as well as land. In 1166, at the command of Henry II, following the example of Louis VII of France, a levy of 2d in the pound for the first year and a penny in the pound in each of the four following years of all movables was made in answer to an appeal for the relief of the Holy Land. Every man was to assess himself and put his payments into a

[1] *Chronica Rogeri de Houeden*, ed. W. Stubbs (*RS*, 1870), iii. 294–8.

chest provided for the purpose in each parish. A similar method was used in 1188, again for the assistance of the crusade, but with the addition of a jury of assessment if any individual was thought to have made a false return. In 1193–4 these precedents were followed in raising the money for the King's ransom, and in 1203 and 1207 for the raising of a general tax for government purposes.[1]

The Church was in a difficulty about its own property and revenues. On the one hand the holding of land was, in most cases, acknowledged as carrying with it certain feudal obligations, on the other, much of the income of churches and clergy could be regarded as alms given for the support of the services and other work of the church and therefore not properly to be diverted to any secular ends.

2

The first attempt at royal or papal taxation in the time of Henry III arose out of a scheme proposed by Pope Honorius III that one prebend in every cathedral and prebendal church, a fixed payment proportioned to their resources from every monastery, and perpetual gifts from each bishop, should be set aside to provide an income for the officers of the papal court so that the fees charged by them and the gratuities that they demanded might be drastically reduced. This proposal was considered by two assemblies in 1226 to the first of which were summoned the bishops, deans, archdeacons, abbots, and conventual priors, and to the second the same persons and also proctors from the cathedrals and other collegiate churches and monasteries. With the support of the King it was turned down.[2] At the same time Henry had succeeded in getting from the pope an order that the archbishops, bishops, provosts, and other prelates and rectors of churches should provide him with a caritative

[1] S. K. Mitchell, *Taxation in Medieval England* (Yale, 1951), 114–34.

[2] W. E. Lunt, *Financial Relations of the papacy with England to 1327* (Cambridge, Mass., 1939), 178–86.

subsidy, and each bishop was asked to put the mandate into effect in his diocese.[1] The chapter of Salisbury, considering the difficulties that might arise if there were not some uniformity of reply asked their bishop to induce the archbishop to summon proctors representing all the churches concerned to appear before him and agree on a common reply. An assembly of this kind was held in London on 14 October 1226, and eventually a grant of a sixteenth was agreed. The archdeacons attended as did the representatives of the cathedrals and monasteries, but not those of the lower clergy, unless they had instructed the archdeacons to represent them.[2]

In 1240 the legate Otto was charged with the collection of a subsidy demanded by Gregory IX to finance him in his conflict with the Emperor Frederic II. The bishops seem to have done their best to put the legate off, and eventually, according to Matthew Paris, said to him "we have archdeacons under us who know the capacity of the beneficed clergy subject to them, whereas we do not. This business touches all and all therefore ought to be summoned. It is neither fitting nor expedient to reply without them." Professor Lunt and others doubt the authenticity of this reply, but whether Paris was right or not the legate did issue a formal summons to the bishops requiring them to cite the deans, archdeacons, abbots, abbesses, priors and prioresses and chapters of cathedrals and other churches to appear before him, and also with the help of the archdeacons to admonish and persuade the lesser deans, rectors and vicars to give a liberal aid. Here we see a definite voice allowed to the lower clergy in their diocesan assemblies.[3]

[1] Id., 187f.

[2] *Vetus registrum Sarisberiense*, ed. W. H. Rich Jones (*RS*, 1884), ii. 55–76; cf. K. Major, *Acta Stephani Langton* (CY, 1950), 106–8, 112f.

[3] Lunt, op. cit., 197–205; cf. id. "The consent of the English lower clergy to taxation during the reign of Henry III", in *Persecution and Liberty: Essays in honor of George Lincoln Burr* (New York, 1932), 126–32; *Matthaei Parisiensis, monachi sancti Albani, chronica majora*, ed. H. R. Luard (*RS*, 1872–83), iv. 37.

It is probable that local consent of this kind was also obtained in 1247 when another papal legate was told by the bishops that they would acquire a reputation as robbers and rouse rebellion among the lower clergy if they agreed to a subsidy without consultation with them, but offered to try to secure assent to a grant of 11,000 marks.[1]

In 1250 Henry III induced Pope Innocent IV to give him a tenth of ecclesiastical revenues for three years to finance a crusade, and with a little difficulty persuaded the bishops to confirm it.[2] But in 1254 when he asked directly for further aid the bishops said that they could do nothing without the consent of their clergy, and so were directed to consult with the abbots, priors, and clergy of their dioceses, and to have representatives appointed to attend the great council at Westminster on 26 April. At that meeting the clergy offered to appropriate to the King's new business in Gascony the proceeds of one of the years of the papal tenth, but with conditions attached which made the grant ineffective.[3] Almost at once the King's attention was diverted from Gascony by the papal offer of the crown of Sicily to his younger son Edmund, the price being Henry's support for the Pope against Manfred, illegitimate son of the Emperor. In 1255 Alexander IV commuted Henry's crusading vow to the Sicilian expedition and authorized the use for it of the money granted by Innocent for the crusade. New papal collectors were sent to England who attempted unsuccessfully to impose a new assessment of clerical incomes. This attempt was finally defeated in an assembly, whether provincial or national is not clear, which contained bishops, abbots, priors, archdeacons, deans of cathedrals, proctors of cathedral chapters, and three or four proctors of the lower clergy of each archdeaconry, the first recorded instance of the attendance

[1] Paris, *Chron. majora*, iv. 599f, 622f; vi. 145; Lunt, *Financial Relations*, 220–5; *Consent*, 136f.

[2] Lunt, *Financial Relations*, 255; id. *The Valuation of Norwich* (Oxford, 1926), 52–95.

[3] Lunt, *Consent*, 143; *Valuation*, 62, cf. 186.

of the lower clergy at a provincial or national convocation.[1] They were not summoned to the assemblies held in 1257 about a further papal grant to the crown, nor apparently to an assembly in 1267 when a grant to the King of a triennial tenth was imposed by papal authority and further tenth asked for by the King refused.

In 1269 a clerical assembly at the New Temple at the time of the October parliament was presented with a royal request for a subsidy. There were present nine bishops, and proctors of the abbots, priors, rectors, and vicars of all the dioceses of England and Wales except Bangor and St Asaph. The subsidy was refused, the clergy appealing to the canonical prohibition of the Fourth Lateran, as well as alleging the many exactions from which they and the bishops had suffered in recent times.[2] In the following year Henry III summoned a council of the archbishops, bishops, and prelates at which he asked for a subsidy for himself and the Lord Edward for the crusade. Those present made an immediate grant of a twentieth of personal property of themselves and of the villeins on their demesnes but it was only after diocesan assemblies had been summoned and there had been much discussion with the lower clergy that the grant was extended to them.[3]

We must add to these meetings held in connection with taxation a number of other ecclesiastical assemblies in this reign. First, there are some which seem to fit the concept of an ecclesiastical council as envisaged by the canon law. We know of two clear cut provincial councils of the province of Canterbury, from which legislation proceeded, those held by

[1] *Annales monastici*, ed. H. R. Luard (*RS*, 1864–9), i. 351, 360–3; Paris, *Chron. majora*, v. 524–7, 532; vi. 314; cf. Lunt, *Consent*, 145.

[2] D. Wilkins, *Concilia Magnae Britanniae et Hiberniae* (London, 1737), ii. 19f; cf. Lunt, *Consent*, 161.

[3] *Historical papers and letters from the northern registers*, ed. J. Raine (*RS*, 1873), 24, 38; *Royal and other historical letters illustrative of the reign of Henry III*, ed. W. W. Shirley (*RS*, 1862–8), ii. 336; Wilkins, op. cit., ii. 21; *CPR* (*1266–72*), 431, 508, 513, 536; *The register of Walter Giffard*, ed. W. Brown (*SS*, 1904), 211.

Stephen Langton at Oxford in 1222,[1] and by Boniface of Savoy at Lambeth in 1261.[2] With these should be grouped the legatine councils held by Otto in 1237,[3] and Ottobuono in 1265 and 1268.[4] Unfortunately we have no information about the composition of the 1222 council. Archbishop Boniface was directed by the Pope to summon to his council, in addition to the bishops, the religious and secular prelates, exempt and non-exempt, and this almost certainly included the cathedral chapters. Otto's council was attended by the archbishops, bishops, abbots priors, deans, and archdeacons, and it is probable that the same persons are intended by the rather vague terms used to describe the composition of the councils of Ottobuono. On the whole the composition of this type of council, whether legatine or provincial, is similar to that of earlier times. It did not include any representation of the lower clergy.

Side by side with these formal assemblies can be discovered several others which were concerned with ecclesiastical or mixed business. During the vacancy at Canterbury in 1233 a royal mandate was issued warning all bishops who were about to meet at Gloucester on the morrow of St Katharine that, as they loved their baronies, they should not presume to hold a council touching anything belonging to the crown, or affecting the King's person or his estate or the estate of his council. It is possible that this referred either to attempts being made by certain bishops to mediate between the King and the Earl Marshal, or to the King's attacks on the Bishop of Carlisle.[5] Again in 1241 Henry III directed Letters

[1] *Ann. mon.*, ii. 84, iii. 76, iv. 62, 115; cf. C. R. Cheney, "Legislation of the medieval English Church", *EHR* L. (1935), 389–98.

[2] Gervase of Canterbury, ii. 212; cf. Cheney, op. cit., 405.

[3] *Ann. mon.* i. 105, ii. 318; cf. D. M. Williamson, "Aspects of the legation of Cardinal Otto in England 1237–41", *EHR* lxiv. (1949), 145–73.

[4] F. Barlow, *Durham Annals and Documents of the 13th century* (*SS*, 1945), 193f; *Ann. mon.* iii. 106, iv. 215; Wilkins, op. cit., ii. 1–19; cf. R. Graham, "Letters of Cardinal Ottoboni", *EHR* xv. (1900), 119.

[5] *CPR* (*1232–47*), 33; cf. F. M. Powicke, *Henry III and the Lord Edward* (Oxford, 1947) i., 133f.

patent to the Archbishop of York and other bishops about to assemble in council at Oxford, saying that he had appointed Geoffrey de Langel to appeal against anything that they might decree against the crown and the royal dignity. This probably concerns the council which sent representatives to the emperor to implore him to lay aside his hostility to the Roman Church and assist the election of a new pope.[1] At about the same time Bishop Grosseteste of Lincoln was excommunicated by the Prior and chapter of Canterbury for having summoned an assembly of the bishops of the province, during the vacancy of the archbishopric, without having consulted them.[2] In 1250 and 1251 there were various episcopal assemblies in connection with the financial straits of Archbishop Boniface.[3] In 1258 clerical assemblies took place in connection with the baronial reform movement,[4] and in 1271, during the vacancy after the death of Boniface the Bishop of Winchester presided over a meeting of bishops at Reading at which the question whether they ought to obey the Prior and chapter of Canterbury was discussed and a memorandum of agreement drawn up.[5]

Clearly it was the need to obtain consent to taxation which began to bring the lower clergy into closer relation to the provincial and national assemblies. We have found only two occasions on which they were actually summoned to attend, but there were other times when a grant was only made after consultation with them in diocesan and local assemblies. When the pope commanded the clergy to pay a tax they eventually complied in every instance except one (1244), but they asserted a right to be consulted about the amount and method of assessment. When the king asked for a tax they

[1] *CPR* (*1232–47*), 267; Wilkins, op. cit., i. 682; cf. Paris, *Chron. majora*, iv. 173.

[2] M. M. Morgan, "The Excommunication of Grosseteste in 1243", *EHR* lvii. (1942), 247–50.

[3] Lunt, *Financial Relations*, 225–7.

[4] *Ann. mon.*, i. 438, iii. 208; Paris, *Chron. majora*, v. 707; cf. Cheney, op. cit., 402.

[5] *HMC. Report xiv. App. 8*, 195; cf. *Ann. mon.*, iv. 460.

had a clear power of refusal which they sometimes exercised, though only once, apparently, did they quote the Lateran prohibition as a support.

3

The reign of King Edward I falls conveniently into two parts with the division coming in the year 1292. From the point of view of political history the first twenty years are the great constructive period. When Edward, with the support of his great minister Robert Burnell, was making full use of the ideas and experience that he had gained during the Baronial Revolt, in Gascony, and on the crusade. It coincides with the Canterbury episcopates of the Dominican Robert Kilwardby, from 1272 to 1278, and the Franciscan, John Pecham from 1279 to 1292, a time of some conflict over the limits of ecclesiastical and secular jurisdiction, but conflict which did not seriously harm the personal relationships between the King and the archbishops.

The six years of Kilwardby are of comparatively little importance for our present purpose and we may pass immediately to the thirteen years of Pecham. This Archbishop arrived at Dover from Rome on 3 June 1279 and immediately instructed the Bishop of London to summon the other bishops to meet him at Reading on 29 July to discuss certain urgent matters affecting the whole province.[1] These turned out to be the application of recent ecclesiastical legislation against pluralism, and the increasing use of royal prohibitions to impede ecclesiastical jurisdiction. The first of these affected the crown closely, as well as the second, because many of the king's clerks were supported financially by benefices which they held in plurality and in absence. At the Reading meeting Pecham had read a number of earlier decrees bearing on these matters and promulgated certain additions of his

[1] On the Council of Reading see D. L. Douie, *Archbishop Pecham* (Oxford, 1950), 95ff; W. T. Waugh, "Archbishop Peckham and Pluralities", *EHR* xxviii. (1913), 625–35; Cheney, op. cit., 407ff.

own. In the matter of pluralities at least he was acting under explicit papal instructions. A group of royal clerks, possibly with wider support, attacked the assembly as having been irregularly called, and pointed to the exclusion of those of the clergy who were vitally concerned in these matters.[1] On pluralities the Archbishop himself realized that there were difficulties and was prepared to suggest modification to the Pope, but on prohibitions he was apparently compelled to make a partial withdrawal at the Michaelmas parliament of 1279,[2] though he returned to the subject in the provincial council held at Lambeth in October 1281.

The citation to the Council of Lambeth, and the descriptions of it, leave no doubt that Pecham was here performing one of the canonical duties of a metropolitan.[3] The constitutions issued at the council are among the most important in the medieval English Church, and they cover a wide range of subjects, many of them of a purely spiritual character. There were summoned to the council, in addition to the bishops, abbots and elective priors, exempt and non-exempt, the deans of cathedral and collegiate churches, archdeacons

[1] H. Cole, *Documents illustrative of English history in the Thirteenth and Fourteenth centuries selected from the Records of the Department of the Queen's Remembrancer of the Exchequer* (London, 1844), 362–70. In my more detailed study I shall argue that the council was irregular in its summons and composition. The two documents printed by Cole on pp. 369ff warn us that it is dangerous to speak of a conflict of Church and State at this period without a careful definition of terms. Churchmen, clerks, were to be found in the service of the government as well as in that of the ecclesiastical institution. Archdeaconries, prebends, and other lesser benefices were often held by clerks whose main occupation was the work of some department of State. The first of the two documents shows what the royal clerks thought of themselves, and though, like others, they may have exaggerated their own importance yet their self-estimate was not unreasonable. The second shows that they were capable of taking a stand upon both the custom of the realm and canonical principle. Cf. F. M. Powicke, *The Thirteenth Century* (Oxford, 1953), 459f and note. Sir Maurice Powicke seems to have been the first to draw attention to the importance of this material. Cf. also Lecture 5 below.

[2] *CCR (1272–9)*, 582.

[3] On the Council of Lambeth see Douie, op. cit., ch. iii; H. Johnstone, "Archbishop Pecham and the Council of Lambeth of 1281", in *Essays . . . presented to T. F. Tout* (Manchester, 1925), 171–88; cf. Cheney, op. cit., 407f.

and proctors of chapters, and the Archbishop ordered proceedings to be taken against those who had absented themselves. After the council he replied to two royal letters which had warned the Archbishop and bishops to attempt nothing against the King or the rights that he and his predecessors had enjoyed by ancient and approved custom. Pecham expounded quietly but firmly the superiority of the spiritual to the temporal power and its right to judge in cases on the borderline between the two. Edward seems to have made no answer, and the Lambeth decrees were allowed to stand.[1]

At the end of Pecham's life, in February 1292, we find him holding another provincial council, this time under papal direction and to discuss ways and means of defending the Holy Land and recovering what had been lost there. Its composition was similar to that of the 1281 council.[2]

On three occasions the Archbishop had to deal with royal requests for a subsidy. At the end of 1279 he wrote to the bishops that they should assemble their clergy and put before them the King's needs and urge them to make a grant on the plea that it was canonical for churches to aid their patrons in need. After some considerable delay, a grant of a fifteenth for three years was made, but the details of the procedure by which it was achieved are obscure.[3]

In 1282 the Welsh war raised further financial problems which Edward tried to meet by summoning two mixed assemblies of clergy and laity at York and Northampton. Representatives of the shires and boroughs were summoned through the sheriffs, and the clergy through the two archbishops.[4] The laity granted a thirteenth but the clergy

[1] *Registrum epistolarum fratris Johannis Peckham, archiepiscopi Cantuariensis*, ed. C. T. Martin (*RS*, 1882–5), i. 235f, 242.

[2] *Bartholomaei de Cotton, monachi Norwicensis, historia Anglicana*, ed. H. R. Luard (*RS*, 1859), 199–210; F. Barlow, op. cit., 201f, 232; K. Hampe, "Briefe zur Geschichte des 13. Jahrhunderts aus einer Durhamer Handschrift", in *Neues Archiv*, xxiv. (1899), 519–22.

[3] *Registrum epp. Peckham*, i. 78, 87–9, 145.

[4] F. Palgrave, *The parliamentary writs and writs of military summons* (London, 1827–34), i. 10.

declined to do anything on that occasion, apparently on the ground that the greater part of them had not been summoned.[1] Other reasons are said to have been given which have not been recorded in detail and it is likely that one of them was an objection to the form of summons which included the words *venire faciatis*, a normal form of citation to a secular court.[2] The result of this protest was that Pecham immediately cited the clergy to appear at the New Temple on 9 May 1283. The bishops, abbots, and priors exempt and non-exempt, deans of cathedral and collegiate churches, and archdeacons were to appear in person. The bishops were also to assemble their clergy beforehand and have the royal request expounded to them, so that there should come to the New Temple two proctors for the clergy of each diocese and one for the chapter of each cathedral or collegiate church, "who have full and explicit power of treating of the aforesaid matters with us and our brethren, and of consenting to those things which the community of the clergy shall provide to the honour of the church, the consolation of the Lord King, and the peace of the realm"[3]. This assembly is momentous as providing the form in which the Canterbury Convocation eventually came to be summoned.

In the parliament of July 1290, the laity granted to the King a fifteenth of movables, and it is probable that the clergy were asked for a tenth. At least Pecham summoned a clerical assembly which made such a grant at Ely on 20 October. The bishops, archdeacons, and proctors of the abbots, priors and lower clergy are alone mentioned in the surviving records.[4]

[1] *Registrum epp. Peckham*, ii. 508. [2] See Lecture 4 below, 92 ff.

[3] *Registrum epp. Peckham*, ii. 508f: "qui plenam et expressam potestatem habeant una nobiscum et confratribus super premissis tractandi; et consentiendi hiis, que ibidem ad honorem ecclesie, consolationem domini regis et pacem regni cleri communitas providebit."

[4] *MS. Christ Church Canterbury, Register I*, f 162 v., printed in W. Wake, *The State of the Church and Clergy of England in their Councils, Synods, Convocations, Conventions, and other Publick Assemblies* (London, 1703), Appendix 20, n. xxxii.

In addition to these there were other assemblies in this period about which we are very partially informed. What strikes the attention is the frequency with which the bishops are found meeting in the spring and the autumn. We have records of such assemblies in May 1280, February 1282, before May 1283, November 1285, February and October 1286, May 1287, May and September 1288, and January 1290. It looks as though a twice yearly bishops' meeting was part of the normal organization of the province of Canterbury, though the influence of sessions of parliament should not be overlooked.

We have spoken almost entirely of the province of Canterbury because the York records now and for some time after are very thin. We can say, however, that there the 1280 grant was made by diocesan assemblies. In 1283 a grant appears to have been promised by the bishops, religious and proctors of the cathedrals only, and was not carried into effect.[1] In 1286 there were first diocesan assemblies, followed by a provincial assembly at which the clergy of each diocese were to be represented either by their bishop or by proctors.[2] A similar representation was ordered for Durham and Carlisle in 1290, when the diocese of York was to send proctors for the clergy of each archdeaconry.[3]

4

By contrast with the first twenty years of the reign the last fifteen are dark indeed. Edward was faced by the French attempt to evict him from his possessions in Gascony, by the revolt against his overlordship in Scotland, and for a time also by rebellion in Wales. These external troubles brought with them all the financial problems that arise from continued war, and also provoked outbursts of baronial opposi-

[1] T. Rymer and R. Sanderson, *Foedera* (ed. A. Clarke and F. Holbrooke, London, 1816–30), i. 673; cf. *The Register of John le Romeyn*, ed. W. Brown (*SS*, 1913–19), i. 82.

[2] *Register of le Romeyn*, ii. 82f, 85f, i. 22.

[3] Id., i. 33f, ii. 93–5.

tion at home. Edward was growing old when these things happened. In 1292 he was fifty-three and, at the time of his death in 1307, sixty-eight, a very good age for a medieval king. He was extraordinarily active to the very end, both physically and mentally, but it would be surprising if age had not had some effect on the sharpening of the Plantagenet temper and obstinancy. He also had the misfortune in this same period to have to deal with a pope, Boniface VIII, of whom it has been written that:

> He saw the papacy threatened in its grip upon Europe, faced by new states that questioned its control while as yet little able to provide much direction of their own: and he played high, seeking to restore papal claims to a reality, fuller perhaps than they had ever had.[1]

In England Boniface had a loyal servant in Robert Winchelsey, Archbishop of Canterbury from 1294 to 1313, a man for whom papal decrees ranked higher than the needs of the state, and, probably for this reason, one of the few whom Edward's magnanimity failed to include. Probably some allowance should also be made for growing bitterness in Edward's dealings with the clergy and the papacy. He had set his heart on the crusade, as Henry V was to do after him. In the case of both kings the French war was an obstacle to be cleared out of the way before the real work could be begun, and for Edward there were the additional aggravations of Wales and Scotland, and the refusal to help him on the part of those upon whom he felt himself entitled to rely.[2]

The war with France broke out before Winchelsey's arrival in England, and in August of 1294 Edward issued writs for a national assembly of the clergy at Westminster in September, the precedent of 1283 apparently being taken as the model for the secular clergy, but with writs sent direct to sixty-seven

[1] T. S. R. Boase, *Boniface VIII* (London, 1933), 377f.

[2] I am particularly indebted to Sir Maurice Powicke for putting this point to me.

abbots and the Master-General of the Order of Sempringham.[1] The presence of proctors of the lower clergy was still sufficiently unusual to attract the notice of the Worcester annalist.[2] Edward addressed the assembly on his need for help and then Oliver Sutton, Bishop of Lincoln, who seems to have taken the lead, asked for time to consider, and the assembly divided into groups, probably the bishops, the religious, and the secular clergy. The latter sent the Dean of St Paul's to ask for more information about the King's wishes, but when he had a stroke and died on the way, they offered a grant of two-tenths which was rejected as insufficient. They tried to hold out at this point but were forced to capitulate by threat of outlawry, and the King, having got his way by a grant of half their annual income for one year, promised redress of various grievances.[3]

Need for further supplies caused Edward to summon a representative parliament in November 1295, one which included knights of the shire, citizens and burgesses. It seems to have been his design to embrace all the main tax-paying sections of the population in one assembly, and to incorporate in parliament a clerical element such as he had summoned to Westminster in the previous year. His writ was sent to the two archbishops and all the bishops individually, and to sixty-seven abbots and three other leading religious. It began with the maxim from Justinian *quod omnes tangit ab omnibus approbetur* and went on to speak of the threat to all from the French. The ecclesiastics were ordered to be at Westminster on the Sunday after Martinmas to treat ordain and execute measures of defence. The bishops, in a clause introduced by the word *premiumientes* were ordered to bring with them the dean or prior of their cathedral, the archdeacons, one proctor representing the cathedral chapter and two representing the

[1] Palgrave, op. cit., i. 25f.

[2] *Ann. mon.* iv. 517: "et clerus ibi similiter habuit procuratores."

[3] The three chief accounts of the assembly are in Cotton, 248–50; H. Rothwell, *The Chronicle of Walter of Guisborough* (*CS*, 1956), 249f; and *Flores historiarum*, ed. H. R. Luard (*RS*, 1890), iii. 90.

clergy of the diocese.[1] When the assembly met, Winchelsey, after consultation with the clergy, offered a tenth, but Edward was not satisfied and sent some of the judges who threatened the clergy and demanded the names of those who were leading the opposition. This Winchelsey refused to give, but he reminded the prelates that without help the King could not defend himself and them. They then raised two objections. First that it was morally wrong to give support to a king in a war against other Christians, and second that they had no money left as a result of Edward's recent exactions. Eventually the Archbishop repeated the offer of a tenth with a promise of a further subsidy if the war continued in the following year. Edward accepted the offer and the assembly dispersed.[2] The evidence of this grant is of particular interest as showing Winchelsey's attitude before the complications introduced by *Clericis laicos* and that he was more appreciative of the King's difficulties than might appear later.

In the autumn of 1296 a further request for a subsidy became necessary. Parliament was summoned to Bury St Edmunds with a clerical representation as in 1295,[3] Edward, no doubt, expecting that the clergy would redeem their promise. But in February 1296, the Pope had issued the bull *Clericis laicos*.[4] In it he referred to the frequent demands made by secular authorities for grants from ecclesiastical revenues, and said that many ecclesiastics had feared the temporal more than the eternal majesty and had acquiesced in such grants without obtaining the authority of the apostolic see. He went on to pronounce sentence of excommunication *ipso facto* against all who agreed to or exacted such grants without papal leave. The bull caused consternation among the English clergy. Although it was not published in England until January 1297, it appears to have been known earlier and to have affected the discussions at the Bury parlia-

[1] Palgrave, op. cit., i. 30f.
[2] *Ann. mon.*, iv. 524.
[3] Palgrave, op. cit., i. 47f.
[4] See above, Lecture 2, 58f.

ment.[1] Royal permission was obtained for an adjournment to January when, after anxious discussion the clergy said that they could see no way round the papal prohibition, but asked that they might send special messengers to the Pope to get permission for a grant or at least directions as to what they were to do.[2] This Edward refused to allow, and on 30 January, declared the clergy outlawed.[3] A further clerical assembly in March debated the matter again, and there were not lacking those who said that necessity overrode the papal prohibition. The king seems to have suggested that a fine for being received back into his protection was a way out of the difficulty and to have sent a message that if this was done he would no longer care about the subsidy. Winchelsey, supported by Oliver Sutton, said that he could not accept this solution for himself, but that everyone must follow his own conscience, and he let it be understood that he would not punish those who submitted to the King.[4] By Easter almost all the clergy had made their peace with Edward on the terms he proposed.[5]

At this point the situation began to change in various respects. From February onwards opposition to the King on the part of a section of the baronage headed by the Earl Marshal and the Constable steadily grew.[6] Then, in the late spring, Winchelsey became aware that the Pope, in reply to petitions from the French clergy, had said that he had no intended to prevent subsidies from being given to kings when

[1] The principal accounts of this assembly are in Cotton, 314; Gervase of Canterbury (continuator), ii. 315; and the Peterborough Chronicle printed by V. H. Galbraith in *EHR* lviii. (1943), 64. On this occasion and in subsequent meetings the clerical assembly, at the Archbishop's command, divided for discussion into four groups, (*a*) the Archbishop, bishops, and proctors of absent bishops, (*b*) the religious, (*c*) the dignitaries, deans, and archdeacons, (*d*) the proctors of the clergy.

[2] The principal accounts are given by Cotton, 317; *Flores*, iii. 99; and Walter of Guisborough, 287.

[3] Cotton, 318f; *Ann. mon.*, iv. 530.

[4] Cotton, 322f; *Flores*, iii. 100; *Ann. mon.*, iii. 406, iv. 531; Galbraith, op. cit., 66.

[5] *CPR* (*1292–1301*), 235–8; *Flores*, iii. 291.

[6] Powicke, *The Thirteenth Century*, 666, 678.

their country was in danger, and that the French bishops had voted to their King a double tenth for two years.[1] In July a reconciliation took place between Edward and the Archbishop, and at some point the King, who was already preparing to leave for Flanders, offered to confirm the charters, Magna Carta and the Charter of the Forest, in return for a grant. For this purpose Winchelsey summoned an assembly containing the lower clergy to meet in August but unexpectedly met a firm resistance. He was told that the clergy could not make a grant of this kind without papal permission and further that it was neither right nor proper that the prelates should discuss the common business without the lay magnates.[2] This was probably a reference to the refusal of the two earls and their following to take part in the grant of a tax in parliament in July, and suggests that some of the clergy had already made common cause with them. A message was sent to the King to say that the clergy had hopes of persuading the Pope to allow them to make a grant if the King was willing that they should send to Rome. This, however, Edward again refused to permit, and before he sailed for Flanders ordered an immediate levy on ecclesiastical possessions.[3] Within a month, however, the Scottish victory at Stirling Bridge placed the regency council at the mercy of the opposition, and a confirmation of the charters was forced with additions which limited the King severely in the matter of taxes and aids.[4] This was followed immediately by a further application for help and this time a clerical assembly in November granted a tenth. Winchelsey wrote to the Pope to explain that he and the other prelates and clergy had come to the conclusion that the imminent danger to church and realm justified them, and that they had made the grant without any sort of lay compulsion.[5] On Edward's return in

[1] *Registrum Roberti Winchelsey*, ed. R. Graham (*CY*, 1952–6), 176–9; *Ann. mon.*, iv. 531; Boase, op. cit., 149.

[2] *Registrum Winchelsey*, 184, 189.

[3] Palgrave, op. cit., i. 396.

[4] Stubbs, *Select Charters*, 491.

[5] *Registrum Winchelsey*, 198f, 528–31.

1298, however, the clergy in another assembly in June made it plain that they were not prepared to go beyond what they had done in the emergency of the previous November without explicit papal permission.[1]

From 1298 to the end of the reign interest centres on the King's attempts to recover the concessions made in the 1297 Confirmation of the Charters, and there seems to be little doubt that rightly or wrongly he came to regard Winchelsey as the chief leader of opposition to him in this matter. Suspicion of Edward's intentions mounted to such an extent that he found it expedient to summon a parliament to meet in London in March 1300, and to this the lower clergy were summoned by the *premunientes* clause as in 1295.[2] When it met Edward agreed to the document known as the *Articuli super cartas* by which he was bound without question to the whole text of the charters. On the other hand his prerogative was guarded in a saving clause, and he was not compelled to repeat the additions made in 1297. A grant of a twentieth was made by the laity.[3]

In 1301 at the parliament held at Lincoln, to which the lower clergy were not summoned, a bill of twelve articles was presented on behalf of the whole community by a knight, Henry of Keighley, behind whom stood, so it was thought, Winchelsey, the bishops and lay magnates. The twelfth article stated that the prelates did not and could not make any grant from their goods or the goods of the clergy without papal approval, and to this the reply was entered *Non placuit regi set communitas procerum approbavit.*[4] Edward no longer had the support of the lay magnates against the clergy, as he had had in 1296 and the early part of 1297.

The King now seems to have decided that his best course was to revert to his father's policy. In February 1301,

[1] Id., 260–2, 536f.

[2] Palgrave, op. cit., i. 82–5.

[3] H. Rothwell, "Edward I and the struggle for the Charters 1297–1305", in *Studies in Medieval History presented to F. M. Powicke* (Oxford, 1948), 324f.

[4] Palgrave, op. cit., i. 104f; *Flores*, iii. 109; Powicke, op. cit., 704.

Boniface VIII had imposed upon the clergy a tenth for three years, and in March 1302 he was persuaded to grant half the proceeds of this to the King. The Pope's death in October 1303, enabled Edward to take a good deal more than his share, and this, with customs, dues and tallages, probably met his needs until 1306.[1] He held a parliament in February 1305, to which the lower clergy were summoned by the *premunientes* clause,[2] and in which he clearly expected trouble from the Archbishop and others, trouble which was diverted by an attack made by the laity upon the monks, particularly the Cistercians, who sent large sums of money out of the country to alien mother houses.[3] Edward's position was now much stronger than four years earlier. The new Pope, Clement V had, as Archbishop of Bordeaux, been his subject in Gascony and showed himself willing to oblige. In August 1305, Clement imposed upon the clergy an annual tenth for seven years, a small portion of which was to go to the young Prince Edward and Queen Margaret, and the rest to the King.[4] In 1306 he suspended Winchelsey from his office and summoned him to the curia to answer complaints laid by the King.[5] The Archbishop was still at the papal court when Edward died in July 1307.

The first twelve years of Winchelsey's pontificate were so much dominated by political crises that there was little opportunity for the normal ecclesiastical business of a provincial council and it is not surprising that we have nothing to set beside Pecham's two great assemblies of Reading and Lambeth. There were, however, two important developments. First the frequent meetings in the years 1294 to 1302 had formalized the composition of the clerical assembly summoned for the purpose of taxation and had also led the same body to discuss points in the relations of church

[1] Lunt, *Financial Relations*, 366–79. [2] Palgrave, op. cit., i. 137.
[3] F. W. Maitland, *Memoranda de Parliamento 1305* (*RS*, 1893), xxxiv, 127, 213.
[4] Lunt, *Financial Relations*, 382–4.
[5] *Registrum Winchelsey*, xxi; *Flores*, iii. 127; *CCR* (*1302–1307*), 430.

and state, constitutional procedure and ecclesiastical discipline, which arose out of the conflicts over taxation. This clerical assembly had come to consist of the archbishop, the bishops, abbots and priors, deans of cathedrals, and other collegiate churches, one proctor for each chapter, and two for the clergy of each diocese, except that occasionally the Welsh dioceses were represented by only one. Something similar seems to have happened in the Northern Province, but the records there are very sparse for this period.

Second there was the King's attempt to include the clergy as a whole with the wider lay representation in parliament. The commons spiritual were summoned with the commons temporal in 1295, 1300, and 1305. They were not summoned provincially through the archbishop, but through their diocesans, and those called were the deans and archdeacons, one proctor for the chapter and two for the clergy of each diocese. The more important abbots and priors were summoned directly by royal writ. There is therefore this difference, that the taxing assembly or convocation, as it began to be called, was summoned by the archbishop at the King's request or to consider a matter put to the archbishop by the King. The clergy came to parliament by royal command, though when there they seem frequently to have met as a distinct estate under the archbishop's presidency. The further development of these two forms of assembly, and their effect upon the provincial council will be the subject of the next lecture.

LECTURE 4

21 February 1960

COUNCIL, CONVOCATION, AND PARLIAMENT

There never was wanting a supply of persons duly qualified and somewhat eager to serve the state and hold the benefices of the church.

F. W. Maitland.

1

ECCLESIASTICALLY the first seven years of the reign of Edward II have their centre of interest in the trial of the Knights Templar.[1] This Order had fallen into some discredit, a scheme for its amalgamation with the Hospitallers had been sharply rejected by its head, and Philip IV of France, who had had the amalgamation much at heart, seems to have been prepared to use the most fantastic charges of heresy and apostasy to compass its ruin. He succeeded in having the matter taken up by Clement V who, in August 1308, appointed commissions of inquiry in various countries and ordered the summoning of provincial councils to investigate the charges locally. The results of these investigations were to be presented at a General Council to meet at Vienne in October 1310, but later postponed to 1311. In consequence of these directions Winchelsey, whose suspension had been removed at the beginning of the new reign, held a provincial council in London which met for about three weeks in November and December 1309, then again in September, October, and November 1310, and April to July 1311. To it were summoned the bishops, abbots, priors, deans, provosts, archpriests, archdeacons, chapters, colleges, and the clergy of every diocese, exempt and non-exempt. In preparation the bishops were directed to hold local assemblies of the clergy and religious of their dioceses.[2]

Although proceedings against the Templars were instituted with the knowledge and assistance of Edward II nevertheless

[1] The best study of the proceedings against the Templars in England is C. Perkins, "The Trial of the Knights Templars in England", *EHR* xxiv. (1909), 432–47.

[2] The *acta* of the Council begin on p. 1004 of *Registrum Winchelsey* but break off. A fuller account is in *MS. Christ Church Canterbury, Register Q*, ff 48–50, reprinted in Wilkins, op. cit., ii. 312–14.

on the second day of the council three knights appeared and presented on the King's behalf a document which warned the bishops not to attempt anything to the harm of the crown or against approved usages and customs. The council was clearly expected to and did consider other matters besides the charges against the Templars. These did not, however, in Winchelsey's view include taxation, for when in the autumn of 1310 the government in London asked for an advance in the payment of the triennial tenth imposed by the Pope, to meet the expenses of the war in Scotland, he summoned a special assembly to meet three weeks after the adjournment of the provincial council. The citation to this assembly mentions only the bishops, chapters, and clergy.[1] The procedure of it, however, followed closely the legal forms for the opening of a provincial council, and it is referred to repeatedly in one document as *provinciale concilium*.[2] In the following year Edward asked for a further subsidy of 12d. in the mark and also asked that the provincial council should examine certain articles of dispute between himself and the King of France touching his status in the Duchy of Aquitaine. What was done about these two requests does not appear.[3]

At York also provincial councils were held in May 1310 and May to July 1311.[4] The lower clergy were not summoned to these, and it is therefore all the more significant that by a special citation they were directed to attend on the first day of the adjourned council, i.e. 24 May 1311, to deal with the royal request for a subsidy for the Scottish war. They are mentioned as present in the *acta* for the first and third days only, and the reply to the King says that the clergy discussed

[1] *The Register of Walter de Stapeldon Bishop of Exeter*, ed. F. C. Hingeston-Randolph (London and Exeter, 1892), 119.

[2] Id., 120; cf. MS. *Register of John Dalderby, Bishop of Lincoln* (Lincoln episcopal registers iii), ii. f 173, to which Professor Cheney has drawn my attention.

[3] *CPR* (*1307–14*), 338, 341.

[4] *The register of William Greenfield*, ed. W. Brown and A. Hamilton Thompson (*SS*, 1931–40), iv. 329–33, 366–9; *The Records of the Northern Convocation*, ed. G. W. Kitchin (*SS*, 1907), 35–47.

the request for three days and finally gave to the bishops by common consent a reply in writing excusing themselves from granting an aid. They gave various reasons, including *Clericis laicos*, and said that they would be willing to help if they had papal permission and after there had been discussion and agreement *in communi parliamento cleri et regni Angliae*.[1]

The lower clergy were summoned to the parliament of August 1311, by the *premunientes* clause,[2] but when that parliament was prorogued in October instead of the *premunientes* writs were addressed to the two archbishops directing them to summon the clergy of their whole province.[3] Winchelsey took exception to the form of the writ, but a conciliatory letter from the King induced him to do as asked. He was unable to be present himself, and the terms in which he commissioned the Bishops of Salisbury and Chichester to to act for him indicated that he regarded the clergy as being in parliament under his authority. In fact nothing was done on this occasion,[4] and for the further prorogation the *premunientes* clause was used.[5] In April 1312 a provincial council of Canterbury met, with a full representation of the lower clergy probably because it was desired to impose a tax for certain church purposes,[6] and in 1313 Winchelsey also summoned a provincial council. The citation to this is of particular interest for in it he says that he proposes to celebrate a provincial council *secundum quod exigunt statuta canonica* at a time when the bishops will be in London for parliament but on the morning before the parliament begins. Only the bishops are cited, but they are to tell the deans and priors and chapters of their cathedrals that if they come to the council they will be admitted *iuxta iuris exigenciam*, a clear

[1] *Letters from Northern Registers*, 210.
[2] *RDP*, 205*.
[3] Palgrave, op. cit., ii. 57; cf. M. V. Clarke, *Medieval Representation and Consent* (London, 1936), 131f.
[4] Palgrave, op. cit., ii. 58; *Registrum Simonis de Gandavo*, ed. C. T. Flower and M. C. B. Dawes (*CY*, 1934), 410, 417f.
[5] *RDP*, 211.
[6] *Registrum R. Winchelsey*, 1247; *Registrum S. de Gandavo*, 421.

reference to the decretal *Etsi membra*.[1] The Archbishop himself was too ill to attend and died before the proceedings were finished. In June, during the vacancy, Edward II tried to get for himself the proceeds of the tax imposed by the council of April 1312, but at least one bishop replied that as the money had been granted by a provincial council for the needs of the church it could not be given to the King without the consent of another such council.[2]

2

Winchelsey was succeeded by Walter Reynolds, Bishop of Worcester, who had long been closely associated with the King and was forced by him into the archbishopric against the wishes of the Prior and chapter of Canterbury and to the great disgust of the Church at large. Trouble was not long delayed. Edward decided that he must make a determined attempt to settle the Scottish question and began to collect an army at Newcastle. To finance it he proposed to hold a parliament at Westminster on 17 May. The clergy of the Canterbury province were summoned by the *premunientes* clause but Edward also wrote to Reynolds requiring him to appear personally at Westminster before certain of the King's *fideles* to treat with them concerning the raising of a suitable aid from the clergy of the province as had been agreed by the clergy and community of the realm at the last parliament (Easter, 1314), and as he should be required by the said *fideles*. He was also to cause to appear, *venire faciatis*, before the same persons his suffragans, the deans, abbots, priors, archdeacons, chapters, and clergy of the province.[3] Reynolds acted upon this letter and issued his citation.[4] When the assembly met he was faced by a strong protest from the

[1] *Registrum S. de Gandavo*, 444; cf. Lecture 2, 80f.

[2] *PRO. Ancient Correspondence*, xxxiv. n 51. Letter of the Bishop of Salisbury, 28 June 1313.

[3] Palgrave, op. cit., ii. 122.

[4] *Registrum S. de Gandavo*, 483f.

clergy.[1] They said that the form of the citation, with its recitation of the royal letter, was a violation of the principle that the clergy of the province or kingdom ought not by law and were not accustomed to be summoned by royal authority, and that this matter had been discussed in a provincial council by Archbishop Winchelsey and it had been agreed that these royal mandates were prejudicial to the liberties of the Church. Their implication was that the King could command the archbishop to assemble the clergy as often as he pleased, and this was a dangerous precedent. Morevoer, the writ was very like the ordinary *venire faciatis* used in secular courts, which entailed severe penalties for failure to obey. Then objection was taken to the place of meeting as Westminster was outside the Archbishop's jurisdiction and he had no right to summon his subjects there. Also it was noted that although lay persons could not be judges in ecclesiastical causes yet the mandate required the bishops and clergy to appear *coram dilectis et fidelibus domini nostri regis*, and these persons had no ecclesiastical authority. In addition to all this the representation was incomplete because priors who governed houses with no abbot over them had not been summoned, nor had the convents of abbots and priors been cited, and abbots could not bind their convents. Finally the clergy fell back on the prohibitions of *clericis laicos*, and expressed the hope that the Archbishop would secure the recall of the royal letter and cancel his citation.

Reynolds saw that it was useless to try to proceed, and so, on the excuse that the citation had not reached certain persons and that it would be improper to act with an incomplete attendance, he issued a fresh citation for another assembly,[2] this time including the conventual priors and proctors of the convents, to meet before himself at St Paul's

[1] *MS. Christ Church Canterbury Register I*, ff 328 v.– 329 v., printed in Wilkins, op. cit., ii. 442.

[2] *MS. Register of Walter Reynolds, Archbishop of Canterbury*, ff 105 v., 106; cf. Wilkins, op. cit., ii. 444. The bishops seem to have continued to meet and to have discussed the matrimonial case of the Earl of Warenne.

on 8 July. What happened then we do not know. It is probable that a similar trouble arose at York. Archbishop Greenfield also had to issue a second citation, but in the North, where the danger from the Scots was more obvious, a grant was made.[1]

The *premunientes* clause was included in the writs of summons for the parliaments at York in September 1314, and Westminster, 1315, and in each case the Archbishop of Canterbury was asked to issue a provincial summons as well, the *venire faciatis* form being used, but with the notable omission of any requirement that the clergy should appear before the King or his ministers.[2] Reynold's letter of summons to the Westminster parliament does not in fact require appearance either before the King and his ministers or before himself, and the Bishops of Exeter and Salisbury seem to have regarded this with suspicion.[3] Bishop Stapeldon's register has, indeed, a record of a meeting at the house of the Carmelites in London on 3 March 1315 at which certain protests were laid before the Archbishop by the bishops and clergy.[4] These covered many of the points made in the previous year, but are much sharper in tone. The Archbishop had required the clergy to appear in a secular court. Nevertheless the clergy present offered to do what they could and as far as the canons allowed and without prejudice to the interests of those who were absent, and they proceeded to make a grant of a tenth, but they asked that in future mandates due order and canon law be observed and formally protested that they would not be able to obey many more mandates of the present kind without harm to the freedom of the Church and danger to their status.

In spite of all this the clergy were summoned to the

[1] *Register of W. Greenfield*, v. 574–7, 140; *MS. Durham Cathedral Priory Register II*, f xxvii *v.*, xxviii *v.*; *Registrum palatinum Dunelmense*, ed. T. D. Hardy (*RS*, 1873–8), I. 577f, 636f, 641.

[2] Palgrave, op. cit., ii. 128, 138.

[3] *Register of W. de Stapeldon*, 121f; *Registrum S. de Gandavo*, 551.

[4] *Register of W. de Stapeldon*, 122. The protest is also in *MS. Christ Church Canterbury Register I*, f 333 v.

parliament at Lincoln in 1316 by both the *premunientes* clause and the provincial *venire faciatis* writ.[1] Reynolds was ill and could not attend. In his absence the clergy, probably with the encouragement of Stapeldon and other bishops, made it plain that they could not commit themselves in that assembly, though they were prepared to make a provisional grant subject to confirmation by separate provincial convocations. The King, therefore, asked that this should be done,[2] and it is probable that in due course the grant of a tenth was confirmed.

To the parliaments at Lincoln and York, 1318, the clergy were summoned by the *premunientes* clause, but without any additional provincial writ.[3] At York a subsidy was asked for and the Canterbury clergy at least again said that they could only decide in an assembly of their own.[4] In the following year their resistance forced the Archbishop and bishops to appeal to the Pope in connection with taxation, and John XXII imposed a tenth upon the Canterbury province, to bring it into line with a grant already made by the York clergy who were now suffering directly from the Scottish invasion.[5] This encouraged the King to approach the Pope directly and to secure the imposition of a second tenth.[6]

It was, no doubt, the existence of these two grants which caused the *premunientes* clause to be omitted from the writs for the parliaments of January and October 1320,[7] the first omission since 1309. The clause reappeared in the writs for the Westminster parliament of July 1321, and for this the provincial writ *venire faciatis* also reappears, though only

[1] Palgrave, op. cit., ii. 154.
[2] *MS. Register of Walter Reynolds*, f 73; Wilkins, op. cit., ii. 456; *CCR (1313–18)*, 325.
[3] Palgrave, op. cit., ii. 172, 182.
[4] *CCR (1318–23)*, 30; Rymer, *Foedera*, ii. 379.
[5] *Registrum Radulphi Baldock, Gilberti Segrave, Ricardi Newport, et Stephani Gravesend episcoporum Londoniensium*, ed. R. C. Fowler (*CY*, 1911), 207–9; *MS. Register of W. Reynolds*, f 225 v.; Wilkins, op. cit., ii. 492; cf. Lunt, *Financial Relations*, 408.
[6] *Registrum S. Gravesend*, 223–5; Lunt, op. cit., 409.
[7] Palgrave, op. cit., ii. 215, 219.

apparently addressed to the Archbishop of Canterbury.[1] Neither seems to have been particularly successful as later in the year the absence of the clergy from that parliament was made a ground for attacking the validity of the sentence passed in it against the Despensers.[2] For the York parliament of 1322 both *premunientes* and *venire faciatis* were used.[3] The York clergy, who had been summoned not by *venire faciatis*, but by another royal letter to the Archbishop, granted the King a subsidy of 5d. in the mark,[4] but the Canterbury clergy refused to act, alleging that they could not be required by law to meet outside their own province.[5]

After this Edward and his advisers seem to have realized that it was a waste of time to try to induce the clergy to make a grant in parliament, and in November 1322, he wrote to Reynolds to say that the lay commons had made a grant and asked him to summon a provincial council of the prelates and clergy at Lincoln as soon as possible to make one also, since the defence of the realm against the Scots was as much the concern of the clergy as of anybody.[6] Reynolds in carrying out this request was, perhaps, careless in that he summoned the clergy only to discuss with him and not to appear before him,[7] and this gave them the opportunity to protest, as they had done in 1314, against being summoned by royal authority. Their reply to the King's request for aid was that the Pope had only just granted him what was understood to be a sufficient subsidy and that they could not make a further grant without offence to and contempt of the

[1] Id., 234, 236.

[2] A note in the register of Bishop Martival of Salisbury (ii. f 121 v., cf. Clarke op. cit., 138 n 1) shows that the Archbishop's provincial citation was regarded as improper, as in 1314.

[3] Palgrave, op. cit., ii. 247. Apparently the *venire faciatis* was addressed to Reynolds alone, and not to Melton of York.

[4] *MS. Register of William Melton, Archbishop of York*, f 461 v.; Wilkins, op. cit., ii. 514.

[5] *MS. Register of Roger Martival*, ii. f 135 v.

[6] *CCR (1318–23)*, 686; Rymer, *Foedera*, ii. 500.

[7] *MS. Register of R. Martival*, ii. f 143.

apostolic see.[1] The *premunientes* clause and *venire faciatis* were used in the summons to the parliament of February 1324,[2] at which the King asked clergy and people for a subsidy to help in ransoming John of Brittany, but did not get it. The centre of interest of the parliament seems to have been his attempt to arraign Bishop Orleton of Hereford for high treason.[3] In the following year *premunientes* without the provincial writ was used in summoning the last parliament held before Edward's deposition.[4]

The expression provincial council was perhaps used rather loosely in the royal letter of November 1322, and the assembly summoned by Reynolds does not bear many of the marks of a canonical *provinciale concilium.* That such councils were not held during this period seems to be established by a letter which Reynolds wrote to the King, almost certainly in the year 1326.[5] In it he said that during the whole of his archiepiscopate he had not once celebrated a provincial council, although he was much pressed to do so, and ought, by the canons, to hold one every year. He gave as his reason for this failure that the King was much occupied with the Scottish war and unwilling for such a council to meet without his assent. Reynolds said that he was being pressed very hard to summon such a council because of the failure to get any attention paid to clerical grievances otherwise, and he besought the King to direct the chancellor and council to give favourable attention to these grievances as he was

[1] The repetition, *mutatis mutandis*, of the 1314 grounds appears only in the *MS. British Museum, Cotton Faustina A.* 5, f 3, from which it is printed in a misleading form by Wilkins, op. cit., ii. 517–19. The *Deliberatio* and the schedule of complaints against lay attacks on the Church are found also in *MS. Christ Church Canterbury Register I*, f 386, and in *MS. British Museum Cotton Vespasian E xxi* f 52, printed in Palgrave, op. cit., ii. 283.

[2] Palgrave, op. cit., ii 290.

[3] *Adae Murimuth continuatio chronicarum*, ed. E. M. Thompson (*RS*, 1889), 43; *Johannis de Trokelowe et Henrici de Blaneforde, monachorum S. Albani . . . chronica et annales*, ed. H. Riley (*RS*, 1886), 140.

[4] Palgrave, op. cit., ii. 334.

[5] *PRO Ancient Correspondence*, xlix, n 92; cf. *EHR*, liv (1939), 491; lix (1944), 340. Mr Pantin kindly lent me his transcript of this letter.

reluctant to summon a general council without the royal assent.

The York assemblies are now much better documented than before and it is possible to say that in the North also provincial councils seem to have been lacking. Archbishop Greenfield, in 1314, produced a formula for dealing with taxation, which was followed both by the Dean and chapter of York during the vacancy and by Archbishop Melton. It began with a recital of the King's need and request and then continued "which business cannot be performed without the summons of the prelates and clergy of our city, diocese and province",[1] and then went on to cite the bishops and clergy to appear on a stated day.

To the second half of this reign most probably belongs the document called the *Modus tenendi parliamentum.*[2] If so it is ironical that a text which lays such emphasis on the place of the proctors of the clergy in parliament should have appeared at a time when the clergy were beginning to make it plain that they would not tax themselves in parliament, as seems to have been Edward I's design. It is not easy to distinguish what was readiness to use any excuse to avoid taxation, what was personal opposition to Reynolds, and what was defence of the principle of ecclesiastical independence. No doubt all these motives worked together, and Reynold's weakness and stupidity caused him more than once to provide occasion for a valid protest. That something more than mere selfishness was involved is probably indicated by the support given to these protests by Stapeldon and by two or three others of the more moderate bishops who normally served the King but could on occasion resist him on what seem to have

[1] *Register of W. Greenfield*, v. 141: "quod absque convocacione prelatorum et cleri nostrarum civitatis, diocesis, et provincie non poterit hujusmodi negocium adimpleri."

[2] The fullest and most important study of this document and its setting is Miss Clarke's *Medieval Representation and Consent*, but cf. also V. H. Galbraith, "The *Modus Tenendi Parliamentum*" in the *Journal of the Warburg and Courtauld Institutes*, xvi. (1953), 81–99.

been grounds of genuine constitutional principle.[1] Such, for instance, seem to have been Stapeldon and Cobham's insistence that the sentence against the Despensers should only be revoked in time of parliament as it had been passed in time of parliament.[2]

The conflicts that we have summarized lend some significance to a change in the wording of the provincial writ when it was issued again, in Edward II's name, on 3 December 1326, for a prorogation of parliament to January 1327.[3] This was the assembly in which the King was deposed. The change is the omission of the objectionable words *venire faciatis* and the consequent recasting of the phrase in which they occurred. This had run: "vobis mandamus rogantes quatinus decanos etc. . . . ad dictos diem et locum venire faciatis". The new form was: "vobis mandamus firmiter injungentes quod premuniri faciatis priores decanos etc. . . . quod iidem priores decani etc. . . . sint in dicto die apud dictum locum", a change which brought it much closer to the wording of the *premunientes* clause itself against which no objection seems to have been taken. This was the first concession made by the new government to clerical sensitivities, and the new wording was followed consistently until the writ ceased to be issued after March 1340.

3

The situation was also eased somewhat by the death of Reynolds in November 1327. During the short pontificate of his successor, Simon Mepham, 1328–33, two provincial councils in the full canonical sense were summoned. To the first, in 1329, which issued an important set of constitutions, were cited precisely the same selection of people as had by now come to constitute the taxing assembly of the province,

[1] Cf. Clarke, op. cit., 133ff.
[2] *Register of W. de Stapeldon*, 441; *The Register of Thomas de Cobham, Bishop of Worcester*, ed. E. H. Pearce (Worcs. Hist. Soc., 1930), 117, 119.
[3] Palgrave, op. cit., ii. 352f.

i.e. including representatives of the lower clergy.[1] The second, in September 1332, was similarly composed, and seems to have been occasioned by Mepham's attempt to make a visitation of the diocese of Exeter.[2] Beside these, in April 1330, we must set a convocation type of assembly which refused a royal request for a subsidy on the ground, among others, that it was understood that the Pope had imposed a tax upon the English Church for the King's benefit.[3] This proved to be true and the clergy had to pay a tenth for four years.[4] Before this assembly the clergy had been summoned to parliament both by the *premunientes* and by the provincial writ in its new form, but the prelates had said that they could do nothing in the absence of the archbishop.[5] The clergy were summoned to the parliaments or councils of February, April, July, and October 1328, March and November 1330, September 1331 and March 1332.[6] They were not summoned in September and December 1332 and January 1333. The provincial writ in support of the *premunientes* clause was issued for February, July, and October 1328, March 1330, and March 1332.[7]

Archbishop Mepham was followed by a much stronger and more able personality in John Stratford, 1333–48. Stratford had been a professor of canon law at Oxford, the revered master of the most prominent English canonist of the fourteenth century, John of Athon. In the middle years of Edward II he had entered the royal service, and in 1323 when sent to the papal court to press for the appointment of

[1] *The Register of John De Grandisson, Bishop of Exeter*, ed. F. C. Hingeston-Randolph (London and Exeter, 1894), 446–52; *Chronicles of the reigns of Edward I and Edward II*, ed. W. Stubbs (*RS*, 1882–3), i. 344; *Murimuth*, 59.

[2] *The Register of Ralph of Shrewsbury, Bishop of Bath and Wells*, ed. T. S. Holmes (Somerset Record Soc., 1896), 103–5; *Murimuth*, 66; *Chron. of Edw. I and II*, i. 356f.

[3] *MS. Register of Henry Burghersh, Bishop of Lincoln* (Lincoln episcopal registers v.) f 429; *Chron. of Edw. I and II*, i. 348.

[4] *Literae Cantuarienses*, ed. J. B. Sheppard (*RS*, 1887–9), i. 322–33.

[5] *RDP*, 391, 394; Rymer, *Foedera*, ii. 783.

[6] *RDP*, 378, 381, 384, 386, 391, 397, 403, 408.

[7] Id., 380, 386, 389, 394, 411.

a royal nominee to the see of Winchester had secured the bishopric for himself. In 1326–7 he took a leading part in the process of the deposition of Edward II and, except for a brief period, remained a close friend and trusted adviser of Edward III until his death in 1348. Being a lawyer he showed a more than usual care for legal forms. At the end of July 1334, he received three royal writs. One was the normal summons to parliament, with the *premunientes* clause. The second was the provincial writ, and the third was a letter which expounded the King's troubles in Scotland and Ireland and asked for a convocation to be summoned to consider an aid.[1] In his citation the Archbishop writes of his desire to spare the clergy from vexatious expense, of the pressing needs of the realm, and of the King's insistence by letter and by word of mouth that the clergy should be assembled. He then sets out the first and third of the three writs already mentioned, and to comply with the first summons the bishops and clergy to appear before him in St Paul's on the day fixed for parliament, 19 September, and to comply with the other orders them to appear before him in the same place a week later on the 26th.[2] On one or other of these occasions a grant was made.[3]

From February 1334, onwards to the present time, the *premunientes* clause has always been included in the writs summoning the bishops to parliament. The provincial writ in support of it was issued in February and September 1334, May 1335, March and September 1336, March 1337, February 1339, and January and March 1340.[4] We have no record of what Stratford did in 1335. In March 1336 he summoned the clergy to appear before himself in St Paul's and a tenth was voted to the King.[5] In September he was directed by writ to summon the bishops and clergy to meet

[1] Id., 427f, 430. [2] *MS. Register of H. Burghersh*, f 481.
[3] Rymer, *Foedera*, ii. 897; cf. *Register of J. de Grandisson*, 789.
[4] *RDP*, 425, 430, 446, 456, 463, 473, 503, 509, 518.
[5] *MS. Register of H. Burghersh*, f 523 v.; *Register of Ralph of Shrewsbury*, 331.

at Leicester, a week after the date fixed for the parliament at Nottingham. This he did and again a tenth was granted.[1] In September-October 1337, again at the royal direction, a convocation was held a week after the opening of a parliament, and a grant of a tenth for three years was made.[2] A convocation not connected with a parliament was assembled in October 1338, to consider a request that the second year of the triennial tenth be anticipated and a fourth year added.[3]

Down to this point little difficulty had arisen. The King and the Archbishop worked together and found the clergy amenable. A pattern of parliament and associated convocation seems to have been taking shape. But the war with France which broke out in 1337 brought extra needs and disturbed the harmony. Stratford himself went to Flanders with the King, and in their absence early in 1339 the government, fearing a French invasion, ordered local assemblies for the raising, equipping, and financing of troops, and the bishops were directed to assemble their clergy for this purpose. When news of this reached the Archbishop at Antwerp he wrote a strong letter to his suffragans in which he said that the laudable custom hitherto observed was that in the summoning of the clergy of the diocese or province of Canterbury at the King's mandate for the making of a subsidy to the King or realm, letters ought to be addressed to the Archbishop or his vicar-general, so that no reply should be made to the King, particularly in difficult matters, without discussion and consent by all the clergy of the province. He went on to condemn the procedure which had now been followed, as he said without the King's knowledge, and urged the bishops to be vigilant particularly in parliament.[4]

[1] *RDP*, 463; *MS. Register of H. Burghersh*, f 539 v.; *Register of Ralph of Shrewsbury*, 331.

[2] *RDP*, 481 f; *Register of Ralph of Shrewsbury*, 336–8.

[3] *RDP*, 496; *Register of J. de Grandisson*, 60; *CFR*, v. 98.

[4] The only copy known to survive is that addressed to the Bishop of Bath and Wells (full text in H. E. Reynolds, *Wells Cathedral*, n.pl., n.d., Appendix M. 151; abridged version in *Register of Ralph of Shrewsbury*, 357), but as there is no obvious reason why he alone of the suffragans

Stratford seems to have become increasingly doubtful about the conduct of the war, and about the burdens which were being imposed upon the clergy in the shape of purveyance and other extraordinary forms of taxation. He himself returned to England in advance of the King in the autumn of 1339, and in the following summer unsuccessfully tried to persuade Edward not to go back to Flanders. At the same time he resigned his post as Chancellor. Matters came to a head at the end of 1340 when the King unexpectedly returned to England, dismissed most of the ministers and accused them of failing to provide proper support for his army. The Archbishop, who was understood to be the real object of the attack, withdrew to Canterbury where, on 29 December, he preached a sermon in which he blamed himself for having devoted his whole time to secular affairs since he became Archbishop, and in particular for the oppressions of the clergy and community of England and the procuring of subsidies and tenths for the King. He asked pardon of those present and declared that he was now ready with all his might to protect the rights and liberties of the Church, to assist the clergy and community in parliament, and, laying aside all secular matters, to perform his pastoral office.[1]

Eventually after a pamphlet warfare and scenes in parliament the King and the Archbishop were reconciled in the summer.[2] It is, however, some indication of a genuine change in Stratford that on 23 July he issued a citation for a provincial council to meet at St Paul's on 19 October.[3] In it he says that although the canons require metropolitans to hold a provincial council each year he has been unable to do so,

---

should have been selected as the recipient it may be surmised that the letter was addressed to others also.

[1] H. Wharton, *Anglia Sacra* (London, 1691), i. 21.

[2] On the conflict in general see G. T. Lapsley, *Crown, Community and Parliament in the later Middle Ages*, ed. H. M. Cam and G. Barraclough (Oxford, 1951), 231–72.

[3] *Register of J. de Grandisson*, 968–71; cf. *Murimuth*, 122, 223.

but now the opportunity has come, and so, following in the steps of the ancient fathers he has, with the assent of a majority of his suffragans decreed that a council be summoned. To it the bishops are cited *peremptorie et precise*. The deans and priors of cathedrals, abbots, elective priors, archdeacons, chapters, convents, colleges and the clergy of each diocese are to be premonished to come if they think fit, or if they think they are concerned in the business or if they have matters to be dealt with by the council. The exempt were also to be informed that if it seemed to them expedient they should attend, without prejudice to their privileges, from which the Archbishop did not intend to derogate. Moreover each bishop was to deliberate with the clergy and religious of his diocese about matters needing reform and to draw up a written list of *reformanda* for the council.

Here we see a very careful observance of the prescriptions of the canon law, and a marked difference from the convocation type of assembly which the Archbishop had summoned in his first six years. The contrast was to be made even more pointed a year later. On 23 August 1342, Stratford sent out another citation for a provincial council to deal with matter left over from the previous year.[1] It was to meet at St Paul's on 14 October and the form of summons was similar to that of 1341. On August 28 he sent out a citation, enclosing a royal writ, for a convocation to meet at St Paul's on 9 October.[2] The same persons were summoned as to the provincial council, but whereas there the lesser prelates and lower clergy had the option of attending or not, for this assembly their attendance was compulsory. The provincial council issued in the publication of provincial constitutions,[3] the convocation made a grant of a tenth to the King.[4] Nothing could show more clearly that at this date, in the eyes of an expert lawyer and administrator, there were two

[1] *MS. Register of Thomas Beck, Bishop of Lincoln* (Lincoln episcopal registers vii.), f 1.

[2] Id., f 2 v.

[3] Id., f 39; Wilkins, op. cit., ii. 702.

[4] *CFR*, v. 312.

distinct bodies with different functions, but it might also have been surmised that the close similarity in composition would eventually blur the distinction. Moreover the gradual separation of the clerical taxing assembly, or convocation, from parliament assisted such a development. We have seen how the clergy established their right to be separately summoned for taxation and summoned by their own ecclesiastical superiors, and we have also observed how the provincial writ ceased to be issued after 1340. At about the same time a number of the religious began to deny any obligation to attend parliament and their denial was accepted in practice by the King [1] though seculars who tried to follow this example were not so successful.[2] The problem of the attendance of the proctors of the lower clergy at parliament in obedience to the *premunientes* clause is likely to remain in obscurity. The evidence for any period is fragmentary, and scraps of information which indicate that proctors were in places appointed for parliament can be found through the fourteenth century and into the fifteenth,[3] but whether any individuals attended or not it is plain from the mid-fourteenth century that for practical purposes the clergy in parliament consisted only of the bishops and some abbots and priors.[4] They had the responsibility for seeing that clerical interests were pressed in that assembly, but they had no power to commit the clergy as a whole there. The clergy were repre-

[1] *RDP*, 528f; 533, 535, 554; cf. *CCR* (*1341–3*), 269.

[2] In October 1339, January and March 1340, and May 1341, the clergy of the diocese of York asserted that they were not bound to attend any assembly held outside their own province, and appointed proctors to present their excuses for not going to parliament (*PRO. Parliamentary Proxies*, files 21, n 1025, 22, nn 1046, 1098, 23, n 1113). In January 1352, they are found appointing proctors in the ordinary way for the parliament at Westminster (id., file 25, n 1235). In May 1344 the chapter of York seem to have given their proctors two forms of proxy one of which was the normal appointment, but the other copied the language of the clergy's protest of 1339–41, but by March 1348 they are again appointing in the normal way (id. file 23, nn 1146, 1147, file 24, n 1200).

[3] I shall discuss this extremely perplexing evidence more fully in my larger work.

[4] Cf. A. M. Reich, *The Parliamentary Abbots to 1470* (Berkeley, 1941).

sented in convocation and were subject to the provincial council and it is to this growing together of these two assemblies that we must now turn.

4

The beginning of a fusion between them can be seen in 1356. At the November parliament of the previous year the prelates and clergy present discussed various matters relating to Church and realm and decided that provincial councils should be summoned.[1] In consequence Archbishop Islip, 1349–66, issued his citation in January for his council to meet at St Paul's in May.[2] In it he referred to the requirements of the canons and the manifest needs of the Church which had been discussed in parliament. The bishops were to cite the abbots and priors, including the exempt or at least those of them whose monasteries held non-exempt benefices in the province, the deans and provosts of cathedral and collegiate churches, the archdeacons, colleges and convents by one proctor and the clergy of each diocese by two. Canonical penalties would be taken against absentees. All who had grievances which required correction by the council would be heard and justice done to them. When the council met [3] royal representatives attended and prohibited it from doing anything to the prejudice of the King or the law of the realm, and then Sir Walter Manny expounded the King's needs and asked for a grant of six-tenths to be paid within three years. After some days of discussion the clergy presented a statement of grievances, mostly relating to other financial burdens laid on them such as the procurations of papal nuncios, a heavy tax on wool and a decline in the value of benefices. They also complained that grievances presented to

[1] This is made plain in Archbishop Thoresby's citation to the York provincial council, in *MS. Register of Gilbert Welton, Bishop of Carlisle*, p. 26.

[2] *MS. Register of Simon Islep, Archbishop of Canterbury*, f 111.

[3] Id., f 117. Apart from a fragment in Winchelsey's register (see above note 2) these are the earliest formal *acta* to survive in the archbishops' registers.

the King in the previous year had not been amended although the tenth granted conditionally on their correction had been collected. At last the bishops persuaded the clergy to make a fresh grant of a tenth, half to be paid in November 1356 and the other half in June of the following year. It is probable that at this assembly the clergy also presented a petition against the mendicant friars. Archbishop Thoresby of York summoned his provincial council to meet in June. Its composition was similar to that of Canterbury and it made a grant in the same terms.[1] He also summoned provincial councils in May 1357 at which the grant of the second half-tenth was confirmed,[2] and in February 1360 at which another tenth was granted.[3] At Canterbury both these matters were dealt with in what was definitely a convocation.

In January 1370 Archbishop Whittlesey, 1368–74, held an assembly which, if one were to judge simply from the citation, would be called a convocation. Indeed in his register the document is described as *Mandatum pro convocacione episcoporum et cleri Cantuariensis provincie*, and the *acta* are similarly headed *Convocacio cleri provincie Cantuariensis*, but in the body of the Acts the registrar repeatedly writes of the assembly as *concilium* or *concilium sive convocacio*, and, what is more important, the Archbishop in the commissions issued by him on 26 and 31 January, when he could not be present, says: *in concilio sive convocacione provinciali*. Eventually a triennial tenth was granted.[4] The citation for the corresponding assembly at York suggests a convocation rather than a provincial council.[5] In 1371 the situation is reversed. York is clearly a provincial council,[6] Canterbury a convocation.[7] In December

[1] *MS. Register of G. Welton*, p. 26; *CFR*, vii. 16, 40f.

[2] *MS. Register of John Thoresby, Archbishop of York*, de suffraganeis, f 1; *CFR*, vii. 40f.

[3] *MS. Register of Thomas Hatfield, Bishop of Durham*, p. 93ff; *CFR*, vii. 123.

[4] *MS. Register of William Whittlesey, Archbishop of Canterbury*, ff 17 v.–18 v., citations, and ff. 22 v.–24, *acta*.

[5] *MS. Register of Thomas Hatfield*, f 48 v.

[6] *MS. Register of Thomas Appleby, Bishop of Carlisle*, 227.

[7] *MS. Register of W. Whittlesey*, ff 40 v.–43.

1373 again Archbishop Whittlesey's commission to preside in his absence speaks of *in concilio sive convocacione provinciali*.[1]

The convocations of Archbishop Sudbury, 1375–81, contain no such references, but give all the appearances of being routine meetings for the purpose of granting taxes. The citation shows a strong tendency towards becoming a stereotyped form. Throughout the decade between 1373 and 1383 an introduction beginning with the words *Ingens et indissimulata negotiorum necessitas* is used.[2] This is followed by the recitation of the royal writ, and then detailed directions about the persons to be summoned, which again seems to be becoming common form. All the more significant therefore is the convocation held by Archbishop Courtenay, 1381–96, at Oxford in November 1382 and adjourned to Blackfriars, London, in February 1383. It was summoned by a citation of the kind just described. The *acta* are headed *Convocatio Prelatorum et Cleri Cantuariensis Provincie*, and throughout the registrar refers to the assembly as *convocatio*. But the Archbishop, in opening the meeting declared the causes for its summons to be fourfold: (1) the extirpation of heretics in the province; (2) *pro delictis et excessibus corrigendis;* (3) *pro injuriis Ecclesie sancte illatis reformandis;* (4) for the granting of a competent subsidy to avoid and repel the dangers which notoriously threatened the Church, King and realm of England. Most of the time of the convocation was occupied by exposing of heresy in the University, and the recantations made by Philip Repingdon, John Ashton and others. A half-tenth was granted to the King. At the London session Courtenay was unable himself to preside and appointed the Bishops of London and Winchester to do so in his place. In his commission to this effect he writes of the assembly as *concilium nostrum provinciale seu convocationem prelatorum et cleri nostre Cantuariensis provincie*.[3]

[1] Id., f 64 v.

[2] It appears for the first time in January 1370 (*Whittlesey*, f 17 v.) and was used for eleven out of the fourteen convocations between that date and December 1383.

[3] *MS. Register of William Courtenay, Archbishop of Canterbury*, ff 33–5.

Fourteen years later the representatives of this University who appeared in convocation to present complaints against the Chancellor are said to have done so *coram domino consilium suum provinciale unacum dictis epsicopis et prelatis solempniter celebrante.*[1] In 1398 the one convocation held by Roger Walden, during his short tenure of the see of Canterbury (1398–9), both issued a constitution for the observance of the feasts of certain saints, and made a grant to the King.[2] In January 1401, convocation met both to deal with the heresy of William Sawtre and to make a grant to the King. In the *acta* Archbishop Arundel (1396–1414) is said to have expounded *causas et negotia celebrationis sui concilii provincialis* (*convocacionis cleri vulgariter nuncupati*) *videlicet pro defectibus eiusdem provincie tam in clero quam in populo juxta juris exigenciam canonice reformandis.*[3] Heresy and schism caused the spiritual side of these meetings to become more prominent in Arundel's time, and the assemblies that he held seem to be described indifferently as convocation or provincial council. Oxford, 1407,[4] and London, 1408 [5] and 1409,[6] for example, were all without doubt provincial councils in the canonical sense. Constitutions were made at Oxford and promulgated at London in 1409. The business of the papal schism was discussed and proctors appointed to represent the province at the General Council. The Oxford assembly is spoken of as a *convocatio* in the citation and as a *provinciale concilium* in later references. The others are generally *convocatio*. That there was felt to be something which might appear strange to foreigners about the prominence of the lower clergy in these gatherings is suggested by the way in which they are referred to in the

[1] *MS. Register of Thomas Arundel, Archbishop of Canterbury*, i. f 45.

[2] *Wykeham's Register*, ed. T. F. Kirby (Hampshire Record Soc., 1896–9), ii. 481, 607. The dates in this edition are not always reliable, but in this instance the entries are confirmed by other as yet unpublished registers.

[3] *MS. Register of T. Arundel*, ii. f 178; cf. Wilkins, op. cit., iii. 254.

[4] *MS. Register of Richard Clifford, Bishop of London*, f 23; *MS. Register of Robert Hallum, Bishop of Salisbury, Memoranda*, ff 52 v.–53.

[5] *MS. Register of T. Arundel*, i. ff 71–4.

[6] Id., ii. ff 7–13.

formal documents which the proctors were to take with them to the General Council as evidence of their credentials. Both are in the name of the archbishop, bishops, abbots, priors, deans of cathedrals, archdeacons, and other prelates of the whole Canterbury province, and these distinguished persons say that they have appointed certain proctors *de nostrorum communicato et deliberato consensu et assensu pro nobis et quolibet nostrum, ac toto clero provincie antedicte ipsius cleri consilio interveniente.*[1] The formula used by Arundel in promulgating his constitutions with penalties for infringement attached, is also interesting: *de consilio et assensu omnium suffraganeorum nostrorum, et aliorum praelatorum in hac cleri convocatione praesentium, et procuratorum absentium, atque ad instantem petitionem procuratorum totius cleri nostrae Cantuariensis provinciae.*[2]

Under Archbishop Chichele (1414–43) *convocatio* and *concilium provinciale* seem to be completely interchangeable terms and no distinction in use can be made on the ground of the business done. A subsidy may be granted to the king in a *concilium provinciale* [3] and heresy dealt with in a *convocatio.*[4] This means that the attendance of the lesser prelates and lower clergy at a provincial council which we saw at an earlier period to be spasmodic and optional, the bishops alone being required to attend, has now, under the influence of the taxing assembly, become formalized and made a regular part of the council. Penalties are pronounced, and sometimes put into effect, against those who refuse to attend.[5] A consequence of this is that the counsel which the clergy gave to the bishops in a *concilium provinciale*, is now also influenced by the right of consent which they had in the matter of taxation. In 1342 Archbishop Stratford was careful to specify the consent of his suffragans only in promulgating his constitutions.[6] The evidence does not appear to exist to

[1] Wilkins, op. cit., iii. 313.
[2] Id., iii. 315.
[3] *The Register of Henry Chichele, Archbishop of Canterbury*, ed. E. F. Jacob (*CY*, 1938–47), iii. 25–7, 33, 45.
[4] Id., iii. 10–19, 81–8.
[5] Id., iii. 26, 30–2, 104, 267.
[6] Wilkins, op. cit., ii. 702

enable us to trace a development in the next fifty years, but in 1391 Courtenay publishes a constitution *de consilio suffraganeorum nostrorum ac cleri nostrae provinciae Cantuariensis pariter et assensu in concilio nostro provinciali.*[1] The passages quoted earlier from Arundel are more on the old lines, but with Chichele consent seems to become the usual thing. In 1415 his two ordinances about the observance of certain feasts are *de expresso consensu fratrum nostrorum et cleri antedicti* and *dicti provincialis concilii auctoritate.*[2] In 1421 he sends to the Bishop of London the ordinance for the promotion of Oxford and Cambridge graduates, made in convocation *de vestro ac ceterorum venerabilium confratrum nostrorum aliorumque prelatorum et cleri provincie antedicte consensu pariter et assensu.*[3]

In the province of York the development, though much less well documented, seems to have been similar,[4] and the place which the lower clergy came to occupy is sufficiently indicated by the important decision taken in September 1462, that all the provincial constitutions of Canterbury which were not repugnant or prejudicial to those of York, should be allowed to have effect in the Northern Province. This decision was taken by the *prelati et clerus* in convocation.[5]

We are now in a position to check the truth of the statement which I quoted from a legal text-book at the end of the second lecture: "The Convocation in its origin was for the purpose of taxation and no other; it was altogether unlike the Convocation of the foreign synods, collected to declare what was the doctrine, or what should be the discipline of the Church."[6] We can see that the institution which from the

[1] Id., iii. 214.

[2] *Register of H. Chichele*, iii. 9.

[3] Id., iii. 73.

[4] I hope to deal more fully with York in my later work. The Surtees Society volume *The Records of the Northern Convocation* is so badly edited as to be an inadequate guide to the history of the Convocation of York in the Middle Ages.

[5] *MS. Register of William Booth, Archbishop of York*, f 342 v. (there are two folios numbered 342 in this register, and this entry begins on the first of them); Wilkins, op. cit., iii. 580.

[6] Above, p. 60.

fifteenth century to the present day has been known as convocation, has a double root. It is the ancient provincial council whose membership has been greatly expanded and formalized by its fusion with a body which came into existence for the purpose of obtaining clerical consent to taxation. The clergy refused to tax themselves in parliament, and although they continued to be summoned to that assembly, and sometimes seem to have attended, the crown accepted the necessity of causing them to be specially summoned in an assembly of their own. Once the fusion between provincial council and taxing assembly had taken place the right of giving and withholding consent which was there in respect of taxation began to extend to other business also, and so in course of time led to a state of things which Edmund Gibson described in 1702 in these words:

> The greatest Power enjoy'd by the *English* Clergy in a Provincial Synod, beyond the Presbyters of other Nations, is, a *Negative* upon the Metropolitan and Bishops, none of whose Resolutions, either in part or in whole, can be pas'd into Synodical-Acts without the previous Approbation of the Inferior Clergy.[1]

[1] E. Gibson, *Synodus Anglicana: or The Constitution and Proceedings of an English Convocation, shown . . . to be agreeable to the Principles of an Episcopal Church* (London, 1702), 172.

LECTURE 5

1 May 1960

SECULARS AND RELIGIOUS IN CONVOCATION

Let be rehersed also to my lordes these monkes, chanons, and religious men, the lawes that commaunde them to go the straite way that leadeth vnto heuen, leauyng the brode way of the worlde; that commandeth them nat to turmoile them selfe in busynes, nother secular nor other; that commaunde that they sewe nat in princis courtes for erthly thynges.

John Colet, *Convocation Sermon*, 1512.

IN THE middle years of the fourteenth century, 1350–80, the fusion of provincial council and taxing assembly which we have been concerned to trace in the two preceding chapters, seemed almost to have resulted in the provincial council losing many of its most characteristic functions. Taxation and related problems almost monopolized the attention of the assemblies of this period and the archbishops seem to have legislated by constitutions issued outside the meetings of councils.[1] In the last twenty years of the century, however, the rise of Lollardy and the existence of the papal schism brought forward again the more definitely ecclesiastical business, and under Archbishops Courtenay, Arundel, and Chichele, for half a century the Canterbury Convocation [2] was more active in legislative and judicial work than ever before. In the second half of the fifteenth century although judicial and legislative acts still occurred from time to time taxation again resumed its dominance.

As was shown in the second lecture the judicial functions of a provincial synod were prominent in the canon law. One of principal purposes of such a synod was the investigation and correction of faults in the province, and although the

[1] W. L. Warren, "A reappraisal of Simon Sudbury", *JEH*, x. (1959), 146. Islip's constitutions seem to have no connection with any meeting of Convocation, but Sudbury's reissue of one of them seems to have been preceded by discussion with his suffragans at the Gloucester Parliament of November 1378 (*Wykeham's Register*, 307).

[2] A typographical problem arises over the point at which one should begin to treat the words "convocation" and "parliament" as signifying established institutions in English society. The achievement of that status may be placed somewhere in the course of the fourteenth century but cannot be ascribed to any particular date, so that there must always be something arbitrary in the decision to use capital letters for these bodies. The convention adopted in the present work is to use capitals from the beginning of this lecture except in quotations, where the usage of the original author will be followed.

cognizance of the *maiores causae* had passed to the papal court, there were still many matters which could be and were brought before the synods. The papacy itself might on occasion direct provincial councils to deal with them as was the case with the charges brought against the Templars in the time of Archbishop Winchelsey. The first Convocation held by William Courtenay after his translation from London to Canterbury was summoned to Oxford for the express purpose of dealing with heresy in the University [1] and in January 1401, the trial of two heretics took place before Archbishop Arundel in Convocation.[2] Archbishop Chichele in 1416 issued a constitution which directed that inquisition be made about heretics in every deanery twice a year, and that the bishops, if after the trial of persons so discovered they did not hand them over to the secular arm, should keep them in custody until the next Convocation when they should be produced before the archbishop with a record of measures taken.[3] In the years following a number of suspected heretics appeared before Convocation in consequence of this ordinance. Professor Jacob points out that in Convocation the procedure resembled that followed in the case of deliberation about a money grant.[4] When William Russell was tried in 1426 Chichele consulted the council as to what should be done and the lower clergy retired to their usual place of meeting in the undercroft of the chapter house of St Paul's to deliberate and formulate their reply which was presented by William Lyndwode their Prolocutor.[5] Nevertheless just as the canonists had recognized the difficulty of dealing with any lengthy or complicated case in a council so we find cases such as that of William Taylor, begun in Convocation but continued before a special tribunal which appears to be in some sense representative of Convocation.[6] In 1463 we also find two cases, one of forgery and one of saying mass when

[1] *MS. Register of W. Courtenay*, f 33; Wilkins, op. cit., iii. 172.
[2] Wilkins, op. cit., iii. 254–63.
[3] *Register of Henry Chichele*, iii. 18f.
[4] Id., i. cxxxvi.
[5] Id., iii. 175.
[6] Id., i. cxxxvi.

not in priest's orders, begun in Convocation but transmitted to the respective diocesans for settlement,[1] and in 1487 the case of William Symonds, the priest who coached Lambert Simnel to play his part as the pretended Earl of Warwick, was begun in Convocation but settled elsewhere.[2] Books were also censured and condemned in Convocation, as in March 1413, when the offending treatises were burnt at St Paul's Cross while the Archbishop expounded to the people the reasons for their condemnation,[3] a foretaste of the more extensive condemnation of books under Henry VIII.

Heresy produced legislation as in the case of the important series of constitutions issued by the Convocation of January 1409, to regulate teaching and preaching,[4] and in Chichele's constitution of 1416, already mentioned. Ordinances were also made to promote the observance of the feasts of certain saints in the province,[5] to deal with the recurrent problem of extravagance in clerical attire,[6] and to regulate the mass of stipendiary chaplains who were financially and in other ways prejudicing the position of the parochial clergy.[7]

The papal schism and the conciliar movement which resulted from it occupied much of the time of Convocation in the early years of the fifteenth century. Representatives had to be sent to the Council of Constance, and the payment of their expenses arranged, and the policy to be put forward

[1] *Registrum Thome Bourgchier Cantuariensis Archiepiscopi*, ed. F. R. H. du Boulay (*CY*, 1957), xxx.

[2] *MS. Register of John Morton, Archbishop of Canterbury*, f 34; Wilkins, op. cit., iii. 618.

[3] *MS. Register of T. Arundel*, ii. f 25 v.

[4] Wilkins, op. cit., iii. 314–19.

[5] Those of Chichele's time have been discussed by Professor Jacob (*Register of Henry Chichele*, i. cxliv–cxlvi). To them may be added March 1413, Feasts of St George and St Dunstan (*MS. Register of T. Arundel*, ii. ff 26 v., 27), October 1444, Translation of St Edward the Confessor (Wilkins, op. cit., iii. 540), March–November 1481, Visitation of the Blessed Virgin Mary, Feasts of St Osmund, St Frideswide and St Etheldreda (*MS. Register of James Goldwell, Bishop of Norwich*, ff 237, 238), February 1487, the Transfiguration (*MS. Register of Thomas Langton Bishop of Salisbury*, f 23).

[6] *Registrum T. Bourgchier*, 109–11.

[7] *Register of Henry Chichele*, i. cxlviii–clii.

had to be agreed.[1] Similar problems arose in connection with the Councils of Pisa and Basle.[2]

At York, too, in the early years of the century Convocations were held in connection with the schism, and ambassadors appointed to go to the Council of Constance,[3] as later to the other councils.[4] Heresy does not seem to have attracted so much attention in the north as in the south but there was one notable trial of friar Thomas Richmond in July and August 1426.[5] From time to time constitutions were made,[6] and we have already seen that in 1462 all the provincial constitutions of Canterbury which were not repugnant to those of York were accepted in the north.[7] This provision is, however, an indication that York was definitely taking second place to Canterbury. It became increasingly rare for the Archbishop to attend meetings of Convocation, and frequently the sole records of these are the citation, a commission to certain persons to preside in the Archbishop's absence, and a letter from the presidents to the Archbishop recording the terms of the grant that had been made. In 1530 Bishop Tunstal of Durham reminded Cardinal Wolsey that it was the custom to see first what the province of Canterbury decided, and then for York to consent or dissent as the case might be.[8] It seems likely that in 1530 the custom was already of very long standing.

A list which was apparently drawn up for the guidance of the Dean and chapter as keepers of the spiritualities in the vacancy following the death of Archbishop Bowet in October 1423 tells us the composition of the York Convocation at that date.[9] The province had for some time now consisted of only

[1] Wilkins, op. cit., iii. 306–11.
[2] *Register of Henry Chichele*, iii. 221, 232–51, 263–70, 282f.
[3] *Records of the Northern Convocation*, 127–35.
[4] Id., 142–5, 174f.
[5] Id., 146–72. The vernacular document on 160–72 should have been printed where the words, "Here follows a confession in English", stand on p. 158.
[6] Id., 183–203.
[7] See above, Lecture IV, p. 111.
[8] A. F. Pollard, *Wolsey* (London, 1929), 292.
[9] *MS. York Sede Vacante Register*, f 361 v.

three dioceses,[1] but the representation was on a much fuller basis than in Canterbury. Not only were there proctors for the clergy of each archdeaconry, but the officials of the archdeacons also attended and areas of peculiar jurisdiction such as Allerton and Howden were represented. Compared with a similar list for about fifty years earlier[2] it shows a smaller number but in neither case can the list be regarded as wholly accurate.

	c. 1376	*c.* 1424
Bishops	3	3
Religious	62	52
Deans, provosts, and other dignitaries of chapters	9	2
Archdeacons, keepers of spiritualities, and their officials	20	19
Proctors of chapters	6	5
Proctors of the clergy	24	20
	124	101

For the province of Canterbury only one similar document survives and this appears to have been written in connection with the Convocation held in February 1453.[3] It does not include the bishops, the diocese of Llandaff is wholly omitted and there is no mention of the proctors for the clergy of the diocese of Lincoln.

Religious[4]	296
Deans of cathedrals	11
Archdeacons	51
Proctors of cathedral chapters	11
Masters of hospitals, etc.	9
Proctors of the clergy	32
	410

[1] In the first half of the fourteenth century the diocese of Whithorn, Candida Casa or Galloway, as it was variously called, was still reckoned as part of the province and its bishop attended provincial synods from time to time. Cf. R. Brentano, *York Metropolitan Jurisdiction and Papal Judges Delegate (1279–96)* (Berkeley, 1959), 94–108.

[2] *MS. Register of Alexander Neville, Archbishop of York*, f 109 v.

[3] *MS. Register of John Kemp, Archbishop of Canterbury*, ff 229–32.

[4] Here as in the York figures the priors and proctors of chapters of the monastic cathedrals are reckoned among the religious.

If we add the eighteen bishops, the two proctors for the diocese of Lincoln, and an estimate of nine religious and five seculars from Llandaff we arrive at a total of 444 members for the Convocation of Canterbury in the mid-fifteenth century. As in the case of York the figures must be regarded as approximate, for such of the diocesan returns as survive show some variation from year to year.

Very little information is available to show the internal working of the Convocation of York at this period, but for Canterbury there unfolds in connection with a side-issue of taxation a curious story which illuminates significantly the relative interests and influence of the different sections of Convocation. In order to appreciate it some understanding of the procedure which followed the granting of a subsidy is necessary.

The amount of the grant together with the date on which it was due, any exemptions from it and any provisos attached to it, were embodied in a formal document which the Archbishop delivered to the Chancery where it was enrolled and then passed to the Exchequer for action. Writs were issued from the Exchequer to each bishop for his diocese, and to the Abbot of St Albans for his exempt jurisdiction, requiring them to appoint collectors and to certify the Treasurer and Barons of the Exchequer of the names of those appointed. It seems to have been usual for bishops to appoint some of the religious in their dioceses for this purpose, the advantage being that a monastery had the staff and a safe deposit and could do the work more expeditiously and satisfactorily than any private individual. In some cases, and particularly in the dioceses of Worcester and Hereford, a bishop might spare the monasteries actually situated in his diocese but appoint the abbot or prior of a house which had appropriated churches in the diocese.[1]

[1] *MS. Register of Thomas Polton, Bishop of Worcester*, f 89, the Prior of Maxstoke in the diocese of Coventry and Lichfield is appointed in January 1431; f 97 v., the Prior of Kenilworth, Coventry, and Lichfield diocese, and the Abbot of Oseney, Lincoln diocese, are appointed in

Monasteries understandably found this work a tiresome burden and one which, if they had to collect in a diocese some distance away, might prove very expensive. The problem was raised in Convocation, probably in 1417, and it was then agreed that religious should not be appointed collectors outside the archdeaconries in which their monasteries lay,[1] but this agreement does not seem to have been much respected by the bishops and in May 1421 the abbots and priors of the realm asked the Commons in Parliament to petition the King for a statute to protect them in this matter.[2] Such a statute was duly passed, but with the proviso that it last only until the Parliament to be held after the King's return to England, and the death of Henry V in the following year brought it to an end. A similar petition was presented by the Commons in the Parliament held in 1435 when the reply was:

> The Kyng will, for as moche as the deputyng of the collectours . . . belongeth to the saide Archebishoppes and Bishoppes, that the matier contyned in this saide petition be committed to theym to putte such remedie thereynne as may be thought best after their wysdoms and discrecions.[3]

October 1431. Other monasteries used in this way by the Bishops of Worcester in the course of the next fifty years were Coventry cathedral priory, Chester abbey, and Lilleshall abbey in Coventry and Lichfield diocese, Clifford priory in Hereford diocese, Biddlesden abbey and Eynsham abbey in Lincoln diocese, Walden abbey in London diocese, Reading abbey and Maiden Bradley priory in Salisbury diocese, and Bath cathedral priory in Bath and Wells diocese (*MS. Registers of Thomas Bourgchier, John Carpenter and John Alcock, Bishops of Worcester*).

Between 1412 and 1485 Bishops of Hereford on a number of occasions appointed the Prior and convent of Lanthony by Gloucester, in the Worcester diocese, to be collectors. They also used for this purpose on occasion the Abbot of Gloucester and the Prior of St Oswald's, Gloucester, and the Abbots of Reading, Tintern, and Shrewsbury. (*PRO. MS. C. 115, Registers of Lanthony Priory, A. 3 and A. 11; Registers of Robert Mascall, Thomas Spafford, John Stanbury and Thomas Myllyng, Bishops of Hereford*, Cantilupe and *CY* societies).

[1] *PRO. C. 115, A. 3*, f 105 v. Undated letter from Chichele to the Bishop of Bath and Wells. Its position suggests that *in ultima convocatione* refers to 1417, as the document which follows is dated Friday in Easter week, 7 Henry V.

[2] *Rotuli parliamentorum* (London, 1783–1832), iv. 131.

[3] Id., iv. 493; H. L. Gray, *The influence of the commons on early legislation* (Harvard, 1932), 296.

The same reply was given when the matter was raised again in 1449,[1] and it is not evident that the wisdom and discretion of the bishops found a remedy for the complaint. In consequence some houses tried to protect themselves by securing from the Chancery letters patent which excused them from collecting subsidies outside their own dioceses.

This particular issue was, however, subordinate to the more fundamental one of the right of monasteries to secure exemption from collecting at all, and in the fifteenth century it is apparent that a large number of houses obtained, no doubt at a price, letters patent giving them that exemption. It does not seem possible to trace the issue of such letters earlier than the reign of Richard II. In 1380 they were granted to the Abbots of Waltham, Holy Cross, and St Albans, and in 1397 to the Abbot of Stratford Langthorne.[2] Such grants became more frequent under the Lancastrians, and there can be little doubt that the financial necessities of the government in the first half of the fifteenth century gave an impetus to such a means of obtaining both ready cash and spiritual credit.

The effect of these exemptions is to be seen in numerous cases in the courts of the Exchequer and Exchequer Chamber [3] of which the common pattern is as follows. A bishop certifies the Exchequer that he has appointed a particular abbot and his convent as collectors of a subsidy, but on the day appointed for payment no money is forthcoming from that diocese. A writ is then issued to the sheriff of the county in which the abbey is situated ordering him to distrain upon the abbot's goods and to cause him to appear in the Exchequer to account for his failure to collect. The Abbot duly appears and pleads that he has letters patent from the King which excuse him from being appointed collector of any

[1] *Rotuli parliamentorum*, v. 151.

[2] For Waltham and Stratford see *PRO. King's Remembrancer Memoranda Roll*, 21 Henry VI, Hilary Term Communia mm. 15 and 16. For St Albans see below.

[3] Chiefly between the years 1430 and 1460.

subsidy to the crown by Convocation. At this the King's attorney points out that the Convocation grant in question included a proviso that such letters patent were to be of no avail, and a long argument ensues as to which holds good the exemption or the proviso. Often such cases were adjourned from term to term, sometimes for two or more years, and in the meantime the King's revenue went uncollected in that diocese until at last the Exchequer ordered the sheriff collect and this in its turn caused further difficulty as the Convocation usually stipulated that grants should not be collected by laymen.

With such an outline in mind we may now look at the story in more detail, beginning with the case of the priory of Wymondham.[1] This house was a Norfolk dependency of St Albans and in 1380 Bishop Despencer of Norwich appointed the Prior collector of a subsidy in the archdeaconries of Norwich and Norfolk. When the first payment was due and not paid a writ of *distringas* was issued against the Prior and resulted in the appearance before the great council of the Abbot of St Albans who claimed that the Prior was removable at his will and not subject to the Bishop of Norwich, and to make his point recalled the prior to the mother house. A fresh writ, therefore, was issued to the Bishop requiring him to appoint other collectors, but he claimed that the Prior was subject to him, being sufficiently independent of the Abbot to be required by law to attend the Norwich diocesan synods and to have a common seal for himself and his convent under which they acquired land and carried on cases in both the secular and ecclesiastical courts. The inconvenience caused to the King by the non-collection of the subsidy was then pointed out and the Bishop was asked to appoint other collectors without prejudice to the final settlement of the case. When he tried further to excuse himself another writ commanded him to have the subsidy collected under pain of

[1] *Gesta abbatum monasterii sancti Albani*, ed. H. T. Riley (*RS*, 1867–9), iii. 123–34. Wymondham became an abbey in 1449.

contempt, and at that point he seems to have given in. The Abbot of St Albans tried to ensure himself against a repetition of the affair by obtaining from the King for himself and the priors of cells subject to him and their successors a general exemption from collecting subsidies.[1]

The author of the *Gesta Abbatum* represents this affair as part of a general attack by all the bishops on those monasteries which were exempt from ordinary diocesan and provincial jurisdiction.[2] The problem of such exemptions was one of the great questions under discussion at this time and during the period of the conciliar movement, and the exempt religious were highly sensitive to any encroachment upon their liberties by the bishops. Although, strictly speaking, the collection of subsidies was more of a temporal than a spiritual matter, controlled by the Crown and Convocation rather than by the pope, there is no doubt that such acts as those of Bishop Despencer were regarded as part of concerted attack upon all the privileges of the exempt.

The matter does not seem to have been taken up in Convocation itself until 1413 when the grant made in May of that year contained the proviso that no one who had been lawfully appointed a collector should be excused by reason of any privilege or exemption even granted or to be granted by the King.[3] A similar provision was made in the following year in Archbishop Chichele's first Convocation [4] when, so the St Albans chronicler Thomas Walsingham tells us, the annulling of privileges granted by the pope to the exempt was discussed. "This beginning of signs", writes Walsingham, "did the new metropolitan to show his ill will."[5] This proviso was repeated in the grants made in 1415, 1416, and 1417.[6] It did not appear in 1419 and 1421 but came back in 1425

[1] Id., iii. 134.
[2] Id., iii. 395.
[3] *MS. Register of T. Arundel*, ii. f 27.
[4] *Register of Henry Chichele*, iii. 315.
[5] *Thomas Walsingham . . . Historia Anglicana*, ed. H. T. Riley (*RS*, 1863–4), ii. 302.
[6] *Register of Henry Chichele*, iii., 6, 27, 45.

and was included in the terms of the five grants made between that date and 1433.[1]

Meanwhile, however, there had been further trouble and St Albans was again the centre of it. The letters patent granted by Richard II in 1380 had been confirmed by Henry IV in 1404,[2] but in spite of that in January 1416 Dr Matthew Ashton, Archbishop Chichele's keeper of the spiritualities during the vacancy of the see of Norwich, nominated the Prior of Wymondham as collector of a tenth together with the Prior of Walsingham. A protest was quickly made and before the end of the month Ashton had nominated another collector in his place.[3] In 1424–25 a similar incident occurred when during the attempted translation of Bishop Fleming of Lincoln to the archbishopric of York, which happened to coincide with Chichele's metropolitical visitation of the diocese of Lincoln, one of the Archbishop's clerks nominated the Abbot of St Albans collector of a tenth in the counties of Hertford and Buckingham. The Abbot at once appealed to the Chancery and obtained exemption but nevertheless the Archbishop proceeded to certify the Exchequer of the nomination and was only persuaded to withdraw it when the Abbot produced a letter of Archbishop Reynolds testifying in general to the exempt status of St Albans.[4]

In 1432, however, began the most serious case, from the St Albans point of view.[5] In that year Bishop Alnwick in the course of his visitation of the diocese of Norwich came to Binham priory which, like Wymondham, was a dependency

[1] Id., iii. 114, 180, 210, 215, 227, 236, 251.

[2] *PRO, K. R. Mem. Roll*, 12 Henry VI, Mich. Term, Communia, m. 11.

[3] *Register of Henry Chichele*, iii. 395–7.

[4] *Annales monasterii sancti Albani a Johanne Amundesham monacho ut videtur conscripti*, ed. H. T. Riley (*RS*, 1870–1), i. 195–204. The first pages of this account are a parody of the first two chapters of the Book of Job, with Archbishop Chichele in the place of God, one of his clerks as Satan, and the Abbot of St Albans as Job.

[5] Id., i. 300–69. This very full account of the affair includes a copy of the formal record of the process in the Exchequer which is to be found on *K.R. Mem. Roll*, 12 Henry VI, Mich. Term, Communia, m. 11.

of St Albans. The Prior, fearing that his liberties would be infringed, ignored the Bishop's presence in the neighbourhood, and his failure to show the customary courtesies was made the most of by the local inhabitants. It was this incident which, according to the St Albans version, moved the Bishop in October of the following year, 1433, to nominate the Prior as collector in the archdeaconries of Norwich and Norfolk of the half tenth granted by Convocation in September 1432. The Prior refused to accept the nomination, and the Bishop's messenger returned to his master with the story that the epsicopal letters had been trampled underfoot, but Alnwick nevertheless informed the Exchequer of the appointment. At this stage the Abbot of St Albans intervened and, a personal interview with the Bishop and the aid of the Dukes of Gloucester and Bedford being of no avail, he obtained various writs from the Chancery. Even these failed and eventually the sheriff of Norfolk distrained upon the Prior for his failure to collect. The case came to the court of the Exchequer in the Michaelmas Term 1433, and after discussion there the advice of the other justices and of the serjeants was sought in the Exchequer Chamber.[1] As the Abbot claimed that he had vindicated his position by protesting in Convocation against the terms of the grant it was decided to ask the Archbishop for an official account of what had happened. Chichele replied in January 1434 that the grant had been made with the proviso that exemptions by reason of royal privileges should not be allowed, that the Abbot of St Albans had protested verbally that this proviso was contrary to the liberties of his house but had made no mention of the priories or cells of the abbey, and as the protest was not in writing it

[1] Such seems to be the implication of Amundesham's statement that the St Albans representatives appeared "coram Baronibus in Curia, assistentibus eisdem Baronibus ibidem Justiciariis Domini Regis de utroque Banco, ac servientibus Domini Regis ad legem, necnon Attornato ejusdem Domini Regis", i. 326, cf. 328. On the Exchequer Chamber see the two volumes edited by Dr M. Hemmant, *Select Cases in the Exchequer Chamber*, vols. li and lxiv of the Selden Society publications, 1933 and 1945.

was, according to his judgement, invalid by ecclesiastical law. The case then dragged on through the Easter, Trinity, and Michaelmas terms after which the Barons, seeing that no speedy decision was to be expected ordered the sheriff of Norfolk to collect the half-tenth.

At one stage the case engaged the attention of the highest officers of the land. The St Albans chronicle contains a long account of one of the sessions, presumably of the Exchequer Chamber, at which were present not only the judges and the two parties, the Bishop and the Abbot, but also the Chancellor and the Treasurer and the two archbishops. After the lawyers had been ordered to withdraw the Archbishop of York, John Kemp, put arguments against the Abbot. He maintained that it was part of the legal rights of a bishop to be able to appoint any suitable person within his diocese as a collector, and pointed out that if the King could exempt one he could exempt all and then the burden of collecting would fall on the bishop himself, which would be absurd. Kemp also argued that if the King violated the conditions on which a parliamentary grant was made then the grant was automatically annulled, and he maintained that the same principle applied to convocation grants, the proviso in question being a condition attached to the grant. The Archbishop was followed by the Bishop of Norwich who said that the Prior of Binham, though summoned to Convocation where his privilege was called in question, did not appear to defend his exemption and so had lost the right to object. The Abbot's protest could not be taken as an adequate substitute because (*a*) it was oral and not written, (*b*) he mentioned only himself and his church and not its dependencies, (*c*) the Prior had pleaded various other cases in his own person and therefore he and not his Abbot ought to appear and plead in Convocation. Bishop Alnwick further argued that he who abuses a liberty given him loses it and that the Prior of Binham, did, in the person of his Abbot, so abuse the privilege of exemption because the Abbot of St Albans always collected his own tenths and accounted for them to the Exchequer thus acting against his privileges.

Abbot Whethamstede replied to most of these points in detail, but tried at the same time to go to the root of the whole conflict by raising the fundamental question of the authority of Convocation in relation to the Crown. In England, he said, the King has the same power in temporal matters as the pope has in spiritual; but the pope can exempt a place or a college from diocesan jurisdiction, and the King has likewise power to exempt from temporal jurisdiction. The matter of the collecting of tenths is one of temporal jurisdiction for it is done by virtue of a royal writ. The King of England knows no superior in temporal matters, but he would be acknowledging such if he allowed his grants to be restricted in this way. In particular reply to the Bishop of Norwich Whethamstede enlarged on the relation between the temporal and spiritual powers. According to the teaching of Hugh of St Victor each had its own sphere and neither could without guilt usurp the place of the other. "Although, therefore, Convocation may act against the King in matters which pertain to spiritual rule, since it is bound to live according to the laws of the Church, it should never do so in those which belong to the earthly power for the latter knows no superior to itself within this realm."[1] Throughout his speech the Abbot recurred again and again to the theme that the collection of convocation grants was a temporal matter and that if the King allowed privileges granted by him in this respect to be annulled by act of Convocation his prerogative would suffer thereby.

We shall return to this argument later. For the moment it is to be noted that although the case, like so many others of its kind, has no formal conclusion the St Albans chronicler

[1] "Licet igitur Convocatio agere posset contra Regem in hiis que pertinent ad spirituali regimen, cum teneatur vivere secundum leges Ecclesiie, nequaquam tamen in hiis quae pertinent ad potestatem terrenam, cum in hac infra regnum non novit se superiorem habere." *Amundesham*, i. 353.

regarded it as a victory for his side, and says that judgement would have been given for the Prior but for the displeasure of the archbishops and bishops of England, who, with the Chancellor and Treasurer of the realm, supported the Bishop of Norwich.

At one point in the story, namely in respect of the Convocation which met in November and December 1433, it is possible to compare both the official record of proceedings in Archbishop Chichele's register [1] and an informal account in the St Albans chronicle. Evidently the Binham case was under discussion in Convocation and Amundesham suggests that the bishops had decided to claim that the Abbot had made no protest at the last Convocation but were foiled when he produced a statement of what had occurred, signed by the clerk of the Convocation, and had it read by the Prolocutor of the lower House, Thomas Bekynton. On the next day the Abbot found the Archbishop and bishops conferring privately, and we are to infer that they were preparing Chichele's answer to the enquiry sent from the Exchequer Chamber, for we are told that this reply was eventually rejected by the judges as being *ex parte*. The Abbot decided to seek the support of the Lower House and presented a petition that they should do nothing contrary to his liberties. The Prolocutor began to take a vote on this, which was apparently done by asking each member in turn for his opinion. It quickly became apparent, however, that there was a majority against the Abbot who then addressed protests to both Houses in turn and finally, when the objectionable proviso was included in a new grant, made a third protest which he asked the clerk of the Convocation to put into writing. This, no doubt, is what Chichele's register records as happening on 17 December 1433, when it says that there were various claims and disagreements about the immunity and privileges of the exempt concerning the collection of subsidies and tenths, and that the protagonists of the religious were the

[1] *Register of Henry Chichele*, iii. 251.

Abbots of Westminster, St Albans, and Waltham Holy Cross. Notwithstanding these protests the proviso was included in the terms of the grant made in December 1433, but the affair seems to have had some effect, as the grant of November-December 1435 contains no such proviso, and that of April-May 1437 contains the statement that the clergy do not by this grant intend to prejudice or harm any ecclesiastical person excused or privileged by letters patent of the King.[1]

This abatement of the attack was, however, only temporary. The old proviso reappeared in the grant made in November-December 1439,[2] and in December 1441 Alnwick's successor at Norwich, Bishop Thomas Broun, obtained a charter from the King to the effect that no one in his diocese who was appointed by him a collector of tenths should be excused this duty, all royal privileges notwithstanding.[3] In 1441, also occurred the Prior of Leeds' case,[4] to which Professor Plucknett has drawn attention.[5] This was in essence similar to that of the Prior of Binham. The Prior of Leeds, having been nominated by the Archbishop of Canterbury as a collector in his diocese pleaded letters patent exempting him from such obligations, and the case came before the Barons of the Exchequer and was referred by them to the Exchequer Chamber. Again the principle was not decided but the tenth was eventually collected by the appropriate sheriffs.

The grant made by Convocation in April 1442 contained an extension of the now usual proviso, to the effect that

> after the ordinary of a place shall have appointed any regular person as collector of the tenth or moiety of the tenth within the diocese, and shall have certified the Treasurer and Barons of the Exchequer of his name, he shall in no wise be bound to

[1] Id., iii. 260. [2] Id., iii. 288.
[3] *MS. Register of Thomas Broun, Bishop of Norwich*, f. 90 v.
[4] Hemmant, op. cit., li. 84–95.
[5] T. F. T. Plucknett, "The Lancastrian Constitution" in *Tudor Studies presented . . . to A. F. Pollard*, ed. R. W. Seton-Watson (London, 1924), 168–72.

> charge or certify another person as collector, beyond that person so certified by him, any letters of discharge from collection, made by letters patent of the King to any spiritual person within the province of Canterbury, notwithstanding.[1]

In the course of the following year the Abbots of Gloucester, Waltham Holy Cross, and Stratford Langthorne and the Prior of Newark by Guildford were brought before the Exchequer in circumstances similar to those of the Prior of Leeds.[2] When, therefore, the Convocation of October 1444, the first held by Archbishop Stafford, included in its grant a proviso similar to that of April 1442, it is not surprising that we read of a formal protest being made by the Abbot of Gloucester, the Prior of St Bartholomew in Smithfield, and Dr William Albon, the Proctor of the Abbot and monastery of St Albans and its cells.[3] There was some discussion and witnesses were called but the *acta* of the Convocation contain no conclusion to the discussion though the proviso appears in the form of the grant as sent to the King.[4]

The proviso was repeated in the Convocation grants of June-July 1446 and July 1449.[5] This last Convocation, however, produced another expedient which suggests that interest had now moved from the principle of monastic exemption to the question of the loss of revenue caused by it, and here we must note the development of another form of exemption, namely the issue to certain religious houses of letters patent exempting them from paying subsidies. It is difficult to be sure how extensive this practice had been. Certainly the Houses of the Order of Sempringham were thus exempt and some fifteen or twenty other religious houses, although their names suggest that it was on the whole the poorer communities which were thus privileged and that the loss of revenue to the crown may not have been very con-

[1] *CFR* xvii. 245.
[2] *K.R. Mem. Roll*, 21 Henry VI, Hilary Term, Communia, mm. 15, 16, 19, Mich. Term, Communia, mm. 6, 14.
[3] In *MS. Register of T. Arundel*, ii. f. 30 v.
[4] *CFR*, xvii. 312.
[5] *CFR*, xviii. 63, 141.

siderable.[1] The year 1449, was, however a year of crisis. In April the war with France broke out again and the French rapidly overran Normandy. In October Rouen surrendered and by August 1450 Cherbourg, the last English stronghold had gone and Charles VII was threatening an invasion of England. "In the meanwhile", writes Dr Stubbs, "England was suffering the first throes of the great struggle in which her medieval life seems to close."[2]

Parliament met in February 1449 and granted a half-tenth and a fifteenth, and continued tunnage and poundage for five years. In June it met again, at Winchester on account of the plague, and continued the wool subsidy for four years and renewed the tax on aliens. The Commons also tried to tax the clergy by granting a subsidy of a noble from each stipendiary priest in consideration of a general pardon, but the King sent the bill to Convocation, telling the clergy that it was for them to bestow the subsidy. If they would grant the noble he would issue the pardon.[3] Convocation met at St Paul's from 1st to 28th July and made four grants. The first three are set out in the certificate sent by the Archbishop to the King, and are (1) a tenth of all ecclesiastical goods, benefices and possessions of the province, assessed and not assessed, with certain specified exceptions; (2) the 6s. 8d. on stipendiary chaplains, asked for in Parliament, again with certain exceptions; and (3) a fourth part of a tenth over and above the whole tenth, on all goods and possessions of all persons exempted by royal letters from the collection of tenths.[4] The fourth is recorded in another letter from the Archbishop to the King dated 12 October 1449, and consisted of a grant to the Archbishop for the defence of the Church, of 2s. in the pound of all goods and possessions of religious men and others who by royal letters had obtained exemption

[1] A list can be constructed from the numerous cases on the *K.R. Mem. Roll* for 32 Henry VI.

[2] W. Stubbs, *The Constitutional History of England* (3rd edn., Oxford, 1884), iii. 146.

[3] *Rotuli parliamentorum*, v. 141–3, 152f.

[4] *CFR*, xviii. 139.

from contributing with others of the clergy to a tenth. This grant the Archbishop himself passed on to the King for the defence of the realm and Church.[1] Thus all forms of exemption were defeated. The tenth was to be paid in two parts at the Feast of the Annunciation 1450 and 1451. Convocation met again in November 1449, and sat until July 1450 when a further tenth was granted, to be paid at the Annunciation, 1452 and 1453, another grant of a quarter-tenth was imposed on persons exempt from collecting; and a second 2s. in the pound on the goods of those exempt from paying tenths was made to the Archbishop and by him passed on to the King.[2] These measures were repeated in the Convocation of February-March 1453. Two-tenths were granted, payable at Martinmas each year from 1453 to 1456; an additional half-tenth was imposed on those exempt from being collectors; and 4s. in the pound payable to the Archbishop in annual instalments of 1s. at Martinmas each year from 1453-1456, was imposed on those exempt from paying tenths, and again granted by the Archbishop to the Crown.[3] This time, however, there were provisos attached to the last two grants to the effect that if the holders of letters patent of exemption surrendered them before the Feast of the Assumption 1453, they should be quit, and should only pay the normal tenths. It appears that a number of houses, including the whole Order of Sempringham, did so surrender their privileges.[4]

[1] *K.R. Mem. Roll*, 28 Henry VI, Easter term, Communia, m. 10 d.; *CFR xviii.* 141, which records this grant, does not say that it was made to the Archbishop.

[2] *CFR* xviii. 165.

[3] *CFR* xix. 32; *K.R. Mem. Roll*, 32 Henry VI, Mich. Term, Communia, m. 1 d. It may be observed that on what appears to be the next occasion that a subsidy was granted to the Archbishop a proviso was inserted to the effect that he must not alienate the grant to anyone in such wise that collectors of it might be constrained to account to the royal Exchequer, *Registrum T. Bourgchier*, 114, cf. 145. On the general subject of such grants see F. R. H. du Boulay, "Charitable subsidies granted to the archbishop of Canterbury, 1300–1489", in *BIHR*, xxiii. (1950), 147–64. Dr du Boulay does not, however, discuss the subsidies of 1449–53.

[4] *K.R. Mem. Roll*, 32 Henry VI, Mich. Term, Communia m. 30. The roll for this term records some seventy cases arising out of these grants.

Others found that their exemptions had been annulled by the general Act of Resumption passed in the Parliament which met at Leicester 1450.[1]

Some exemptions, however, remained and we find that in the Convocation grants of July 1461, November 1462, July 1463, and June 1468, the old proviso against those who claimed to be exempt from collecting, is repeated.[2] In February 1472 an extra half-tenth was imposed upon those who refused to collect.[3] The Convocations of 1473 and 1475 omitted these provisos. The Convocations of 1478 and 1481 returned to the 1444 formula [4] but the solution of February 1472 reappears in 1484,[5] and in 1487 with the addition that the person refusing was to be compelled to collect as well as to pay the extra half-tenth.[6] This was repeated in 1491.[7] The Convocation of 1489 apparently attached no provisos to its grant of 25,000 l.[8] In 1495 the extra charge was not made but any person claiming exemption was to be compelled to collect at his own expense.[9]

This story of the exemptions and the attacks upon them suggests that in the mid-fifteenth century the division of interest in Convocation was not, as at some earlier and later times, one between the Upper and the Lower Houses, but between seculars and religious, and in order to investigate this a little further it will be profitable to consider such information as can be gathered about the persons who composed the Convocation. Of the bishops it is unnecessary

[1] Stubbs, op. cit., iii. 154.

[2] *CFR* xx. 32, 84, 118, 223.

[3] *Registra quorundam abbatum monasterii S. Albani, qui saeculo XVmo floruere*, ed. H. T. Riley (*RS*, 1872–3), ii. 139.

[4] *K.R. Mem. Roll*, 18 Edward IV, Mich. Term, Communia, m. 35; *Registrum Thome Bourgchier*, 141.

[5] *PRO Fine Roll*, 1 Richard III, m. 18. I am grateful to the officers of the PRO for having allowed me to consult the as yet unpublished calendar of the Fine Rolls for this period.

[6] *PRO Fine Roll*, 2 Henry VII, m. 15 [3].

[7] *PRO Fine Roll*, 7 Henry VII, m. 22 [7].

[8] *Registrum Thome Myllyng Episcopi Herefordensis 1474–1492*, ed. A. T. Bannister (Cantilupe and *CY* societies, 1919), 117–23; *PRO Fine Roll*, 4 Henry VII, m. 17 [3].

[9] *PRO Fine Roll*, 11 Henry VI, m. 18 [3].

to say much. Archbishops Stafford, Kemp, and Bourgchier were all in their time Chancellor of England, and of the rest we may quote Professor Hamilton Thompson's dictum that "no appointment of a bishop, at any rate to the more important sees, was made without respect to his possible services to the government".[1] The bishops, in addition to having their own interest as the persons required to appoint collectors, were also, for the most part, in a position to appreciate fully the loss to the crown revenue which resulted from these various exemptions.

It is rather the Lower House whose members require investigation,[2] and here it is proper to begin by considering the Prolocutors, the Convocation equivalent of the Speaker of the House of Commons. The Convocation records are not full enough to provide a complete list, but we have a number of names, and it is suitable to begin with William Lyndewood who was Prolocutor in 1419, 1421, 1424, 1425, and 1426, for his is one of the great names in the history of the canon law in England.[3] At this time he was Official of the court of Canterbury, and already employed in those parts of the government service which required clerks trained in the canon and civil laws. In 1433 he was to be Keeper of the Privy Seal, and was to be a diplomatic representative of the English government in Portugal and in the Low Countries. In 1428 Lyndewood seems to have shared the position as Prolocutor with Reginald Kentwode who was Dean of St Paul's, and also a prominent civil lawyer employed in government business.[4] Thomas Bekynton was Prolocutor in

[1] A. Hamilton Thompson, *The English clergy and their organization in the later Middle Ages* (Oxford, 1947), 15.

[2] The section which follows depends very largely upon information about English graduates in the Middle Ages collected by Dr A. B. Emden. Much of this is now published in his *A Biographical Register of the University of Oxford to A.D. 1500* (Oxford, 1957–9). Dr Emden has been most generous in answering my questions on frequent occasions during the last ten years.

[3] Emden, op. cit., ii. 1191f.

[4] *Register of Henry Chichele*, iii. 185; Emden, op. cit., ii. 1039f.

1433, 1434, and 1438. He had succeeded Lyndewood as Official of the court of Canterbury, was employed a good deal in embassies to France between 1432 and 1442, was King's Secretary about 1439, and Keeper of the Privy Seal about 1443 in which year he became Bishop of Bath and Wells.[1] In the Convocation of 1438 he was followed as Prolocutor by Mr John Lyndfeld, the Dean of the Arches.[2] In 1439 Mr Richard Andrew, Official of the court of Canterbury, was Prolocutor. He was later private secretary to King Henry VI, and Dean of York.[3] William Byconyll, Official of the court of Canterbury, was Prolocutor in 1444. He also was an eminent lawyer.[4] Mr John Stokes was Prolocutor in 1453, 1460, and 1463, a protégé of Archbishop Bourgchier, whom we find as vicar-general at Worcester during the whole of Bourgchier's nine years' episcopate there. In 1445 Bourgchier, having been translated to Ely, made Stokes Archdeacon of Ely. Archbishop Stafford called him to be Auditor of Causes in 1448–9, and Bourgchier made him Official of the court of Canterbury in 1460. He died in 1466 as Archdeacon of Ely and Precentor of Salisbury, a lawyer of considerable eminence.[5] William Pykenham, Chancellor of the Archbishop, doctor of canon and civil law, Archdeacon of Suffolk and Prebendary of St Paul's, was Prolocutor in 1481.[6] The last two Prolocutors of the century known to us, Masters Thomas Cooke [7] and Humphrey Hawardyn,[8] were both Auditors of Causes to the Archbishop. It is plain that throughout the period with which we are concerned the deliberations of the Lower House were presided over by one of the Archbishop's legal staff, a man trained in the construction and interpretation of documents, a man in the

[1] Emden, op. cit., i. 157–9.

[2] Id., ii. 1190. The evidence does not seem to me to support the statement that Lyndfeld was Prolocutor in 1425.

[3] Id., i. 34f.

[4] Id., i. 330f.

[5] Id., iii. 1782.

[6] Id., iii. 1530f.

[7] *MS. Register of John Morton, Archbishop of Canterbury*, f 34; I. J. Churchill, *Canterbury Administration* (London, 1933), ii. 243.

[8] Emden, op. cit., ii. 887f.

confidence of the Archbishop, and one who was generally familiar with the needs and working of the secular government.

The members of the Lower House fall into three classes—the deans and proctors of the secular cathedral chapters, the archdeacons, and the proctors of the clergy. The deans (including the Precentor of St David's but not the Archdeacon of Llandaff, who were the heads of their respective chapters) number eleven, that is omitting the priors of the monastic cathedrals whose interest lay elsewhere. The archdeacons numbered fifty-two, and the proctors of the clergy thirty-six. It is, however, not possible to draw up a complete list for any one Convocation of the fifteenth century. We cannot at present be certain of all the deans and archdeacons at any particular date, the information about the proctors of chapters is spasmodic, and the records of the proctors of the clergy very fragmentary. We can, however, go some way towards constructing a picture of the Lower House at this time. We know the names of most of the deans and archdeacons, and of the sixty Convocations which met between 1401 and 1497. Information appears to survive about some of the diocesan proctors in thirty-seven. For the purpose of this lecture it will suffice to examine one specimen Convocation—that which met in February 1473. The reason for choosing this particular one is that the terms of its grant provided that no member of Lower House appearing in person should be burdened with the duty of collecting the subsidy, and a list of those persons was attached.[1] It contains forty-five names, rather less than half the possible total of the secular clergy and the impression formed by the present writer is that when due allowance has been made for the people who appeared in more than one capacity, forty-five is not much short of the average attendance.

[1] The list can perhaps most conveniently be studied in *The Register of Robert Stillington, Bishop of Bath and Wells, 1466–81*, ed. H. C. Maxwell Lyte (Somerset Record Society, 1937), 98f.

We begin with the Prolocutor John Doggett, a nephew of Archbishop Bourgchier, Fellow and later Provost of King's College, Cambridge, a Prebendary of Lincoln in 1474, ambassador to Pope Sixtus IV and the princes of Sicily, 1479, chaplain to Richard III in 1483, a doctor of canon law of the University of Bologna.[1] He sat in Convocation as Archdeacon of Chichester. Other archdeacons of note present in the Lower House were Thomas Winterbourne, Archdeacon of Canterbury and Dean of St Paul's, Auditor of Causes and Chancellor of the Archbishop;[2] Roger Rotherham, LL.D., Archdeacon of Rochester and of Leicester, Prebendary of Lincoln;[3] John Russell, LL.D., Archdeacon of Berkshire, about to become Keeper of the Privy Seal, Bishop of Rochester and Lincoln, and Chancellor of England;[4] Peter Courtenay, LL.D., Archdeacon of Exeter and Wiltshire, later to be Dean of Windsor, Bishop of Exeter and Winchester, and Keeper of the Privy Seal to Henry VII;[5] John Gunthorp, Archdeacon of Essex and Dean of Wells, and Chaplain to Edward IV;[6] John Morton, LL.D. Archdeacon of Norwich, the future archbishop and cardinal;[7] William Pykenham, Archdeacon of Suffolk, whom we have already seen as Prolocutor in 1481;[8] John Waynflete, Archdeacon of Surrey and Dean of Chichester, probably a relative of Bishop Waynflete of Winchester.[9] There are nine out of the twenty archdeacons who were present and between them they held eleven archdeaconries and three deaneries.

Turning to the twenty-five representatives of the parochial clergy we find that they are not so easy to identify. The proctors of four dioceses are known from the episcopal registers. Bath and Wells was represented by Thomas Overey

[1] Emden, op. cit., i. 582f.

[2] Id., iii. 2060f.

[3] J. Le Neve, *Fasti Ecclesiae Anglicanae*, ed. T. D. Hardy (Oxford, 1854), ii. 61, 169, 580; J. and J. A. Venn, *Alumni Cantabrigienses* (Cambridge, 1922–7), iii. 489. Rotherham was employed with other civil lawyers on a royal commission in 1471, *CPR* (*1467–77*), 317.

[4] Emden, op. cit., iii. 1609–11.

[5] Id., i. 499 f.

[6] Id., ii. 837.

[7] Id., ii. 1318–20.

[8] Id., iii. 1530f.

[9] Id., iii. 2001.

B.C.L., Precentor of Wells and Commissary-General of the Bishop,[1] and by Robert Wilson, D.C.L., Chancellor of Wells.[2] Winchester returned David Husband, Dr of decrees, Canon of Hereford,[3] and William de Laguna, D.C.L. and Rector of Cranleigh.[4] Ely sent Richard Bole, Archdeacon of Ely,[5] and William Malster, B.CN.L., Chancellor of the Archbishop of York in 1455 and Rector of Girton from 1457 till his death in 1492.[6] Worcester returned Mr William Vauce, J.U.B., Dean of Westbury, Chancellor of the Bishop of Worcester and Precentor of Lichfield,[7] and Arnulf Colyns, J.U.B., Vicar of Badminton, and Commissary of the Bishop of Worcester.[8] The high proportion of diocesan officials among these eight elected proctors is in keeping with the evidence for other years. Of the proctors who cannot be so definitely identified with any diocese we may pick a few for comment. Hugh Damlett was Master of Pembroke College, Cambridge, 1447–50 and Rector of St Peter on Cornhill, London, 1447–76.[9] John Crall, D.CN.L., was Rector of St Magnus by London Bridge, 1465–80, Prebendary of St Paul's, 1463, of York, 1467–78, and Archdeacon of Essex from 1478.[10] Edward Shuldham, D.C.L., was only a deacon at the time of this Convocation having been ordained deacon at Lincoln on 22 May 1472, and not being priested until 17 April 1473 at Ely. He was a Canon of Lincoln from 1488–90 and Master of Trinity Hall Cambridge, 1502–3.[11] Thomas Candour, Dr of decrees, was employed in royal commissions to hear cases which involved the civil or canon laws in 1471, 1472, and 1475. He also was a Canon of Lincoln.[12] William Utting, D.D. was Vice-Chancellor of Cambridge University 1467–8, and chaplain to Archbishop Bourgchier. He died in 1482 and is buried in Lambeth parish church.[13]

[1] Id., ii. 1411. [2] Id., iii. 2052. [3] Id., ii. 989.
[4] Id., ii. 1084. [5] Id., i. 213.
[6] From information supplied by Dr Emden.
[7] Emden, op. cit., iii. 1943f. [8] Id., i. 472.
[9] Venn, op. cit., ii. 6. [10] Id., i. 412. [11] Id., iv. 69.
[12] Emden, op. cit., iii. 2158f; *CPR (1467–77)*, 307, 317, 511.
[13] Venn, op. cit., iv. 292.

It is hardly an exaggeration to say that the affairs of the English Church in the fifteenth century were in the hands of a comparatively small official class many of whose members were also intermittently in the royal service or at least had a common interest with the royal clerks. This helps to explain the paradoxical situation in which the King's attorney in the Exchequer is over and over again found arguing for the validity of proviso in a Convocation grant against letters patent issued earlier by the crown.

It is reasonable to surmise that in at least the second half of the fifteenth century affairs in the Lower House of Convocation were in the hands of a comparatively small body of ecclesiastical lawyers and officials many of whom were also familiar with the royal service and the problems of the secular government. If they were concerned to destroy the value of letters patent of exemption it may have been as much to safeguard the royal revenue as to preserve the rights of the bishops. They and the King's attorney who argued in the Exchequer against the validity of his master's grants of exemption, most probably had a common interest. It would be misleading to represent the story of these letters patent as a conflict of Church and State, for to do so would be to ignore the realities of the situation.

Nevertheless a constitutional issue was raised, though not always perceived as such. Professor Plucknett in 1925 drew attention to three cases reported in the Year Books which concern this principle of letters patent versus a Convocation proviso.[1] One is the Prior of Leeds' case which has been mentioned already. The others concerned the Abbot of Waltham in 1480 [2] and the Abbot of Shrewsbury in 1484.[3] Professor Plucknett points out how the arguments in the Leeds case all move within the sphere of private law, the law of contract and of property, and he summarizes them in these words:

[1] Plucknett, op. cit.

[2] *Year Book*, 21 Edward IV, Mich. Term, n 6. It is to be regretted that Dr Hemmant did not include this case in her Selden Society volumes.

[3] Hemmant, op. cit., lxiv. 102–8.

> an act by a representative body which is deliberately made and intended to override a separate arrangement between one of its members and the Crown will only bind that member if he allows it to pass without protesting his exemption. This result is achieved without any considerations of a constitutional nature; it follows from a particular application of the doctrine of estoppel. This is the best that the Year Books of the Lancastrian age have given us in the way of political theory.[1]

He observes, however, that in the Abbot of Waltham's case the constitutional issue was clearly raised.

On that occasion the discussion again moved within the sphere of the law of inheritance until a serjeant called Starkey said:

> It seems to me that the charter should be allowed. As for what has been said about disallowing it on the ground that it must be construed to the King's advantage, you, Sir, are not here to argue for the King's lucre, but to administer justice between the party and the King. . . . And in this case the charter should be allowed: otherwise you will have to affirm that the authority and jurisdiction of Convocation is higher and greater than the authority of the King in his prerogative, of which the contrary is true. The King has exempted the Abbot by these letters patent, and nothing is shown against them save an act made in the Convocation which is below the power and authority of the King.[2]

To these words Professor Plucknett attaches the highest importance. He says that Starkey is the first of the counsel who have been engaged in these cases to realize that the question at the root of them all is that of the Prerogative, and he regards as significant the use of the word "prerogative" to describe that power of the crown which could be ranged against the "authority and jurisdiction" of Convocation. On this point doubts have been raised by S. B. Chrimes who shows reason to think that Starkey was not innovating in this use of the term "prerogative".[3] Where Starkey does appear

[1] Plucknett, op. cit., 180. [2] Id., 173f.

[3] S. B. Chrimes, *English Constitutional Ideas in the Fifteenth Century* (Cambridge, 1936), 41.

important is as the first of the common law counsel engaged in these cases to ask the simple question, Which has the greater authority, the Crown or Convocation? Yet even this must be qualified. Professor Plucknett could be understood as meaning that Starkey raised this as a general constitutional question, and it is therefore unfortunate that in his translation of the serjeant's speech he should have overlooked certain words which seem to limit the application of this issue to temporal matters. The original of the last sentence in the extract quoted above reads:

> Et le Roy ad exempt l'Abbe par ces lettres patentes, *queux sont mere temporel*, & rien est monstre mesque ils serra allowe, forsque un act fait en le convocation qui est desoubs le power & aucthoritie del Roy.[1]

The words italicized, which are not translated by Plucknett, seem to put Starkey's argument on all fours with that of the Abbot of St Albans in the Binham case. The Abbot too had made much of the harm that would be done to the King's prerogative by allowing the proviso, and he too had asserted the superiority of the crown to Convocation, but all this in the limited sphere of temporal affairs. There seems to be no good reason to suppose that Starkey was doing anything more. Nevertheless it is important that even with this limitation the issue of the two authorities should have been so clearly stated. Perhaps if John Whethamstede could have foreseen the question which would confront his successor Richard Whiting nearly a century later he would have been a little more cautious.

[1] Extracts from this case, including part of Starkey's speech, are given in the original French by Chrimes, op. cit., 374.

LECTURE 6

8 May 1960

ONE STATE, ONE CHURCH

That new laws may be made concerning rites and ecclesiastical matters and persons, with regard to the circumstances of outward worship, and promoting order, decency, and edification, besides those delivered by Christ and His Apostles, is a case so evident and agreeable to reason that it would be a glaring proof of prejudice and obstinacy seriously to deny it; but to whom the right of making Ecclesiastical Laws does properly belong, has been eagerly controverted by Divines.

Robert Sanderson, *On Conscience and Human Law.*

1

THE PERIOD upon which we now enter is one in which religious changes and controversies occupy so large a proportion of our history books that it is not easy to speak of Convocation without the whole history of the time. The very isolation of certain events may be thought by some to produce a distortion of the facts, but this is unhappily an inevitable risk in so controversial a period.

The changes which took place between 1530 and 1548 were not altogether unprepared for. The royal control of the appointment of bishops throughout a good deal of the preceding three centuries has often been adduced as a preparation for the Henrician statute, and the case of Richard Hunne [1] in 1514 has rightly been seen as raising issues of the extent of ecclesiastical jurisdiction and the possibilities inherent in the Statute of Praemunire which became prominent fifteen years later. In the last lecture we saw how the financial relations of Crown and Convocation indicated a situation which could easily lead to royal control. There are, however, four other points to which attention should be drawn.

The first of these is that the right of the pope to tax the

[1] Richard Hunne was a well-to-do merchant and freeman of the city of London who was arrested on a charge of heresy. While awaiting trial he was found on Monday, 4 December 1514, hanged in his cell in the Bishop of London's prison. A coroner's jury found a verdict of wilful murder against the Bishop's Chancellor and two of his subordinates. The trial for heresy proceeded in spite of the murder, and Hunne's body, as that of a convicted heretic, was burnt at Smithfield on 20 December. It was believed at the time that the accusation of heresy was made in revenge for actions of Hunne's in refusing a mortuary due to his parish priest, and in accusing the latter of having offended against the Statutes of Praemunire. For a full account of the case and its influence see A. Ogle, *The Tragedy of the Lollards' Tower* (Oxford, 1949). Some new evidence bearing on the case has been discovered by Mr S. F. C. Milsom, "Richard Hunne's 'Praemunire' ", *EHR* lxxvi. (1961), 80–2.

English clergy, which we saw in earlier lectures to have been often helpful to the Crown in the thirteenth and fourteenth centuries, had in the fifteenth come to be excluded in practice. It is true that an opinion of the judges given in the Exchequer Chamber in Trinity Term 1467, states that "the pope can write to the Bishop of Canterbury and compel him to summon his clergy to grant an aid to defend the Faith",[1] but three years before that, King and Archbishop had regarded Pius II's attempt to impose a tax for the crusade as a serious threat. Bourgchier thought it unwise to summon his Convocation to consider the papal bull as the Pope would be sure to hear of it and be angered by a refusal. Edward IV dreaded "the perille and inconveniencye that myght folowe by thexsample of such imposicion hereafter, whereof the lyke hath not been ofte tymes put in ure in the daies of our noble progenitoris, right lothe to suffer such novelrye to take effect in our daies". A solution was found by the King interposing himself between the clergy and the papacy. Diocesan assemblies were summoned instead of Convocation, and the King's letter together with a memorandum from the Archbishop was laid before the clergy who were urged to make a grant to the King which he might pass on to the Pope as a token of England's good will.[2] In 1481 a similar request for a subsidy to Pope Sixtus IV was laid before Convocation by the papal collector, to the great embarrassment of the Archbishop who adopted the expedient of appointing a committee which did not complete its deliberations before the dissolution of the Convocation.[3] The problem occurred again in 1502 when Alexander VI imposed a tax of a tenth on all churches for the protection of Christendom against the Turks. Henry VII, having, as he said, before his eyes the liberties and immunities of the Church and realm of England, hitherto inviolably observed, and being unwilling to allow novelties which might be used later to the prejudice of the Church, induced the

[1] Hemmant, op. cit., lxiv, 11.

[2] *Registrum T. Bourgchier*, xxx, 117–29.

[3] Id., 136–8, 146–50.

Pope to exempt England from the tax, though he informed the clergy that it would be right that a grant should be made to the crown which might be used to assist in defence against the Turks. This course appears to have been followed, the grant being made in Convocation not, as in 1464, by diocesan assemblies.[1] Two of these three incidents in particular show the immediate and sharp reaction of the English monarchy against the suggestion that the pope had the right to impose a tax upon the clergy of the realm.

The second point concerns the form of citation and the time of holding Convocation. It is a remarkable fact that from 1435 to the death of Henry VII in April 1509, Convocation always met in consequence of a royal writ addressed to the archbishop and incorporated by him in his citation.[2] There were thirty meetings in this period of seventy-four years. In 1510 there was a break when Warham held a Convocation in January for the reform of ecclesiastical abuses,[3] but the royal writ was issued again in the following year for the Convocation which met in connection with the Parliament of 1512–13;[4] in 1514 for the Convocation which was prolonged to coincide with the Parliament of 1515;[5] in 1523 for the Convocation which coincided with the Parliament of that year but was partially superseded by Wolsey's legatine council;[6] and in 1529 for the Convocation which coincided with the Reformation Parliament and made the Submission of the Clergy.[7] In previous lectures we have seen

[1] *MS. Register of Richard Fox, Bishop of Winchester*, i. ff 33–5 v.; cf. *The Registers of Oliver King, Bishop of Bath and Wells, and Hadrian de Castello, Bishop of Bath and Wells, 1503–18*, ed. H. C. Maxwell-Lyte (Somerset Record Society, 1939), 65, 72, 80.

[2] In my fuller study of the medieval convocations I hope to include a table of citations which will supply the evidence for this statement.

[3] *MS. Register of Richard Fitzjames, Bishop of London*, f 10.

[4] Id., f 23 v.

[5] *MS. Register of Richard Mayew, Bishop of Hereford*, f 88. The citation is not given in the printed text of this register.

[6] *MS. Register of John Voysey, Bishop of Exeter*, ii. f 16; cf. Pollard, *Wolsey*, 189–91.

[7] *MS. Register of John Longland, Bishop of Lincoln* (Lincoln episcopal registers xxvi), f 173; cf. Wilkins, op. cit., iii. 717.

something of the close connection of Parliament and Convocation in their early history but during the century from 1380 to 1480 there had been no very exact coincidence in the meeting of the two bodies. This coincidence begins to be noticeable after 1489, and it is probable that by 1529 the issue of a convocation writ together with the parliamentary writs was regarded as normal practice. The form of the writ, beginning with the words *Quibusdam arduis et urgentibus negotiis* first appears in 1397 and, except for October 1419, was used regularly from 1402 onwards, although in 1502 the preamble was lengthened to deal with the special case of the papal tax which has just been mentioned. This aspect of Convocation as an assembly held at the royal request and to consider the king's needs was emphasized by the activities of Wolsey as legate. In 1523 the opening ceremonies had only just been concluded at St Paul's when the whole assembly was summoned to Westminster to join the Convocation of York in the cardinal's legatine council.[1] Five years earlier Wolsey had sharply reminded Warham that it was his business and not the Archbishop of Canterbury's to formulate plans for reform.[2] It seemed as if only the taxing aspect of the provincial Convocation was to survive.

This development, important as it was, must not however be allowed to obscure the third point to which attention is to be drawn, namely the attempts towards reform that were made during Warham's primacy. As has been said in an earlier lecture "pro moribus corrigendis et excessibus reformandis" was the usual plea for the summoning of a provincial council, but in England in the fourteenth and fifteenth centuries reform, in the eyes of churchmen, usually meant resistence to lay encroachments upon ecclesiastical privilege, or else the extirpation of heresy, and indeed these two things were not always very clearly separated, as the

[1] Wilkins, op. cit., iii. 700; H. Ellis, *Original Letters illustrative of English history* (2nd edn. London, 1825), i. 219–23.
[2] Wilkins, op. cit., iii. 660.

Hunne case showed. It is rare, before 1500, to find an English Church council which showed much awareness of the real scandals of ecclesiastical administration, the secularized outlook of the clergy from the bishops downwards, the abuses of the Church courts, and the legalism which dominated both theology and popular religion. With the advent of the sixteenth century there seems to have been both a greater awareness of the need for reform and some attempt to meet it. As regards the awareness one cannot do better than point to the extremely outspoken sermon preached by Colet before the Convocation of 1512.[1] Criticism of the method of appointment of bishops in the English Church has been a constant theme through the centuries, but it is not every preacher who would say to an assembly of bishops: "Because prelates are chosen often time more by favour of men than by the grace of God; therefore truly have we not a few time bishops full little spiritual men, rather worldly than heavenly, davouring more the spirit of this world than the spirit of Christ." Colet went on to speak of the need for bishops to reside in their dioceses, to be careful in ordination and in appointment to office, to spend their income:

> not in costly building, not in sumptuous apparel and pomps, not in feasting and banquetting, not in excess and wantonness, not in enriching of kinsfolk, not in keeping of dogs, but in things profitable and necessary to the church.

And he exhorted them:

> For sooth if you keep the laws, and if you reform first your life to the rules of the Canon laws, then shall ye give us light in the which we may see what is to be done of our parte,—that is to say the light of your good example. And we, seeing our fathers so keeping the laws, will gladly follow the steps of our fathers.

[1] The English text of this sermon is reprinted in J. H. Lupton, *A Life of John Colet D.D.* (London, 1887), 293–304, from which the extracts given here are taken. Mr F. S. Ferguson has very kindly examined the Latin text as printed by Pynson, and tells me that in his opinion the publication of it must be placed between February 1512 and July 1513.

Colet did not want many new laws, but that the existing laws be observed, and he said:

> at the last let be renewed those laws and constitutions of fathers of the celebration of councils, that command provincial councils to be oftener used for the reformation of the church. For there never happeneth nothing more hurtful to the Church of Christ, than the lack both of council general and provincial.

In the Convocation of two years previously Warham had made some beginnings of an attempt at reform. The law requiring chaplains and other stipendiary clergy to attend the choir services of the cathedrals and collegiate churches to which they were attached had been tightened up, and the bishops had been given fresh powers to deal with cases of simony, and to punish those of the clergy who displayed worldliness by elaboration of dress.[1] Warham had also in 1507 issued ordinances for the reform of certain abuses in his own courts.[2] In 1518–19 Wolsey was discussing with the bishops various schemes of reforms, and diocesan synods were held as part of his investigation. Plans for the creation of a dozen new dioceses were mooted as well as other long overdue improvements of organization.[3] In 1527 Warham had made further changes in the Court of Arches,[4] and in the first session of the 1529 Convocation heads of reform among both secular and regular clergy were discussed, and it is possible that ordinances were made restricting the ordination and promotion of clerks, simony, aspects of clerical worldliness, and the condition of monasteries.[5] Slowly, but definitely as it seems, the clergy were beginning to take lay criticisms of the Church seriously, and to recognize the need for something more drastic in the way of reform than had occurred to them hitherto. They were, however,

[1] *Registrum Ricardi Mayew Episcopi Herefordensis*, ed. A. T. Bannister (Cantilupe and *CY* societies, 1919), 106–9.

[2] Wilkins, op. cit., iii. 650.

[3] Id., iii. 661, 715; *Registrum Caroli Bothe Episcopi Herefordensis*, ed. A. T. Bannister (Cantilupe and *CY* societies, 1921), 59 f, 65–8; cf. E. L. Taunton, *Thomas Wolsey Legate and Reformer*, London, 1902, 117–24.

[4] Wilkins, op. cit., iii. 710.

[5] Id., iii. 717.

too late to be able to resist the main force of the attack which was to come upon the right of independent legislation, and this is the fourth point to be emphasized.

The case of Richard Hunne, which has rightly been regarded as of great significance in exacerbating lay feeling against the clergy and the Church courts, was followed in 1515 by the proceedings taken in Convocation against Dr Standish, Warden of the Mendicant Friars, who had attempted to justify an Act of Parliament passed to limit benefit of clergy.[1] The proceedings are not without their obscurities but it seems that Standish was accused of maintaining that a constitution ordained by the pope and clergy does not bind a region where a contrary custom has always prevailed. Standish sought help from the King and a debate took place before Henry and representatives of Parliament together with the justices and the King's counsel both spiritual and temporal. Behind much of the argument lay the question whether laws of the realm were superior to all that part of the ecclesiastical law which was not universally recognized as the law of God. In 1515 the issue was not fought to a finish, but it was raised in a sharper form after 1529.

2

At some stage early in the Parliament which began in the autumn of 1529, a series of complaints against the Church courts was drawn up by members of the Commons who included in what they said the observation that while the lords spiritual had a voice in the making of laws in Parliament, they and the clergy yet claimed to make further laws in Convocation without consulting anyone.[2] In another draft this wording was sharpened:

[1] R. Keilway, *Reports* (edn. of 1688), ff 182 v.–185 v.; Ogle, op. cit., 132–61; Pollard, op. cit., 43–52.

[2] G. R. Elton, "The Commons' Supplication of 1532; Parliamentary Manoeuvres in the Reign of Henry VIII", *EHR*, lxvi. (1951), 507–34. Dr Elton's conclusions have been criticized with some force by Mr J. P. Cooper, "The Supplication against the Ordinaries reconsidered," *EHR*, lxxii. (1957), 616–41.

> the prelattes & ordinaries with the Clergy of this your most excellent Realme have in thayr Convocacyons heretofforе made ordeynyd and Constitutyd dyuers lawse and also do make daylye dyuers lawes and ordenanunces without your Royall assent or knowlage or the assent or consent of Any of your laye Subiectes.

This petition was brought forward in the session which opened in January 1532, and became the document known as the Commons' Supplication against the Ordinaries. It was presented to the King on 18 March and referred by him for answer to the Convocation. On 15 April the Lower House produced replies to some of the complaints, replies which were read by Gardiner, Bishop of Winchester, approved by the Upper House, and assented to by the Lower on 19 April.[1]

On the point of the necessity of the royal assent for canons the answer said that the King must know from his learning that the clergy could not submit the execution of their charges and duty to his royal assent. But if, as heretofore had been done, the King would show them his mind and opinion they would most gladly hear and follow it with all submission and humility. They also asked that both their own laws and the laws of the realm should be conformed to the determination of Scripture and Holy Church.[2] The King, delivering the answer to the Speaker of the House of Commons gave him a lead by saying "We thynke their answere will smally please you, for it semeth to us very slender".[3] At the same time he demanded of the Convocation a second answer. This was given in May, and contained the offer that while Convocation should continue to make ecclesiastical laws they were content to promise "to publish and put forth, as upon the lay subjects, no constitutions, acts or ordinances which they should thereafter make, without his consent required;

[1] Wilkins, op. cit., iii. 748. [2] Id., iii. 750 f.

[3] E. Hall, *The Union of the two noble and illustre famelies of Lancastre & Yorke* (London, 1548), "The Triumphant reigne of Kyng Henry the VIII", f ccv.

and from time to time to suspend such acts and ordinances, thereafter to be made, until they should be authorized by his consent and authority, except they were such as concerned the maintenance of faith and good manners in the Church, or the reformation and correction of sin".[1] This, however, was not satisfactory, and on 10 May Convocation was told that it must agree to three propositions presented on behalf of the King. These were: (1) No constitution or ordinance to be thereafter enacted promulged or put in execution without the King's assent; (2) Existing provincial constitutions to be examined and revised by a commission of thirty-two persons, sixteen from Parliament and sixteen from the clergy; (3) All other constitutions not abrogated by the commission to stand with the King's assent.[2]

On the next day Henry sent for the Speaker and twelve members of the Commons, and informed them that he had just discovered a major constitutional issue:

> We thought that ye clergie of our realme had been our subiectes wholy, but now wee haue well perceived, that thei bee but halfe our subiectes, yea and scace our subiectes: for all the Prelates at their consecracion, make an othe to the Pope, clene contrary to the othe that thei make to vs, so that thei seme to be his subiectes, and not ours, the copie of bothe the othes, I deliver here to you, requiryng you to inuent some ordre, that we bee not thus deluded, of our Spirituall subiectes.[3]

An outbreak of the plague prevented the House from doing more than discuss briefly in tones of horror this discovery when it was reported to them. Meanwhile anxious debate took place in Convocation. Compromises were proposed and discussed with a group of lay peers and counsellors representing the King, and eventually on 15 May the clergy surrendered in the document which we know as the Submission of the Clergy,[4] and which was embodied two years

[1] Wilkins, op. cit., iii. 753f.
[2] Id., iii. 749.
[3] Hall, op. cit., f ccv.
[4] Wilkins, op. cit., iii. 749.

later in 1534 in the Act 25 Henry VIII, cap 19: "The submission of the clergy and restraint of appeals".[1]

Both these documents contain the substance of the three articles presented in the King's name on 10 May. In the submission the clergy undertake not to make any new canons without the royal assent, they ask for a commission to review existing canons and say that those approved by the commission are to be put in force with the royal assent, and they add a parenthesis about convocation which does not seem to appear in the King's three articles nor in any of the earlier documents. It states that Convocation "is, always has been, and must be assembled only by your highness' commandment of writ". The Act recited the substance of the Submission and then, treating it as a petition, proceeded to give the authority of Parliament to it and to impose penalties for transgression. The parenthesis about the summoning of Convocation was cast into a positive form and the historical part of it was dropped, so that it reads "which alway shall be assembled by authority of the king's writ".

The Submission of the clergy on 15 May 1532 was followed immediately by the prorogation of Convocation by virtue of a royal writ. The date fixed for its resumption was 5 November, but before then, in August, Archbishop Warham died. This should have caused the dissolution of the synod, but the King addressed a writ to the Prior and chapter of Canterbury, as guardians of the spiritualities of the vacant see, directing them to prorogue the assembly from 5 November to 5 February 1533.[2] In fact they seem to have sent out a mandate through the Bishop of London in a form similar to that of the summons of a new Convocation.[3] The assembly met on 5 February, and after transacting business for six days was adjourned to 17 March when some of the legal formalities connected with

[1] H. Gee and W. J. Hardy, *Documents illustrative of English Church history* (London, 1910), 176–8, the Submission of 1532, and 195–200, the Statute of 1534. There seems to be no record of the action of the York Convocation.

[2] Wilkins, op. cit., iii. 749.

[3] *MS. Register of Geronimo de Ghinucci, Bishop of Worcester*, f 79.

the opening of a new Convocation took place, after which there was a further adjournment to 26 March.[1] Now the Bishop of London was presiding and there were three days of discussion of the King's divorce. On 30 March Cranmer was consecrated Archbishop of Canterbury and immediately took charge. On that day the Bishops of London, Winchester, and Lincoln presided by virtue of a commission from him, and on the 1 April he presided in person. On 8 April the Convocation was by royal writ prorogued to 7 June, and then by intervals to 4 November 1534.[2] On that date the Lower House, by a majority of thirty-four to five gave a negative answer to the question whether the Roman pontiff has any greater jurisdiction in this realm of England given to him by God in Holy Scripture than any other foreign bishop, and Cranmer gave orders that in future in all forms of proxy drawn up for Convocation the words "apostolicae sedis legatus" were to be omitted from his title, and the word "metropolitanus" substituted.[3] There were then further long prorogations by royal writ to 4 November 1535, February and April 1536, and then, also by writ, the Convocation was dissolved on 24 April.[4]

A new Convocation was summoned for 9 June of the same year, 1536. Now followed an unforeseen consequence of the assumption two years earlier by Henry, of the title of "the only supreme head in earth of the Church of England". At the second session of the new Convocation Master William Petre appeared as proctor for Thomas Cromwell, recently appointed the King's vicar-general for ecclesiastical causes, and demanded that the King, and in consequence his vicar-general, be given "supremus locus in synodo". The remaining sessions, to the dissolution on 20 July, were attended by Cromwell himself.[5] He is usually described as having presided over Convocation, but this is not quite accurate if by preside is meant that he entirely supplanted the Archbishop. The

[1] Wilkins, op. cit., iii. 749.
[2] Id., iii. 756f.
[3] Id., iii. 769. Four members voted for the Pope, and one was "dubitans".
[4] Id., iii. 802f.
[5] Id., iii. 803.

latter was obviously still in charge. On 21 June it was he who laid before the synod a draft sentence of nullity of the King's marriage with Anne Boleyn "in praesentia Thomae Cromwell", and only the Archbishop, bishops, prelates and the Prolocutor are said to have subscribed it. On 23 June the Prolocutor and the clergy are said to have appeared "coram reverendissimo". On 11 and 20 July Cromwell, the Archbishop, and the members of both houses subscribed two papers of conclusions presented by the Bishop of Hereford. On 19 July it is said that an agreement was made between Cromwell and the two houses about the observance of certain feast days.

Convocation did not meet again until May 1539, when again part of the session was attended by Cromwell who this time, in the presence of the bishops, handed to the Prolocutor a schedule of questions concerning the eucharist, clerical marriage, religious vows, and confession, on which their opinion was desired.[1] He does not seem to have been present in April 1540,[2] and by the time of the July session which dealt with the annulment of Henry's marriage with Anne of Cleves,[3] the minister was in prison.

This Convocation was the first to be held without the presence of the religious. The citation, issued on 26 March, had been in the usual form, demanding the attendance of abbots and priors, but Bishop Voysey of Exeter noted at the end of his return "Abbates vel priores nulli sunt in Diocesi Exoniensis",[4] and other bishops no doubt did the like. Bishop Voysey's return consisted of the dean and the four archdeacons, to whom must be added the two proctors for the clergy of the diocese. We may compare this with his return in 1523 when there had been in addition the names of eight abbots and nine priors.[5] The Dissolution in fact removed three quarters of the members of the Canterbury Convocation and half the Convocation of York.

[1] Id., iii. 845. [2] Id., iii. 850. [3] Id., iii. 851.
[4] *MS. Register of John Voysey*, ii. f 80. [5] Id., ii. f 17 v.

The two remaining Convocations of Henry VIII's reign in 1542 and 1545 saw no further constitutional changes.

3

The preamble to the Act in Restraint of Appeals, passed in 1533, sets out a theory of the constitution.[1] Under the King are two bodies, the body spiritual or the English Church which declares and interprets any cause of the law divine or of spiritual learning; and the body temporal which is concerned with the ownership of lands or goods and the keeping of the peace "and both their authorities and jurisdictions do conjoin together in the due administration of justice, the one to help the other". In that year, 1533, it would have been possible to argue that the Submission of 1532 had placed the clergy in Convocation under the Crown but not under Parliament. It is true that in the commission to review the canon law, for which Convocation had asked, half the membership was to be drawn from the two Houses of Parliament, but their recommendations were to be given authority by the King alone, and there was no suggestion that they should be submitted to Parliament, any more than that Parliamentary consent was necessary for the making of new canons.

This balance of powers was upset in 1534 when the Submission was embodied in an Act of Parliament. The subordination of Convocation to Parliament was not merely implied, but, it may be argued, actually contained in the proviso that no canons "shall be made or put into execution within this realm by authority of the convocation of the clergy, which shall be contrariant or repugnant to the king's prerogative royal, or the customs, laws, or statutes of this realm". Those who have studied the relations of Church and State in pre-Reformation England can have little doubt what was in mind here. The Church courts exercised a wide jurisdiction over the laity in matters matrimonial, testamentary

[1] Gee and Hardy, op. cit., 187–95.

and moral. This was to continue, but in determining the content of the law to be applied in this area of what might be called mixed matters the last word was now beyond all doubt to rest with the customs, laws and statutes of the realm. At first probably few men saw much further than that, but within a matter of months there was a new development when a convocation opinion on what might be regarded as a doctrinal matter namely the Scriptural basis of papal authority, was made the foundation of an Act of Parliament,[1] and an extension of this was the Six Articles Act of 1539 which gave statutory authority to convocation opinions on the eucharist, clerical celibacy, religious vows, and confession.[2] Under Edward VI this development received still further extension. With the advent of Elizabeth I, however, there was a reassertion of the theory of the preamble to the Act in Restraint of Appeals. Much of this belongs to the history of Elizabeth's Parliaments, so fully and fascinatingly set out by Sir John Neale, who has shown us how repeatedly the Queen resisted the attempts of the Puritan party in the Commons to carry through legislation affecting the Church. The complement to that picture is the revival of the legislative activity of Convocation, in, for example, the Revision of the Articles of Religion,[3] and the making of canons and constitutions. In 1571 [4] and again in 1597–8 [5] short codes of canons were drawn up with the Queen's knowledge, and the second of these was promulgated under the great seal without reference to Parliament.

These codes seem, however, to have held good for the Queen's lifetime only, so that at the beginning of the new reign it was necessary to review the situation. In 1604 the Canterbury Convocation, sitting under the presidency of Bancroft, then Bishop of London and shortly to be translated

[1] Id., 243f.
[2] Id., 303–19.
[3] E. Cardwell, *Synodalia* (Oxford, 1852), i. 34–52.
[4] Id., i. 111–31; W. E. Collins, *The canons of 1571* (Church Historical Society, xl. 1899).
[5] Cardwell, op. cit., 147–63.

to Canterbury, subscribed the Thirty Nine Articles [1] and embarked upon a fresh revision of the canons. This resulted in the code of 141 canons which, with three or four changes made in the nineteenth century, is still a fundamental and major part of the canon law of the Church of England. The main work of codification is said to have been done by three lawyers, Sir Thomas Ridley, Dr John Cowell, and Sir Edward Stanhope. The code was passed by the Convocation of Canterbury on 25 June 1604, and confirmed on 6 September by Letters Patent issued under the Great Seal.

In his confirmation the King enjoined that the canons be "diligently observed, executed, and equally kept by all our loving Subjects of this our kingdom",[2] not, be it noted, by the clergy only; that in every parish church or chapel they be read through at Divine Service once a year, and that the Book of the Canons be provided at the charge of the parish. James I was premature in enjoining upon all his subjects canons which had been passed for the province of Canterbury only, and this the Yorkists were not slow to point out. After some argument the Convocation of York was allowed to deliberate and to give its assent in 1605.[3] The Puritan party in Parliament violently attacked the canons and introduced a bill to annul the effect of some of them, but though they did not succeed in getting it through, controversy about the status of the code continued. The question at issue came to be whether canons made by Convocation with the royal assent could bind the laity, and ultimately the contention that they could not prevailed. Towards the end of the seventeenth century Chief Justice Holt stated: "Tis very plain that all the clergy are bound by the canons confirmed by the King but they must be confirmed by parliament to bind the laity"[4] and in 1736 Lord Hardwicke enlarged this statement in what is now the *locus classicus* for the subject:

[1] C. Hardwick, *A history of the Articles of Religion* (London, 1884), 230.
[2] Cardwell, op. cit., i. 328. [3] Wilkins, op. cit., iv. 426–8.
[4] *Matthew v. Burdett*, 2 Salkeld, 412.

> We are all of opinion that the Canons of 1603, not having been confirmed by Parliament, do not *proprio vigore* bind the laity; I say *proprio vigore*, by their own force and authority; for there are many provisions contained in these canons, which are declaratory of ancient usage and law of the Church of England, received and allowed here, which, in that respect, and by virtue of such ancient allowance, will bind the laity; but that is an obligation antecedent to, and not arising from, this body of canons.[1]

A different issue was to be raised when next the Convocation made canons. In April 1640 the synods assembled at the same time as Parliament and the royal licence was given to frame canons. On 5 May, before the Canterbury Convocation had reached any conclusion, the Parliament was suddenly dissolved. Immediately question was raised whether the Convocation was dissolved also, and this view was taken by a party in the Lower House. The King consulted legal advisers who gave the following opinion: "The Convocation called by the King's writ under the great seal doth continue until it be dissolved by writ or commission under the great seal, notwithstand the parliament be dissolved". The Convocation, therefore, continued to the twenty-ninth of May and drew up a code of seventeen canons, which received the royal assent and were confirmed by letters patent.[2] Two of the seventeen, in particular, excited fierce criticism from the Puritan party, and a resolution disallowing them was passed in the first session of the Long Parliament. The issue of whether Convocation could continue to sit after Parliament had been dissolved was not settled, but it has since been the practice always to issue the writs for the dissolution of Convocation at the same time as those for the dissolution of Parliament, a practice which has considerable inconvenience, particularly when, as in 1950 and 1951 two dissolutions occur within a short period. Sessions of Convocation have to

[1] *Middleton v. Crofts*, 2 Atkinson, 650. That there are reasons to doubt whether historically this judgement is soundly based is indicated by Dr N. Sykes, *From Sheldon to Secker* (Cambridge, 1959), 203f.

[2] Wilkins, op. cit., iv. 538–42.

be cancelled and the Church is put to the expense of fresh elections. The canons of 1640 have not been held binding by the courts, for they were expressly excepted from the act of 1661 which restored the ecclesiastical law as it had been before the Commonwealth.[1]

We have surveyed a period in which the English provincial synods were definitely subordinated to the authority of the Crown. The Tudor monarchs and the first two Stuarts were all keenly interested in religious matters upon which they had definite, if differing views. From 1558 to the time of the Commonwealth it was the royal policy to protect the Church against any further limitations of its freedom and in particular against parliamentary encroachment upon that liberty of ecclesiastical legislation which remained with the Convocations. It must be remembered, however, that these synods were advantageous to the Crown in another way. The events of the reformation had not taken away the Convocations' right to tax the clergy, even though it had become usual for the clerical subsidy to be confirmed by statute. In 1640 the Convocations not only passed canons after the dissolution of Parliament, they also granted subsidies of four shillings in the pound for four years, and though the yield of a clerical subsidy was not what it had been in earlier times it was still something worth having, and could be got with less trouble and danger than a parliamentary tax. There was therefore an advantage in having the synods meet regularly.

What must principally be borne in mind, however, is that the legislation and the events which have been surveyed in this lecture belong to a view of society which prevailed in England from early times to the middle of the seventeenth century, the view that Church and State are but two aspects of one community and that dissent from neither is to be allowed. This more than anything else gives meaning to the conflicts of jurisdiction and the rivalries of legislative capacity which produced the Reformation Statutes.

[1] 13 Car. 2. c. 12.

LECTURE 7

15 May 1960

SUPPRESSION AND REVIVAL

I mentioned to him how common it was in the world to tell absurd stories of him, and to ascribe to him very strange sayings. JOHNSON. "What do they make me say, Sir?" BOSWELL. "Why, Sir, as an instance very strange indeed (laughing heartily as I spoke), David Hume told me, you said that you would stand before a battery of cannon to restore the Convocation to its full powers." Little did I apprehend that he had actually said this: but I was soon convinced of my error; for with a determined look, he thundered out "And would I not, Sir? Shall the Presbyterian *Kirk* of Scotland have its General Assembly, and the Church of England be denied its Convocation?"

Boswell, *Life of Johnson*, 1763.

1

IN MAY 1661, the assembling of the Convocations after a silence of twenty years marked the re-establishment of the Anglican ecclesiastical polity, and there seemed to be promise of carrying out a more thorough reform and modernization of the Church than had been possible in the troubled years before the Civil War. Revision of the canons as well as of the Prayer Book was discussed.[1] The former came to nothing but the latter issued in our present English Prayer Book, synodically subscribed on 20 December 1661 [2] and imposed by the Act of Uniformity of the following year. Thereafter the Convocations seem to have been allowed to do little business. Those, both clerical and lay, who were responsible for ensuring that the restoration of the monarchy was accompanied by the restoration of the Church seem to have been blind to impossibility of maintaining the unitary system of Church and State to which reference was made at the end of the last lecture. It is fair to add that they were not alone in this, and that the question was which of the various competing systems should be imposed upon the whole country. Dr Bosher, in his study of the making of the Restoration Settlement, has argued with force that the choice which had to be made was between a definite system of Church Order within which a wide range of belief was tolerated, and a rigid system of both doctrine and practice. The former of the two won and, as Dr Bosher writes, because of the stand of the Laudian party "the Church of England, alone among post-Reformation bodies, remained constant in its refusal to commit itself to a rigid system of doctrine and practice, and preserved that tension of authority and

[1] Wilkins, op. cit., iv. 566; Cardwell, op. cit., ii. 642f.
[2] Cardwell, op. cit., ii. 659f.

freedom, of variety and order, which is its unique heritage in the Christian world".[1] This victory was, however, achieved at the cost of allowing the settlement to be imposed by Act of Parliament, and in the belief that religious unity could be enforced upon the whole country, at least to the extent of excluding from public life those who would not conform. Thus the new era was darkened both by the medieval view of a unitary society and by the Erastianism of the preceding century and a half. In consequence the next period in the history of the Convocations is one of disaster.

In 1664 Archbishop Sheldon, by oral agreement with Lord Chancellor Clarendon, surrendered the right of the clergy to tax themselves in Convocation. Dr Sykes has suggested that this agreement was made as the alternative to a revaluation of ecclesiastical benefices such as would increase the proportion of taxation paid by the clergy.[2] If so it was a bargain of extreme short-sightedness, and one which showed little knowledge of the history of the synod. We have seen how large a place the right of consent to taxation occupies among the factors which influenced the development of Convocation, and also the peculiar power it had given to the lower clergy *vis-à-vis*, the bishops. Now the Convocation was of no particular use to the government, and although it continued to be summoned when there was a Parliament, it was, as a rule, quickly prorogued, and the pages of the convocation register between 1664 and 1669 are almost a blank.

When next the Convocation was allowed to discuss serious business, after the Revolution of 1688, it was presented with proposals for substantial changes in the liturgy, as well as in other aspects of Church settlement, in order to try to bring in some at least of the Protestant dissenters.[3] It became quickly apparent, however, that there was disagreement between the two houses. The Lower House, by a small

[1] R. S. Bosher, *The making of the Restoration Settlement* (London, 1951), 277.

[2] N. Sykes, op. cit., 41–3.

[3] Cardwell, op. cit., ii. 692–700.

majority, elected as its Prolocutor Dr Jane, Dean of Gloucester and Regius Professor of Divinity at Oxford, who had been a member of the commission appointed to prepare a revision of the liturgy and had absented himself from the proceedings on the ground that no changes were needed. The opposition of the Lower House to all proposals was such that only a revision of the three State Services for 30 January, 29 May, and 5 November was achieved. Burnet, who then was a keen advocate of the proposals, later thought that their carrying at that time might have made the schism of the Non-Jurors a much bigger separation than was actually the case, as many more persons would have adhered to what they viewed as the old and true Church of England.[1] On the other hand, as Dr Sykes has pointed out, the failure of Convocation to deal with the revision of the canons and of the ecclesiastical courts, which were specifically mentioned in the royal letters of business, did great harm to the Church. He writes: "With the passing of the Toleration Act and the legal protection and recognition thereby given to orthodox Protestant dissenters, the established church was faced by an entirely novel situation, to which the Canons of 1603 were no longer entirely applicable. The omission to revise them at the Restoration was doubly underlined now by the second failure in 1689, with the result that the ecclesiastical canons and courts were alike inadequate to the problems of the post-Revolution era".[2]

The experience of 1689 caused the government to resume the practice of the previous twenty-five years, and Convocation again maintained only a formal existence. But in 1697 a new champion appeared with the publication of the *Letter to a Convocation Man*, in which it was argued that the Convocation has the right not only to meet with every session of Parliament, but also to do business. This was followed by a pamphlet warfare during the next three years, in which

[1] G. Burnet, *History of my own time* (London, 1850 edn.), ch. v. 542.
[2] Sykes, op. cit., 45f.

Francis Atterbury appeared as the chief asserter of the rights of Convocation, and William Wake as his opponent. The issue at that stage was whether the terms of the Submission of the Clergy meant that the Convocations could not make canons without the royal licence, or whether they meant that no business at all could be transacted without royal permission. Dr Sykes sums up the results of this stage of the controversy in these words:

> The historical researches of both parties established the fact that the lower clergy had an undeniable right to represent their grievances to the bishops and to offer their opinions on any matters conductive to the good of religion and the church; whilst it was for the Upper House to determine what, if any, action should be taken. If such action must take the form of canonical enactment, then a royal licence was necessary; but short of this both houses had considerable freedom of deliberation and debate.[1]

A practical achievement was the permission given to the Convocation in 1701 to transact business. But now a new issue arose as Atterbury, backed by a substantial following, argued that the Lower House stood in a similar relation to the Upper as to that in which the House of Commons stands to the House of Lords. In furtherance of this a majority of the Lower House claimed to be able to put their Prolocutor into the chair before his election had been confirmed by the Upper House; to have the right to adjourn themselves by a vote of their own House and to fix their days of meeting at other times than those appointed by the Archbishop; and to have the right to appoint committees of their whole House, and to insist on a conference with the Upper House instead of presenting their answers in writing to documents sent down from the Upper House. The story of the ensuing controversy has been told in more than one recent work and it is therefore unnecessary to repeat it here.[2] Comparative calm prevailed

[1] Id., 47.

[2] The most important accounts are those by Dr Sykes in his three books *Sheldon to Secker*, *William Wake* (Cambridge, 1957), *Edmund Gibson*

after Atterbury entered the Upper House as Bishop of Rochester in 1713, and some progress in business was actually made. Draft canons for regulating the issue of marriage licences in order to prevent clandestine marriages, and draft forms of service for certain occasions not provided for in the Prayer Book were drawn up and, had it not been for the Queen's death, it is likely that they would have received the royal assent. It almost seemed as if the work of revision which had failed in 1661 and 1689 was at last to be taken up again under happier auspices. Even the change of dynasty did not at first darken the picture. In 1715 regulations about the behaviour of the clergy, and a form of service for the consecration of churches and churchyards were prepared,[2] but all was wrecked upon the rock of Bishop Hoadley's doctrinal errors.

In 1710 the Queen, in response to a petition from the Archbishop and bishops, had consulted the judges and the Attorney and Solicitor General as to whether the Convocations still possessed a jurisdiction in matters of heresy. Eight of the twelve judges and the Attorney and Solicitor General replied in the affirmative, and in consequence of this Convocation condemned the Arian doctrine contained in the writings of William Whiston.[3] Benjamin Hoadley had, as early as 1706, made himself objectionable to the Lower House by his views on ecclesiastical authority, and after he had become Bishop of Bangor, roused particular resentment by his sermon on the text "My kingdom is not of this world", preached on 31 March 1717. On 3 May the Lower House drew up to be laid before the bishops on 10 May a representation about Hoadley's sermon and about a book which he had published in the previous year.[4] On 8 May Arch-

(Oxford, 1926); E. F. Carpenter, *Thomas Tenison* (London, 1948), 248–71; G. V. Bennett, *White Kennett* (London, 1957), 26–84.

[1] Cardwell, op. cit., ii. 770–85, 794–815. Some progress had already been made in 1710, id., ii. 724–53.

[2] Id., ii. 816–26.

[3] Id., ii. 753–69.

[4] On the proceedings about Hoadley see Sykes, *William Wake*, i. 141–5.

bishop Wake was sent for to meet Lord Sunderland and certain other members of the administration, and informed that the King was to be advised to issue a writ requiring the prorogation of Convocation, on the 10th. Wake and other bishops had been discussing means by which Hoadley's doctrine might be condemned while at the same time avoiding a personal attack upon him, but now the matter was taken out of their hands. Wake's comment, written a week later to the Archbishop of Dublin, is revealing:

> Your Grace must needs be sensible how hard a game I have to play. The King is a stranger to our constitution; he does nothing but by the advice of others; and I doubt those whom he chiefly relies upon, are far from giving him such advice as they ought to do. It is from hence arise all the difficulties I labour under. Ministers of state mind only what they think will promote their political interests. The service of God and his church is of little weight with them, in comparison of the other; and better twenty convocations were prorogued and bishops and clergy despised who do not think and act as they would have them, than one son of the church (I should have said father) exposed for his faithful service to them, or discouraged from appearing again on the next occasion on their behalf. In the meantime, I will venture to say that in policy, if in nothing else, they should have shewn a little more complaisance to so many bishops of their own side as desired to go on in the defence of the Church of England; the most of whom they have happily disobliged so far as to set them more on their guard than ever they were before, *ne quid detrimenti capiat Ecclesia.*[1]

It quickly became apparent that the government's intention was to prolong the suspension of Convocation indefinitely. The formal sessions continued as before, and at various times in the next thirty-five years attempts were made to have business done. At last in 1741 some further reform of the Church was entered upon, the state of the ecclesiastical courts, qualifications for ordination, the salaries of curates, and clandestine marriages were discussed and legislation contemplated, but for some reason which remains obscure

[1] Quoted by Sykes, *William Wake*, i. 145.

the whole was broken off, and Convocation resumed its sleep.[1] Some picture of it is given in a letter from the Registrar of the diocese of Lincoln to the Bishop's chaplain on 23 May 1761:

Dear S^{r}

You will receive by this same post ye Instrument relating to the Election of Proctors for ye Convocation.

The Notice was much too short, yet we collected together an agreeable sett of clergy, to compliment Mr Cust, and after ye ceremony of the Election was over they had an Hansom Ordinary, and cheerfully were Merry, and drank the health of his Majesty &c—ArchBp. Bp. of ye Diocese, and their Absent representative.

I expected some person deputed by proxy to have come out of Bedfordshire to Lincoln and proposed one of their Body: Upon ye return of ye Monition from Bedford, there was sent an imperfect proxy constituting Dr. Osborn to appear upon ye 21st to vote for the Election of two proctors for ye Diocese but as Dr Osborn did not come nor was it signified to the clergy present whether Dr Osborn would or did offer himself as a candidate they chose Mr Monoux who besides being a prebendary of this Church was recommended by some of the Electors.

This is the 4th Election of this sort I have seen at Lincoln. The Expenses have been Equally paid by the candidates, and I must desire you on behalf of Mr Cust to signify Mr Monoux Election to him and the Expence attending it, which he may pay into your hands and I will refund Mr Cust what he has paid more than his share. I have no reason to believe Mr Monoux will be so ungenteel as not to pay his proportion tho' he was not here and may not thank the Electors for the trust reposed in him.[2]

The bill amounted to £6. 13*s*.

In the previous October Mr Richard Grey, to whom the Registrar had sent a notice of the coming election had replied:

I thank you for the favour of your Letter which I read last night. It is, I think a matter of very little Consequence as things

[1] Sykes, *Sheldon to Secker*, 54f.
[2] Lincoln diocesan archives, Convocation box 4.

> stand at present, who is Proctor for the Clergy in Convocation for the Archdeaconry of Bedford or any other place. I think myself however obliged to you for the notice you have given me in case it might have been of service to know what you have communicated.[1]

This, no doubt, was the general feeling, though there were some who thought otherwise, as the words of Dr Johnson set out at the head of this lecture show.

2

Seventy years passed before any serious attempt was made to change this state of things, and one effect of this long period of silence was that the affairs of the Church passed more and more into the hands of Parliament. Between 1530 and 1760 the average of ecclesiastical statutes was less than two and a half a year. Between 1760 and 1820 it rose to ten. After 1820 the Church experienced the hurricane of reform which swept through most departments of English public life in the mid-nineteenth century and between 1820 and 1870 the annual average of ecclesiastical statutes rose to twenty-five.[2] Ecclesiastical jurisdiction was touched in respect of the Church courts, and the finances and diocesan organization of the Church began to be changed by Act of Parliament. It will be remembered that the suppression of ten Irish bishoprics by Statute was the immediate cause of John Keble's Assize sermon which Newman regarded as the beginning of the Oxford Movement.

It needs to be emphasized, however, that the Tractarians had very little connection with the movement for the revival of Convocation. This was the work of other men, of varied schools of thought, who were in part disturbed by the increase in Parliamentary legislation mentioned above, but

[1] Ibid.

[2] These figures are taken from *The Canon Law of the Church of England, Being the Report of the Archbishop's Commission on Canon Law* (London, 1947), 50.

who also considered that as a result of the repeal of the Test and Corporation Acts in 1828 and Roman Catholic Emancipation in 1829, Parliament was no longer a suitable body to represent the laity of the Church. They accepted the position of religious freedom brought about by those acts, but asked that the Church should also be given a freedom which seemed to them consequential upon it. In June 1830, the Archdeacon of Cleveland, Vernon Harcourt, in a Charge to the clergy of his archdeaconry, advocated the revival of Convocation and the union of the councils of England and Ireland in one National Synod.[1] During the next six years half a dozen pamphlets at least, appeared from the pens of clergymen in parts of the country as widely separated as Gloucester, Lincolnshire, and Montgomeryshire, in one form or another stressing the need for some representative assembly of the Church. The Evangelical Vicar of Cheltenham, the Reverend F. Close, later Dean of Carlisle, wrote of "the absolute necessity of a revival of our legitimate councils".[2]

It is necessary to understand in what form the Convocations existed at this time. Their composition was as it had been since the suppression of the monasteries. The Upper Houses consisted of the diocesan bishops, the Lower of the deans and archdeacons, one proctor for each cathedral chapter, and, in Canterbury, two proctors for the clergy of each diocese. At York there were two proctors for the clergy of each archdeaconry, so that there the proportion of elected members was higher. On the occasion of each new Parliament royal writs were issued for the summoning of a new Convocation and the two archbishops issued their citations which were duly executed in the manner which had been customary since the fourteenth century. In the province of Canterbury the Convocation duly assembled, usually on the

[1] J. B. Sweet, *A memoir of the late Henry Hoare Esq., M.A. with a narrative of the church movements with which he was concerned from 1848 to 1865 and more particularly of the Revival of Convocation* (London, 1689), 25f.

[2] Id., 35.

day after the opening of Parliament, a Latin service was held at St Paul's, a Latin sermon preached, the legal formalities duly carried out. Then the Lower House elected a Prolocutor, after which the assembly moved to Westminster where, after the Dean and chapter had protested the privileges of the Abbey, a Loyal Address was moved and agreed to by both Houses, the Lower House always asserting its independence by altering one word. There was then a prorogation for a few days until the sovereign's reply was received, after which the Archbishop prorogued the Convocation to the first day of each new session of Parliament, and so on until the royal writs for the Dissolution of both assemblies were issued. After the voting of the Loyal Address at the first session, no further business was allowed to be done. At York even less happened. Archbishop Musgrave stated in 1852 that, as far as he could ascertain, since the time of Henry VIII no Archbishop of York had attended his Convocation in person, except in 1689 and 1708, and it seems that none of the other bishops attended, and very few of the clergy. The Archbishop usually appointed a member of the cathedral chapter as his commissioner who opened and prorogued the Convocation, all within a brief time. There was no sermon and no Loyal Address.

By 1837 the movement for the revival had gathered such strength that a considerable number of the clergy of the Northern province determined to elect only such proctors as would appear in person. A strong muster assembled, and as their names were called several of them asserted the right to address the Queen on her accession, in common with their brethren of the South; to proceed to the business of deliberation on matters touching the defence and security of the Church of England, as mentioned in the royal writ; and to petition the Archbishop to intercede with Her Majesty that she would be pleased from time to time to reassemble and convene the several bishops, archdeacons, and proctors in order that they might deliberate and advise. The Archbishop's commissioner, however, refused to hear any of this and formally closed the Convocation, whereupon the disappointed proctors, on the motion of Archdeacon Headlam, adjourned to the Minster Library and adopted an Address and Petition to the crown.[1] Ten years later another attempt was made, this time apparently with the agreement of the aged Archbishop Harcourt, to present a Loyal Address, and a question affecting the election of one of the proctors was also raised, but the death of the Archbishop prevented the business from being completed. His successor, Musgrave, was most unsympathetic, and although, in February 1852, several members notified him on the day before that fixed for the session that they had petitions to present, the session was not opened to hear them. Lord Redesdale raised the matter in the House of Lords and expressed the hope that the Northern Convocation might be allowed the same freedom of meeting and presenting petitions as obtained in Canterbury, but the most he could extract was a promise that the Archbishop would give the matter earnest consideration.[2] In fact Musgrave, to his death in May 1860, resisted all attempts to make his Convocation anything more than a pure formality. In June 1859, the clergy elected a Prolocutor and tried to present him to the Commissioner who refused to take any cognizance of it. Then the Reverend W. Dodd presented a petition from the archdeaconry of Lindisfarne which the Commissioner refused to allow him to read. Dodd, however, had taken legal advice and insisted on his rights by beginning to read the petition aloud, whereupon one of the Commissioners started to read the schedule of prorogation, and the two worthy gentlemen continued for some time reading simultaneously, but Mr Dodd had so worded his petition that he could finish before the end of the schedule of prorogation, as otherwise he would have been out of order. One who was

[1] Id., 42.

[2] *Hansard*, 3rd series, cxxi (1852), col. 420. For the text of the petition see C. Warren, *Synodalia: A Journal of Convocation* (London, 1853), 79f.

present wrote that the Commissioners "concluded a very arbitrary proceeding by accelerating the retirement of the members from their presence, by the intervention of the Verger".[1] In the next year, however, Musgrave was followed by Archbishop Longley, and he in a short time by William Thomson, both of whom were sympathetic to the desire for synodical revival, and in 1861 the York Convocation resumed its active life.

In Canterbury success had been achieved some years earlier. From 1846 there seems to have been increasing public agitation and in November, 1847, the presentation and discussion of petitions (among which was one for the increase of the episcopate and the diaconate) occupied a full day.[2] In the following year the publication of the Reverend William Palmer's *A Plan for the Co-operation of Churchmen*, which had as one of its four objects the restoration of a Church legislature or national synod of some kind, led to the formation of the Bristol Church Union, and similar bodies at Gloucester, Liverpool, Plymouth, Leamington, Warwick, Kenilworth, Stockport, Huntingdon, Beverley, Chester, Manchester, in Dorset, in Leicestershire, and in London.[3] The most active seems to have been a group of clergymen in the archdeaconry of Leicester who on 12 October 1848, held a general clerical meeting in the Bath Rooms at Ashby-de-la-Zouch, and appointed a sub-committee to draw up an address to the Archbishop of Canterbury, asking for the restoration of a synod or representative council of the Church.[4] An address to the Queen was also agreed. These documents came into the hands of an influential layman, Henry Hoare, the banker, and from 1849 he was the real leader of the movement for revival, spending much time and

[1] J. T. Dodd, *Convocation and Edward Dodd's share in its revival* (Oxford, 1931), 31.

[2] *Chronicle of Convocation*, 1–7. The proceedings of Convocation 1847–57 were reprinted and issued in one volume in 1889, and references are to this volume. Sweet, op. cit., 49.

[3] Sweet, op. cit., 60.

[4] Id., 64.

money in obtaining legal opinion upon points of dispute as they arose, in long correspondence with the Archbishop and many others, and in frequent travels to address meetings and arouse support all over the country. He was a man who could deliver to the Archbishop a severe rebuke couched in terms of the deepest respect. From 1851 he worked in close association with Bishop Wilberforce of Oxford who, with the support of Blomfield of London, Philpotts of Exeter, Gilbert of Chichester, and Denison of Salisbury forwarded the movement in the Canterbury Upper House. In the House of Lords, Lords Redesdale, Lyttelton, and Nelson were always ready to ask questions and to press either the government or the Archbishop when occasion served.

Two events in the course of 1850 affected the movement. One was the Gorham judgement delivered by the Judicial Committee of the Privy Council on 8 March, and reversing the judgement of the Court of Arches, on the doctrine of baptism permissible in the Church of England. The controversy resulting from this case confirmed the views of those who were asserting the Church's right to express itself synodically and added to their ranks, but it also had the effect of alienating some of the Evangelicals who had hitherto supported the movement, and from now on the Low Church party led by Lord Shaftesbury could be reckoned among the principal opponents of the revival of Convocation.

The other event of 1850 also affected both supporters and opponents. It was the publication by Cardinal Wiseman of the papal brief establishing the Roman Catholic hierarchy in England. In order to appreciate the excitement roused by this act it is necessary to understand not only the deeply rooted English fear of Rome, but also the interpretation put upon the act by some Roman Catholics. Thus the French periodical *L'Univers*, in a passage which was translated and circulated in this country wrote:

> In the same way as St Gregory transferred the primacy of London to Canterbury, in like manner as Popes Boniface and

> Honorus confirmed the change, so does Pope Pius IX now transfer the primacy of Canterbury to the Archiepiscopal See of Westminster. It is in virtue of authority inherited from his predecessors that the Pope substitutes the See of Southwark for that of London, and that he abolishes all former episcopal sees established in England by the Popes who preceded him in the chair of St Peter. Pius IX distinctly declares it in the brief which creates the new hierarchy.
>
> Consequently, since the promulgation of the Papal brief, the Sees of Canterbury, of York, of London, and any other sees established before this reform, have ceased to exist. The persons who in future may assume the title of Archbishops of Canterbury or Bishop of London, will be nothing less than intruders, schismatic priests, without any spiritual authority.[1]

The papal aggression seemed to Henry Hoare and his friends to make it all the more necessary that the Church of England should be free to express itself and to reform its life through its own properly constituted organs. To others it made more fearful any step that might seem to emancipate the Church from State control and so open the door to possible conflicts of Church and State, and to the influence of Romish tendencies.

There were also some who, while in favour of the revival of synodical government, thought that Convocation was not the right place in which to begin. One of their number wrote to Hoare in 1851, pointing out that the parochial clergy in that assembly were far outnumbered by the ex-officio element all more or less directly appointed by the Crown:

> With a body thus constituted, he said, I have little hope that the Church would have any thing like justice done to her. Doctrine, discipline, every thing would be sacrified to what is called the spirit of the times—Erastianism would rule the day . . . For the present I am for directing our energies towards Diocesan Synods, which, after all, are the older and more legitimate mode of expressing the Church's voice, though, as a matter of convenience, superseded by the Convocation.
>
> In the Diocesan Synod, the parochial clergy would be fairly represented. They are sound, and are to be depended on. The

[1] Id., 253.

> Minister of the day cannot bribe *them* into a betrayal of their Master. And when Diocesan Synods have spoken with sufficient clearness and decision, I think that by that time a sufficient substratum of public opinion (in the best sense) will have been established, without which no body can act, and against which even Convocation itself (if the Minister of the day, thinking he had sufficiently poisoned it, were to allow it to sit in order to carry out *his* views against the Church) would be comparatively powerless.[1]

The unrepresentative character of the Convocations was widely recognized as a difficulty. Some advocated radical reform before they were allowed to do any business, others thought that they should be allowed to continue their formal existence but for practical purposes be superseded by a national assembly on a more representative basis. There was also raised the question of the admission of the laity.

Henry Hoare and his friends fully recognized the need for reform in the constitution of Convocation, but they argued that this must be the work of the synod itself. First let it be restored to life, and then let it set about reforming itself. Only thus could continuity be preserved with the historic representative organs of the English Church, upon which they placed such emphasis.

The advocates of synodical revival were encouraged by the experience of churchmen overseas. The influence exercised upon the English Church by the growth of independent dioceses and provinces in the colonies has not been sufficiently recognized or studied. How such dioceses could be established at all had raised big problems of Church and State, and the way in which they were to be organized created even more difficulties, as the Colenso controversy of the sixties was to show.[2] In 1850 it was Australia which attracted attention.

[1] Id., 308.

[2] The constitutional importance of the Colenso case is at least equal to its doctrinal interest. The clumsiness shown by the Crown lawyers in handling the affairs of the Church in South Africa contributed something to the growing resentment against the Judicial Committee of the Privy Council felt by many churchmen. Bishop Gray's claim to metropolitical authority in South Africa rested in part upon the letters patent issued

In October of that year the bishops of Australia and New Zealand assembled in conference and adopted certain resolutions about the doctrine, law and constitution of the Church in their dioceses.[1] News of this meeting reached England early in 1851 and attracted lively attention. Then in the summer of that year came the diocesan synod held by Bishop Philpotts at Exeter, which issued an important declaration on baptism, and also resolutions about problems facing the Church in that diocese.[2] The summoning of this synod had been the subject of questions in Parliament, and it appears that the law officers of the Crown were consulted as to whether the Submission of the Clergy had been violated. On 25 May Lord John Russell stated, in answer to a question in the House of Commons, that the meeting did not contravene the Act of 25 Henry VIII, though he deprecated the use of the word synod, which he felt liable to misinterpretation.

As regards Convocation some progress was made. At the end of 1850 a Society for the Revival of Convocation had been formed under Hoare's chairmanship, and on 14 January 1851 he presided at a meeting in the Freemasons' Hall in London at which an address to the Queen and a petition to the Archbishop and bishops of the province in synod assembled was drawn up.[3] Convocation had been prorogued from the previous November to 5 February, and there was some doubt whether the presentation of a petition at a prorogued session as distinct from the opening of a new Convocation, would be allowed. The Registrar, on being consulted, said that there were precedents, and so the petition was received formally in each House, but the Arch-

---

to him in 1853 when the see of Cape Town was divided, but the Privy Council decided ten years later, and again in 1865, that the issue of these letters patent had been *ultra vires*. Lord Westbury, who delivered this judgement in 1865 had been Solicitor General in 1853.

[1] R. A. Giles, *The constitutional history of the Australian Church* (London, 1929), 75–82; Sweet, op. cit., 274.

[2] G. C. B. Davies, *Henry Philpotts, Bishop of Exeter, 1778–1869* (London, 1954), 264–86; cf. Sweet, op. cit., 304.

[3] Sweet, op. cit., 255, 261.

bishop then ordered the reading of the prorogation so that no discussion of it was allowed.[1]

In July Lord Redesdale moved in the House of Lords for a copy of the petition to be made available. This was a device for initiating a debate on the general subject of the revival of Convocation, and he, Lords Lyttelton and Nelson and the Bishops of London and Oxford spoke strongly in favour of the revival. The Archbishop of Dublin (Whately) was in favour of providing some form of synodical government for the Church but did not think Convocation suitable for the purpose. The Duke of Argyll, a staunch Presbyterian, who was regarded as one of the chief opponents of Convocation, spoke in deep resentment at any comparison between it and the General Assembly of the Church of Scotland. The Archbishop of Canterbury (Sumner) was also against revival. He thought that Convocation could serve no useful purpose, that if debates were allowed they would manifest and exacerbate disunity in the Church. The Marquess of Lansdowne expressed the government's opposition to revival.[2]

At the session of Convocation in February 1852, petitions that steps should be taken to procure from the Crown the necessary licence for the performance of its constitutional functions, were presented from all twenty-one dioceses. When Wilberforce announced his intention of moving that the Upper House consider the prayer of the petitions, the Queen's Advocate, who was also Vicar-General of the province, interposed saying that he felt it his duty, as legal adviser to the Archbishop, to declare that such a proceeding was without precedent, and cited the statute 25 Henry VIII as forbidding Convocation to do any business whatsoever without the express permission of the Crown. On this he was taken up by Philpotts who forced him to admit that the prohibition of the statute was only against making canons without the Queen's licence, not against doing any business. Wilberforce then proceeded with his motion, consideration of

[1] Id., 280. [2] *Hansard*, 3rd series, cviii (1851), cols. 516ff.

which, after some discussion, was postponed until the next session in August.[1] In fact Convocation was dissolved with Parliament in July and that particular business lapsed with it. The occasion had, however, served to draw out the true meaning of the Submission, and established that the prohibition applied only to the making of canons.

In preparation for the new Convocation the Society for Revival carried out a campaign which resulted in the election of twelve capitular and thirty-four diocesan proctors in favour of revival, as against five and eight opposed to it.[2] The Society also took legal advice on the question of the Archbishop's right to prorogue Convocation on his sole motion *sine consensu fratrum*. A case was prepared and put to three counsel, two of whom, the Attorney-General Sir Frederick Thesiger, and Dr Robert Phillimore gave their opinion that the Archbishop had no such right and advised that if so improperly prorogued the suffragans should formally protest, inform the Lower House, and continue their deliberations. The third, Sir William Page Wood, held that the Archbishop had the right to prorogue on his own authority.[3]

When the Convocation met in November there was an unusually large attendance. In the Upper House Wilberforce moved an amendment to the Loyal Address and secured an insertion which expressed the view that the revival of Convocation would be both desirable and beneficial. He also challenged the Archbishop's right to prorogue without the consent of the other bishops. Sumner refused to give way on this but said that he would be very sorry to exercise the right at any time, except under very peculiar circumstances. The Lower House debated a motion for three days, and a committee of both Houses was appointed to consider certain matters and report in February, to which date the Convocation was prorogued.[4]

[1] Sweet, op. cit., 313–20; *Chronicle of Convocation*, 11.
[2] Sweet, op. cit., 320.
[3] Id., 324–34; Warren, op. cit., 42–9.
[4] *Chronicle of Convocation*, 15f, 41–6, 57f; Warren, op. cit., 117–33;

These proceedings excited alarm in both Houses of Parliament. In the Commons the Home Secretary, Spencer Walpole, tried to minimize the departure from precedent. The only deviation that had occurred had been that the address was debated upon three days instead of upon one, and that a committee had been appointed. The government could not be required to interfere unless the licence of the Crown was desired to make a canon. He added, however, "So long as I have the honour to hold the office I now hold, nothing will induce me to advise the Crown to grant a licence to Convocation to make canons. Nothing would be so detrimental to the Church of England, or so likely to create division in that Church, as to revive Convocation for such a purpose". In the Lords the Earl of Derby assured Lord Shaftesbury that the proceedings of Convocation had gone no further this year than in previous years.[1]

The opponents of revival, who were beginning to lose ground, now decided to attack the appointment of committees which, as it were, kept the synod in being between sessions. In 1853, after the Convocation on 16 February had appointed a committee which was to report in August, the government asked the law officers for their opinion as to the legal position, and on 4 March Lord John Russell had to report that in their opinion there could be no doubt as to the legality of the course pursued. He had also to explain that a prorogation of Convocation was totally different in its nature and effects from a prorogation of Parliament and was, in fact, nothing more than the convocation term for an adjournment.[2]

During that year Wilberforce and Hoare devoted themselves to trying to bring about a change of mind in the Archbishop and in the Prime Minister, Lord Aberdeen.[3] With the latter they were far from being immediately

A. R. Ashwell and R. G. Wilberforce, *Life of the Right Reverend Samuel Wilberforce D.D.* (London, 1880–3), ii. 153f.

[1] *Hansard*, cxxiii (1852), cols. 247, 277.

[2] Id., cxxiv (1853), cols. 977, 1070.

[3] Ashwell and Wilberforce, op. cit., ii. 160–72.

successful, and in the first month of 1854 it seemed that pressure from the other side had carried the day. On 31 January, in the House of Commons Sir John Pakington asked permission to take the unusual course of putting down a question on the first day of the session. He had observed that Convocation was due to reassemble on the following day and had heard a report that in consequence of an interview between certain members of Convocation and the Prime Minister it was intended that Convocation should proceed to business. Lord John Russell replied that the Prime Minister had expressed the view that it would not be desirable to depart from the usual course:

> What he has said is, that it is desirable that the Convocation should be prorogued in the usual manner, and that, therefore, unless a necessity should arise, the interposition of the Crown should not take place. I may say further, though it does not enter into the right hon. Gentleman's question, that if Convocation shall be continued beyond to-morrow, and shall be adjourned to another day, then the Earl of Aberdeen will consider that that case of necessity has arisen, and that the interposition of the Crown should take place.[1]

In fact the Convocation sat only for the one day on 1 February, but it again appointed committees, one of which was to consider the reform of its own constitutions.[2] The work of these committees and the discussions which took place when their reports were presented in Convocation in July seem to have made such an impression as to remove the main episcopal opposition to revival. The brothers Sumner of Canterbury and Winchester were by now converted,[3] and in July Blomfield of London, moving in the House of Lords that copies of the reports be made available, was able to speak with pride of the unanimity and absence of party strife as a happy augury for the revival of Convocation.[4] No

[1] *Hansard*, cxxx (1854), col. 108.
[2] *Chronicle of Convocation*, 112–52.
[3] See P. J. Welch, "The Revival of an Active Convocation of Canterbury (1852–55)", *JEH*, x. (1959), 188–97.
[4] *Hansard*, cxxxv (1854), col. 492.

dissent was expressed, but the opposition had not finished. In February of the following year Lord Shaftesbury endeavoured to embarrass the Archbishop by a question in the House on the eve of the meeting of the new session and asserted, as a matter well known, that Convocation was not authorized to enter upon the discussion of any business without the sanction of Her Majesty.[1] Sumner, however, refused to be moved by this, and Convocation, having discussed the report of its committees further, agreed upon an address to Her Majesty asking that she would grant a licence for it to consider and agree on a canon or constitution to be submitted for her approval for the purpose of modifying the representation of the clergy in the Lower House.[2] Later in the year, however, there was a set-back when the Home Secretary informed the Archbishop that the address had been laid before the Queen and that Her Majesty had not been advised to comply with its prayer.[3] During the next twenty years repeated attempts were made to reform the constitution of the Lower House so as to provide a fuller representation of the parochial clergy, but it was found impossible to move the opposition of the government, and various legal obstacles were put in the way.[4] In fact it was not until 1920 that this reform, so long desired, was obtained.

Nevertheless, in spite of this set-back Convocation continued without further interruption to meet regularly for the discussion of business. It received reports of committees and proved a useful arena for the examination of the many pastoral and legal problems which confronted the Church in the second half of the nineteenth century. It was also able to make certain revisions in the old canons, though a committee which worked for fourteen years on a more general

[1] Id., cxxxvi (1855), col. 1269.
[2] *Chronicle of Convocation*, 199–201.
[3] *Hansard*, cxxxix (1855), col. 2066.
[4] *Chronicle of Convocation* (1866), 225. Cf. *Selected Letters of William Bright, D.D.*, ed. B. J. Kidd (London, 1903), 303. Extract from a letter of 26 January 1900: "As for a more adequate representation of the parochial clergy in Convocation, we know that the lawyers bar the way to it."

reform of the canon law was unable to carry its labours to a conclusion. Amidst much that was valuable, however, two closely connected problems stood out as particularly intractable, the relation of Convocation to Parliament in the matter of legislation, and the association of the laity in some way with its work. The attempts to deal with these problems will be surveyed in the following lecture.

LECTURE 8

22 May 1960

PARLIAMENT, LAITY, AND PROVINCES

This Church, as part of the Universal Church wherein the Lord Jesus Christ has appointed a government in the hands of Church office-bearers, receives from Him, its Divine King and Head, and from Him alone, the right and power subject to no civil authority to legislate, and to adjudicate finally, in all matters of doctrine, worship, government, and discipline in the Church.

11 & 12 George 5. cap. 29
(Church of Scotland Act, 1921).

A right Episcopacy would at once satisfie all just Desires, and Interests of good Bishops, humble Presbyters, and sober People; so as Church-Affairs should be managed neither with Tyranny, Parity, nor Popularity; neither Bishops ejected, nor Presbyters despised, nor People oppressed.

Eikon Basilike.

1

ON 26 FEBRUARY 1861, the Convocation of Canterbury for the first time since its revival, received the royal licence for the revision of a canon, in other words, for legislation. In the Upper House the Bishop of London, Dr Tait, said:

> This is the first time since I became a member of the Convocation that we have met for the distinct transaction of business under the direct authority of the Crown, and it is perhaps scarcely possible to exaggerate the importance which may attach to our proceedings. I confess that I have, if I may venture to say so, on former occasions felt that when assembled in this house there was something of a want of a practical character in our meeting; because, although we knew that it was very desirable that we should have the opportunity of meeting and expressing our opinions, and although we knew also that the opinions so expressed might often be of great influence on the country in general, yet still we did not feel that we were allowed to proceed with any real matter of business. But our meeting to-day is of a totally different character, and we are called upon by the authority of the Crown to discuss a question, in our distinct capacity of an integral portion of this ancient Constitution, and what we may do is as much a matter of distinct business, likely to affect the kingdom generally, as the act of any body distinctly recognised by the Constitution of the country.[1]

The canon under consideration was No. 29 of the code of 1604, which concerns godparents at baptism, and excludes the parents of the infant from performing this office. Application was made for letters of business to revise the canon in order to remove this prohibition and a new form was agreed in appropriate terms. At the end of the canon, however, another change was made. The last words of the old canon

[1] *Chronicle of Convocation* (1861), 346.

read: "neither shall any person be admitted Godfather or Godmother to any Child at Christening or Confirmation, before the said person so undertaking hath received the holy Communion". The title of the canon made it plain that children who were not old enough to be communicants should not be godparents. In debate it was pointed out that as in many churches the communion was celebrated only three times a year a considerable period might elapse between confirmation and reception of communion, during which a person though confirmed and intending to be a communicant would, nevertheless, be prohibited by the canon from being a godparent. To meet this the new version of the canon was made to read: "before the said person so undertaking shall be capable of receiving the Holy Communion." The canon in the new form was duly agreed by both Houses and sent to the Queen for the Royal Assent. After some time had elapsed without any reply an address was agreed, asking respectfully what had happened. To this the Home Secretary replied that the revised canon was ambiguous in its last clause as it might be interpreted to mean that clergymen were authorized to exercise their own judgement as to the capacity to receive holy communion of persons offering themselves as sponsors. In consequence of this the canon was again revised, the final clause was restored to its 1604 form, so that the only change was that explicitly authorized in the letters of business, namely the removal of the prohibition on parents being godparents, and the canon so altered was formally approved by both Houses and re-submitted to the Crown, after which nothing more was heard of it, and so far the royal assent has not been given.[1]

This experience brought home sharply that the grant of the Royal Assent to canons was not to be the formality that the assent to Parliamentary bills had already become, and it may have been the reason why, as it is said, Tait after he had become Archbishop of Canterbury in 1868 preferred

[1] Id. (1865), 1847, 1875; 2403–14.

acts of Parliament to legislation by canon. This has had the unfortunate effect of removing large areas of church business from control by the Convocations and putting it, in effect, in the hands of the House of Commons where the Church has no official spokesman for spiritual matters. It proved, however, even more difficult, as the nineteenth century proceeded, to get ecclesiastical legislation through Parliament at all, and what did get through was extremely slow in its progress. It is said to have taken nine sessions to pass a bill settling the salary of the Archdeacon of Cornwall.[1]

The second half of the nineteenth century saw not only the outburst of troubles and prosecutions which attended the progress of both High Church and Latitudinarian opinion and practice, but also the rise of many problems in the adaptation of church services and organization to the circumstances of the new industrial age, so that the seeming impossibility of securing church legislation without great difficulty and delay was, therefore, a serious matter. The discussion of how best to deal with it naturally became involved with consideration of the place of the laity in Church government.

As has already been indicated there were, among both those who opposed and those who supported the revival of Convocation some who maintained that an assembly which did not include the laity could not function satisfactorily as a central assembly of the Church. The difference between them was whether Convocation should be revived and then reformed, or whether it should be left to continue its merely formal existence, but replaced for all practical purposes by a new council of clergy and laity. The question of the laity was put on the agenda very shortly after the Canterbury synod began again to do business (in February 1857), but the idea of admitting laymen to the convocations did not prove acceptable.

Henry Hoare and his friends in the Society for the Revival

[1] F. A. Iremonger, *William Temple* (London, 1948), 223.

of Convocation were opposed to the admission of the laity to to the synod, but active in promoting lay co-operation at the parochial and ruri-decanal levels. Hoare could, with reason, be claimed as the father of the modern parochial church councils, ruri-decanal and diocesan conferences. His work in this field was widely welcomed, and accustomed the Church to a degree of co-operation between clergy and laity such as had not been seen for centuries. The question of the laity and Convocation could not, however, be postponed indefinitely. Another series of attempts in Convocation led in 1884 to the proposal to set up Houses of Laymen which should meet at the same time as Convocation and should be consulted, more particularly about matters needing Parliamentary legislation. They were expressly excluded from being consulted about "the definition or interpretation of the faith and doctrine of the Church".[1] Archbishop Benson, who was an ardent advocate of the scheme, opened the first session of the Canterbury House of Laymen in January 1886,[2] but York was not able to follow until 1892. Meanwhile there had been proposals for a National Synod of Laymen, and in 1898 provision was made for joint meetings in London of the two provincial Houses of Laymen.

These Houses were essentially advisory bodies to the two Convocations, and more particularly to the two Archbishops. They did useful work in discussing possible parliamentary legislation, and as they included important members of both Houses of Parliament their advice in this field was specially valuable. They also, on occasion, discussed matters which led them into the field of doctrine, as for example in 1897, when both Houses expressed their gratitude to the two Archbishops for their reply to the Pope's condemnation of the

[1] *Chronicle of Convocation* (1877, 1884, and 1885). The necessary resolutions were finally agreed in July 1885. (*Chronicle* XXX, XXXI, 248–65, 270–4.)

[2] A. C. Benson, *The Life of Edward White Benson* (London, 1899), ii. 110; cf. R. Palmer, *Memorials Personal and Political* (London, 1898), ii. 245f.

validity of Anglican Orders.[1] But the voluntary nature of the experiment militated against its real success. The laity had no rights, and in 1902 a Joint Committee of the two Convocations reported that:

> The Church has already been feeling after some method of meeting these altered circumstances. Diocesan, Archidiaconal, Ruridecanal Conferences, Parish Church Councils, and Provincial Houses of Laymen have been called into existence, but they have failed to rouse full enthusiasm, for they have no legal status, they have no power to legislate.[2]

In 1894 Canterbury had 112 and York 107 members in the Houses of Laymen. The average attendance seems to have been at Canterbury twenty, and at York about thirty,[3] a testimony to the small interest that the proceedings aroused.

It is not surprising, therefore, that this state of things was felt to be unsatisfactory, and that in 1898 Archbishop Frederick Temple appointed a Joint Committee to consider the position of the laity. The convener was Mandell Creighton, Bishop of London, and its members included William Stubbs, Bishop of Oxford, John Wordsworth, Bishop of Salisbury, and William Bright, Regius Professor of Ecclesiastical History at Oxford. Unhappily all these, except the Bishop of Salisbury, died before the Committee reported in 1902,[4] and Dr Bright in particular was known to have grave reservations about what was said.[5]

The Report examined the place of the laity in the Early Church, and the Committee summarized its conclusions on that part of the evidence in the following words:

> We believe that there is a primitive distinction between clergy and laity, and that it will continue to the end of the age in

[1] *The Guardian* (1897), 28 April, 668; 12 May, 729.

[2] *The Position of the Laity in the Church, being the Report of the Joint Committee of the Convocation of Canterbury (1902)* (reprinted London, 1952), 54f.

[3] *The Convocation and the Laity, being the Report of the Commission set up by the Church Assembly to consider how the clergy and laity can best be joined together in the synodical government of the Church* (London, 1958), 27; and information supplied by the Secretary of the Church Assembly.

[4] *The Position of the Laity*, iii. f.

[5] *Letters of William Bright*, 302–26.

> which we live. This distinction is involved in the choice and commission of the Apostles: and its continuance is implied in our Lord's words to them connecting their work with His second coming . . . But by distinction we do not understand separation as of bodies with opposing interests. We have no reason to regard the distinction as anything more than a provision for the purpose of developing the fulness of corporate life in the Church which is Christ's body, and for maintaining in it the fulness of truth. Nay, we perceive very clearly, both from the historical and the theological portions of the New Testament, that the ultimate authority and the right of collective action lie with the whole body, the Church. We find, in fact, in this first period traces of the co-operation of clergy and laity in all the three spheres with which our Report is concerned, in legislative functions, in the election of Church officers, and in judicial discipline, and we cannot but conclude that this co-operation belongs to the true ideal of the Church.[1]

The Report then traced the modification of this primitive position brought about by the developments of the Middle Ages. It pointed out that at the Reformation the supremacy and visitatorial power of the Crown, and the right of Parliament to legislate for the Church, were strongly and even arbitrarily asserted, and observed that what was done both by King and Parliament was in a great degree justified by the prevailing conception, which was nearly true in fact, that the Church was co-extensive with the nation. The Committee went on to say:

> As long as Parliament was an assembly of Churchmen, this justification could be put forward with considerable force; but since the Toleration Act of 1689 and the many other changes which have succeeded (some of them with great benefit to the national life), the constitution of Parliament no longer justifies such a claim, and the whole position of the lay members of the Church as such is materially altered . . . the survey of (these changes) forces us to conclude that our laymen have lost the constitutional authority they once had in Church legislation, as well as in most other parts of ecclesiastical administration. In this way also the very important conception that a layman is a

[1] *The Position of the Laity*, 62.

member of the Church, under the discipline of the body, who has responsibilities as well as rights, has been much obscured.[1]

Following this, the Report recommended the formation of a National Council fully representing the clergy and laity of the Church of England, the definition of its powers and method of appointment to be determined by a joint meeting of the members of the two convocations with the provincial Houses of Laymen, with a view to its receiving statutory authority. The immediate result was the establishment in 1903 of a Representative Church Council on these lines which, however, remained a purely deliberative body and consequently could do little in respect of Parliamentary legislation. In 1913, therefore, it recommended the appointment of a commission to survey the relations of Church and State with a view to recommending necessary changes. Thereupon a strong commission was set up, presided over by Lord Selborne, and including his son, Viscount Wolmer, Sir William Anson, A. J. Balfour, Lord Hugh Cecil, Dr W. H. Frere, the Bishop of Oxford (Dr Gore), Lord Parmoor, the Master of Balliol (A. L. Smith), the Dean of Christ Church (Dr T. B. Strong), the Reverend William Temple, the Honourable Edward Wood, later Earl of Halifax, and fourteen other prominent clerics and laymen. In a volume of 300 pages, published in 1916, its principal recommendation was that a Church Council, consisting of the two Convocations together with a House of Laymen, should be given powers to legislate for the Church, such legislation being subject only to the veto of Parliament and of the Crown.[2] It was not proposed to take away by statute the existing legislative powers of Convocation, but it was expected that in course of time these would cease to be used. It was proposed, however, that the constitution of the Lower Houses of Convocation

[1] Id., 63.

[2] *The Archbishops' Committee on Church and State, Report, with Appendices* (London, 1916).

should be reformed in order to provide a majority of elected representatives of the clergy.

Had such a recommendation been made at any other time it is probable that it would have joined the mass of abortive proposals put forward by other ecclesiastical committees and commissions. A perusal of the records of the Church for the last hundred years makes depressing reading, for the same problems have been discussed and argued again and again at intervals of a generation, conclusions have been reached but rarely translated into effect. Moreover it was improbable in the extreme that the Archbishop of Canterbury, Randall Davidson, would look with favour on any such far-reaching changes. That the work of this commission did not prove sterile is due to the mood of enthusiasm for reform generated by the war, and above all the direction of that into the Life and Liberty Movement by William Temple and others. The difference of outlook between Temple and Davidson is expressed sharply in a letter from the former in 1917: "The conception of our leaders that the function of a leader is primarily to keep us all together seems to me disastrous. Is the summons to real adventure to come from those to whom we are looking for guidance or not!"[1] It may be doubted whether the word "adventure" was any part of Davidson's vocabulary.

Constitutional reform was not a primary reason for the foundation of Life and Liberty but was secondary to the purpose of removing numerous abuses which stood in the way of any attempt to make full use of the mood of spiritual enthusiasm and the new moral sense which seemed to have followed the *National Mission* at home, and were reported from the Forces abroad by chaplains such as T. B. Clayton, Studdert Kennedy, Walter Carey, and many others. But, as Dr Iremonger, who was one of the three joint secretaries, has written, "One body blocked all progress, and made swift and decisive action impossible. Not a single reform worth troubling

[1] Iremonger, op. cit., 241.

about could be effected without the consent of Parliament; and to hope that during, or even immediately after, the war a Parliament bewildered and overburdened with the vast problems arising out of it would spare the time—even if the goodwill were there—to discuss such apparent trivialities showed small acquaintance with the history of Church Bills . . . Here, then, was the obvious first step—to go to Parliament and demand freedom for the Church."[1] To some of the founders of the movement this meant disestablishment, others believed that self-government could be achieved without that step, and it was they who carried the day, albeit by imposing a very limited sense on the term self-government. Temple was able to reply to Hensley Henson's accusation of "launching a movement for Disestablishment from within" that their aim was not Disestablishment but self-government.[2]

The Movement had the support of a remarkable range of distinguished men and women in many varied walks of life but it is doubtful whether it would have achieved so much without the personal attraction and abilities of Temple and Dick Sheppard; and it was Temple above all who, by resigning his wealthy West End benefice and devoting himself wholly to the campaign, caught the imagination of Church people and aroused the enthusiasm which carried through at least the greater part of the programme. There were the crowded meetings addressed by him in the Queen's Hall and all about the country, and the individual enthusiasms, such as that of the old lady at Eastbourne who every morning was wheeled up and down the front in a bath-chair, ringing a bicycle bell and displaying a large poster inscribed "Life and Liberty for the Church of England".[3]

The upshot of all this activity was that the proposals of the 1916 Church and State Commission were, with some few alterations, adopted by the Representative Church Council. The convocations approved a constitution for the National Assembly of the Church of England and presented a petition

[1] Id., 222. [2] Id., 223–30. [3] Id., 225f.

to the King that certain powers with regard to legislation be conferred on this body. Again with some small changes these proposals were embodied in the Enabling Act which received the Royal Assent on 23 December 1919. Randall Davidson, who had bowed to the storm, introduced the Second Reading in the House of Lords with the words: "My Lords, I ask your Lordships to give a Second Reading to a Bill to enable the Church of England to do its work properly".[1] The main provisions of the Act are that the Church Assembly may present to Parliament Measures which, in the first instance, are considered by the Ecclesiastical Committee representing both Houses. The Measure together with the Committee's report then lies for forty days on the table of each House, after which a simple resolution assenting to it is proposed, and if passed the Measure then receives the Royal Assent and becomes as much part of the Statute Law of England as any other Act which has passed through the ordinary bill procedure.

Three points in connection with the constitution of the Assembly should be noted. First that it is the creature of the convocations, not of Parliament. Lord Haldane and others made great efforts in the House of Lords to have the constitution set out in a schedule attached to the Enabling Act, but they were defeated.[2] The procedure followed was that recommended by Lord Selborne's Commission which had said:

> It (the Bill) might also contain in a schedule the constitution of the Church Council and its legislative procedure. But this would be objectionable both on theoretical and on practical grounds. For it would mean that the constitution of the Church would be fixed by Parliament; and though Parliament might use its opportunity of framing a Church constitution very sparingly, or might even acquiesce silently in whatever scheme was propounded by the authorities of the Church, it might on the

[1] G. K. A. Bell, *Randall Davidson, Archbishop of Canterbury* (3rd edn., London, 1952), 975.

[2] Id., 973.

> other hand make important modifications in the constitution which could only be rejected by the Church at the price of wrecking the whole scheme, and might under this pressure be accepted by the Church. But such acceptance would be a sacrifice of spiritual independence indefensible and offensive to the sentiments of Churchmen.[1]

The Church Assembly derives its being and its ecclesiastical powers from the ancient synods of these two provinces. It derives only its power of proposing legislation from Parliament.

The second point is that in the constitution the position of the convocations is expressly safeguarded. Section fourteen of the constitution contains the proviso that "it does not belong to the functions of the Assembly to issue any statement purporting to define the doctrine of the Church of England on any question of theology, and no such statement shall be issued by the Assembly". Section fifteen provides that "Nothing in this Constitution shall be deemed to diminish or derogate from any of the powers belonging to the Convocations of the Provinces of Canterbury and York or of any House thereof". Though partly in verbal agreement with the proposals of 1916 these provisos in fact prevent the transfer of function that Lord Selborne's Commission had envisaged.

The third point is that though the lay representatives in the whole hierarchy of councils from the parochial church council up to the Assembly are required to be actual lay communicants, the franchise qualification at the parochial level, on which the hierarchy rests, is that of baptism alone. This matter was hotly debated in 1918–19, and the plea was made for a franchise based upon confirmation. This plea was rejected and every subsequent attempt to make a change has also failed. The defeat of 1919 was the immediate factor causing Dr Gore's resignation of the see of Oxford.[2]

The constitution of the Assembly provided that when it had received statutory powers in regard to legislation it

[1] *Church and State Report 1916*, 61.

[2] Bell, op. cit., 971.

should before entering on any other legislative business, make further provision by passing a Measure declaring that the Convocations of Canterbury and York have power, by canon lawfully passed and promulged, to amend the constitution of the Lower Houses thereof. A Measure to this effect was duly introduced and received the Royal Assent at the end of 1920. In the following year both convocations reformed the constitution of their Lower Houses by canon, the first time, in fact that the composition of those Houses had been regulated in any other way than by the directions given in the Archbishop's citation. The main effect of the change was to provide for a great increase in the number of elected members and some diminution in the ex-officio seats. In the Canterbury Convocation a further change was made in 1936 when representation of the Universities was introduced. The result of this revision has been to change Houses which before 1921 had ex-officio majorities into a state in which Canterbury has 145 elected to 89 ex-officio, and York 71 to 40 ex-officio members.

It was certainly the result of this radical reform as well as of the enthusiasm stirred up by Life and Liberty that in the last thirty years the convocations have been unusually active and have shown no signs whatever of fading into the insignificance envisaged by the 1916 report. A volume of their Acts between 1921 and 1948 runs to 138 pages. Very little of this material is concerned with the revision of canons, for there has developed side by side with that form of legislation another which is called an Act of Convocation. The origin of this is obscure though the term is found in seventeenth-century treatises, but recently an authoritative definition has been given by the Archbishop of Canterbury after taking legal advice.[1] An Act of Convocation is a resolution passed by both Houses, to which the archbishop has given his concurrence and which has been formally declared by him to be an Act of the whole Synod. It has no legal effect such as could be enforced in a court of law, ecclesiastical or otherwise, but

[1] *Chronicle of Convocation* (1959), 159f.

rests solely upon moral authority. It would be fair to say that in the last quarter of a century Acts of Convocation have come to be widely regarded as binding in conscience upon the clergy and are for the most part carefully observed by the bishops in the administration of their dioceses.

The passing of the Enabling Act, certainly eased the situation as far as the time factor in Parliamentary legislation was concerned and a good many long-overdue reforms were made. The Church Assembly Measures passed between 1920 and 1949 fill more than 1,000 pages. But it must be borne in mind that this is all in its nature statute law, and can only be modified by further action in Parliament. In no way was the ultimate legislative control affected by the Enabling Act. That problem was left unsettled. So also was a good part of the problem of the laity, for, in spite of lay membership of the various conferences which mount from the parochial church council up to the Assembly, the right of Convocation within certain fields to legislate by canon without reference to the laity remained unimpaired, as did also the convocation control of relations with other churches.

This exclusion of the laity from certain spheres was thought by many to be inconsistent with the principles laid down in the 1902 Report, and after a debate in the Church Assembly in 1953 another commission was appointed to consider how the laity could best be joined with the clergy in the synodical government of the Church. That commission has suggested that Houses of Laity be added to the two convocations, with rights similar to those now possessed by the existing Lower Houses,[1] but the proposal has not yet been endorsed by either the Assembly or the convocations.

2

It is difficult to avoid the conclusion that the use of the cry "self-government for the Church" by the leaders of the Life

[1] In *The Convocations and the Laity*.

and Liberty Movement was misleading in the extreme,[1] and any who had been so misled must have received a rude shock when the Revised Prayer Book, passed by considerable majorities in both the convocations and the Church Assembly and by more than four-fifths of the elected representatives in the diocesan conferences, was twice rejected by the House of Commons. Preaching at the special service of prayer and dedication held after the passing of the Enabling Act Archbishop Lang had spoken of the great benefit that would come to the life of the Church:

> For the first time, at least since almost primitive ages, the laity in every parish throughout the land are offered vote and voice in the management of their Church; and this not merely as parishioners or as citizens of the nation, but as citizens of the Church; and not merely by the favour of this or that incumbent, but as a right conferred by the whole Church with the concurrence and recognition of the State. In a degree never before possible, every man or woman who professes allegiance to the Church is now invested with a personal responsibility for its welfare, for the success or failure of its Divine Mission.[2]

Within eight years the representatives of the laity chosen on this understanding were told in no uncertain terms that another body had a better right than they to speak on behalf of the laity of the Church of England, and told it by a vote in which the majority of members of Parliament from English constituencies were outvoted by a minority supported by the representatives of Scotland, Wales, and Northern Ireland,[3] and this on a matter which touched the most intimate aspects of the life of the Church, worship and the administration of the sacraments. The fact that many churchmen are now rather relieved that the forms of worship were not standard-

[1] The term "self-government" was evidently being misused in this way as early as 1900, if one may judge from a letter of Dr Bright, in which he writes: "I cannot, I own, attach much practical importance to, or feel much interest in, schemes for Church Reform in the sense of self-government, so long as Establishment lasts, and places us under what is in fact a Parliamentary supremacy." *Letters of William Bright*, 302.

[2] Iremonger, op. cit., 274f.

[3] Bell, op. cit., 1347.

ized in accordance with the pattern of 1927–8, does not alter the effect of the Prayer Book crisis in gravely compromising the standing and prestige of the Church Assembly as representative of the Anglican laity.

The Revised Prayer Book is so far the only major measure of this sort which has been rejected by Parliament, but in other ways the Church Assembly and the convocations have been made to feel that the House of Commons really controls the Church. A small determined group in the House can sometimes virtually dictate the form that a measure shall take, and it is known that already certain persons have undertaken intensive propaganda among members of Parliament with the aim of securing the rejection of some of the measures necessary to prepare the way for the revised canons.

The revision of the canon law has brought home to some churchmen, including the present writer, more forcibly than anything before had done, the stranglehold upon the life of the Church possessed by the House of Commons in virtue of two things, the Act of Submission of the Clergy and the Act of Uniformity to which the Prayer Book is attached. As it turns out only a minority of the new canons will need precedent statutory legislation, but the points at which this is required may well give rise to reflection. Leaving aside the major issues of liturgical revision and the reconstruction of the system of Church courts, we may list a dozen points with which Parliament will have to be asked to concern itself. (1) To require in those who are to be ordained a knowledge of the New Testament in the original Greek, and to give to the bishop a power of dispensing from the knowledge of Greek and Latin in appropriate cases. (2) To allow persons to be ordained on one of the Ember days instead of only on a Sunday or Holy-day. (3) To allow a person by dispensation from the Archbishop of Canterbury to be ordained priest at the age of twenty-three instead of waiting until he is twenty-four. (4) To allow the chief altar in a church to be made of "stone or some other suitable material" and not solely of wood. (5) To allow a bishop to give permission to a Reader to administer the chalice when need arises. (6) To allow the convocations to make regulations that in certain circumstances persons who have not been confirmed may be admitted to Holy Communion. (7) To allow the use of unleavened bread in the Holy Communion after the example of the Last Supper. (8) To provide that persons who are not baptized shall not have the right to be married in church. (9) To allow to a curate a right of appeal to the Archbishop if his bishop takes away his licence. (10) To allow that a minister of the Episcopal Church of Scotland may officiate in an English church or chapel without the permission of the bishop for the same length of time as any other priest or deacon, instead of being limited to one day in three months. (11) To allow the convocations to approve holy days to be observed provincially and the ordinary to approve holy days to be observed locally. (12) To settle what the clergy shall wear in church. It may well be asked whether the parliamentary control of such matters as these is not now an anachronism.

Three chief criticisms may be directed against the present system. First it is wrong in principle. As we have seen in the course of these lectures the Submission of the Clergy and the Act of Uniformity arose from the view that Church and State are one in membership and that the clergy ought not to be allowed to make laws for the laity without the latter's consent. The first of these propositions has been by common consent abandoned in this country. The second still holds good but the right of Parliament to represent the laity has been vitiated by the admission to it of non-Anglicans and non-christians. To the problems arising from this it will be necessary to return presently. The second criticism is that the present system gives far too much power to minorities. The parliamentary control has often been defended on the ground that it protects minorities, and indeed it is sometimes said that without it the Church of England would split into two or three sections. The continuance of the Protestant Episcopal

Church of the United States and other similar parts of the Anglican Communion where the diverse traditions in Anglicanism exist and stay together may give us pause here, but apart from that it must be said that the so-called protection of minorities operates in a very haphazard way. It is no disrespect to the House of Commons to say that very many of its members, including many Anglicans, are ill-informed about Church matters and particularly about the sometimes rather technical and theological issues involved in measures which come from the Church Assembly. The Church has in the House of Commons only one official spokesman and he is there primarily to represent the Church Commissioners whose work, important as it is, is not always directly concerned with theology and worship. The House is therefore very much at the mercy of any group of members who may be disposed to take a particular interest in some Church matter, and also singularly open to the influence of societies and groups outside which can afford to undertake extensive propaganda. Against all this the official voice of the Church has difficulty in making itself heard effectively for as a rule people are more easily stirred up to oppose than to support. Of this the Prayer Book debates provide abundant illustration.

This uncertainty of what will happen to a Church measure in the House of Commons leads to the third criticism of the parliamentary control, namely, that it induces a kind of paralysis in Church life. Any student of the history of the Church of England and its representative organs in the last hundred years must become aware of how many times the same subjects of reform have been raised, considered by committees, reported on, and resolutions about them passed, in some cases in almost every generation, but always without achieving those changes in the law which alone could bring about a settlement. It has been the fortune of the present writer during the last twelve years to sit upon a number of committees and commissions considering such different matters as Divorce and Nullity of Marriage, relations with the Church of South India and with the Methodists, the law relating to ecclesiastical fees and the granting of faculties, the ecclesiastical courts, the association of the laity with the clergy in the synodical government of the Church, and the very miscellaneous set of problems which arise in the course of the revision of the canons. On almost every one of these bodies the question of the parliamentary control has arisen at some stage or other. It has been necessary to consider whether suggestions which otherwise seemed desirable would have any chance of being accepted by the House of Commons. Often the likelihood of opposition there had made it not seem worth while to embark upon the preliminary process of debate in Convocation or the Church Assembly. The present writer has been led to the conviction that the parliamentary control prevents much that would be valuable and widely welcomed in the Church from ever reaching the stage of definite legislative proposal, that it produces a sense of frustration which impedes the work of the Church, and that it causes a number of people, who would gladly be far better employed, to spend much of their time to very little effect in one committee after another, where progress is impeded by statutes, judgements, and a legal tradition which reflect the ideas of a vanished society.[1] Very little worth while reform is likely to come about in the structure, law or liturgy of the Church of England without some serious modification of the parliamentary supremacy as represented by the Submission

[1] In view of my position as secretary of the Canon Law Steering Committee I wish to make it plain that no criticism of the lawyers who have so generously helped the convocations with their advice is intended here. They are bound by the law as it is and by the official interpretations which have been put upon it. The Submission of the Clergy and the Act of Uniformity are now interpreted more rigidly than was the case in the seventeenth century, but that is something which the present generation of lawyers has inherited and does not find it possible to change. It is matter for discussion how far the current legal attitude to problems of Church and State is still dominated by the Roman civil law theory of corporations, as expounded and criticized by J. N. Figgis in *Churches in the Modern State* (London, 1913).

of the Clergy and the Act of Uniformity. As the first quotation set at the head of this lecture shows, Parliament itself has assented to the principle that the Christian Church should be self-governing. It is to be desired that this principle should be translated into practice for the Church of England as it has long been for the Church of Scotland.[1]

In this respect, however, there seems since the war to have been some movement backwards rather than forwards. The Archbishops' Commission on the Relations between Church and State, presided over by Lord Cecil of Chelwood, which reported in 1935, recognized indeed that differences of historical background between England and Scotland were such that the Scottish settlement could not be an exact model for what should be done in England. But the Report went on to say:

> Nevertheless, the Church of Scotland Act and the conditions which it recognized as existing in Scotland, show that a complete spiritual freedom of the Church is not incompatible with Establishment. The Crown in Parliament has solemnly ratified the principles on which the Scottish settlement is explicitly based, and has accepted the relations between the spiritual and the civil power laid down in the Declaratory Articles. It is, therefore, neither illogical nor impracticable to infer that the Crown in Parliament would be willing to consider and to grant to the Church of England what has been, with the full consent of England, freely granted or confirmed to the Church of Scotland. And we cannot believe that what is right for the Church of Scotland is in principle wrong for the Church of England.[2]

By comparison with this the Church Assembly Commission

[1] It is not my intention here to advocate disestablishment. I believe that both Church and State benefit by establishment, and that the disestablishment of the Church of England would be detrimental to the English people and to the cause of Christianity throughout the world. On the other hand I believe that in modern days the terms of the establishment have become in several respects unreasonable, harmful, and offensive, and that the Church should be allowed a freedom of ordering its own faith, life, and worship analogous to that possessed by the other established Church in these islands.

[2] *Church and State* (London, 1936), 55f.

on Church and State appointed in 1949 under the chairmanship of Sir Walter Moberley, is faint-hearted indeed. Its members were not even able to agree that a status similar to that of the Church of Scotland should be the ultimate goal of the Church's long-term policy. They were all agreed that as a policy for the immediate or for any near future it was impracticable, and the few points of difference between England and Scotland which had been mentioned in 1935 were blown up into a series of five arguments held to be decisive against any attempt to imitate the Scottish solution.[1] These arguments must be considered in detail.

> (a) In Scotland the National Church is far more nearly co-extensive with the Christian element in the nation. With the possible exception of the Roman Catholics—and as a nation Scotland is unquestionably Protestant—the members of other religious bodies are relatively few in number. In England there is something like an even balance.

This is no doubt true in fact but its bearing on the question at issue is not immediately obvious. It would appear to be if anything an argument for the disestablishment of the Church of England, certainly not one against it being freed from parliamentary control.

> (b) Within the Church of Scotland there is a much less sharp division on questions of doctrine and worship. The production of an agreed set of Declaratory Articles, setting forth the Church's doctrine, was an essential condition of the 1921 Act. It is more than doubtful whether to-day any such agreed statement could be obtained in the Church of England.

This argument, at first sight much more formidable, will not stand close examination. In the first place it grossly exaggerates the doctrinal content of the nine Declaratory Articles.[2] If one were to substitute for Article II the substance of canons A.1–6 and C.1. clause 1, of the 1959 form of the draft code,

[1] *Church and State* (London, 1952), 27f. [2] See Appendix I.

about which there has been scarcely any controversy;[1] for Article III the historical references appropriate to the Church of England; and for Article VIII some equivalent appropriate to the structure of the Church of England, all of which substitutions would be relatively uncontroversial, there is very little in the rest of the Declaratory Articles to which Anglicans of any but the completely Erastian school of thought could take exception. It is, therefore, highly probable that an agreed statement such as is represented by the Declaratory Articles could be obtained with little difficulty in the Church of England to-day. Moreover the members of the 1949 Commission seem to have been quite unaware of the extent to which old controversies are being undermined by modern developments and of the marked growing together theologically of different schools of thought within the Church in the last twenty years.

> (c) In Scotland there is a less clearly marked line of division between the clergy and laity. The laity's share in Church government is long-established. In England it is new, and perhaps that is why in large sections of the English laity there is an ingrained anti-clericalism to which there is no parallel in Scotland.

Here is something more substantial, something at least of which account must be taken. The place of the laity in the government of the Church is a fundamental question to which we must recur. But assuming for the moment that a satisfactory way of joining together clergy and laity in synodical government is provided then this tradition of anti-clericalism, founded as it is in circumstances wholly different from those of to-day, should not be allowed to hinder the achievement of self-government by the Church.

> (d) In Scotland the General Assembly has a long history and a thoroughly established prestige. In the nature of the case the

[1] See Appendix II. Further support for my argument in this paragraph is to be found in the very general welcome given to the Revised Catechism.

Church Assembly cannot at present make the same claim. It does not yet enjoy a comparable degree of public confidence.

It is difficult to know how to assess this argument. We may agree, and shall suggest later, that some reform in the structure of our assemblies is desirable, but who is to say and how are we to tell when the Church Assembly, or whatever may replace it, enjoys such a degree of public confidence as to warrant that the Church be given its freedom? It might, indeed, be suggested with equal force that the House of Commons no longer has sufficiently the confidence of the Church for it to be able to assert its supremacy effectively, and the widespread use of the 1928 Prayer Book despite its rejection by the Commons would lend support to such a suggestion. There was sufficient confidence in the Assembly before ever it had met, for it to be given the powers conferred by the Enabling Act. Are we to accept that it has gained nothing in public confidence during the forty years of its life?

(e) In Scotland a trenchant assertion of spiritual independence such as that contained in the Declaratory Articles was nothing new; as the 1935 Commission points out, such independence had for long been claimed and explicitly allowed. This has not been so in England. In Scotland precedent favours spiritual independence, in England it does not; and the English are a precedent-loving people, more deeply moved by tradition than by logic.

Again the point is not easy to grasp. The Commission appear to say that the Scots have got what they want because they have consistently claimed it, and that this is an argument for the English not claiming it too. The members might perhaps have recalled the context of the most famous quotation which embodies the word precedent:

It is the land that freemen till,
That sober-suited Freedom chose,
The land, where girt with friends or foes
A man may speak the thing he will:

A land of settled government,
A land of just and old renown,
Where Freedom slowly broadens down
From precedent to precedent.[1]

Apparently in the view of the Commission precedent prevents rather than aids the broadening of Freedom. The implication of what they say is simply that churchmen must be sufficiently determined in asking for what they want.

With one exception it is difficult to regard these arguments as providing a substantial reason why the Church of England should not ask for and expect to be given a freedom of self-government similar to that enjoyed by the Church of Scotland. Undoubtedly the way in which that claim is to be formulated and the circumstances in which it is to be presented will require careful thought, planning and negotiation, and it is not the purpose of these lectures to suggest how or when that should be done. What is urgently needed is a revival from the faint-heartedness of 1949 and a recovery of the spirit of 1935.

3

It is not to be expected that the parliamentary control of the Church will be relaxed unless some provision is made to safeguard the important functions which it is supposed to perform. Few would now contend that one of these is to keep the Church in its place. The clergy are no longer, and are unlikely to become again, an *imperium in imperio* of the kind which provoked the hostility of the lay power in the later Middle Ages, and there is no more reason in principle why the Church of England should be regarded as a potentially dangerous organization needing to be kept under strict control than is the case with any other Christian society in the realm.

A more serious matter is the contention that establishment involves a partnership or contract and that the parliamentary

[1] Tennyson, "You ask me, why, tho' ill at ease".

control ensures that one side shall not be able to make important changes without the consent of the other. This argument would have greater force if it worked both ways, but the fact is that the State does not regard itself as limited by what the Church may approve or disapprove, as recent changes in the law of marriage show. It is obvious that the State must have the right to say that such and such an alteration in the Church makes the continuance of establishment undesirable, but this is not the same as giving to the State a veto on all change. Again, the example of Scotland is relevant, for it is not obvious why what is not thought necessary there should be regarded as essential in England.

The one really substantial point remaining is that the parliamentary control is thought to safeguard for the laity rights in respect of Church government which apart from it they do not possess. These rights amount in fact to a veto on all Church legislation, including a veto on all changes in doctrinal and liturgical formularies. As a matter of practical politics it is highly improbable that Parliament will give up its veto unless it is assured that something similar will continue to be exercised by a really representative body of the Anglican laity. It is important, therefore, to ask what are theologically the proper rights of the laity in respect of Church legislation, and whether what seems to be the requirement of practical politics can be supported in principle. But to answer this question we must begin with a brief consideration of certain aspects of the theology of the Church.

The Church finds its origin in the creative, redeeming, and inspiring work of the Holy Trinity. It is the company of all those children of God to whom the saving work of Christ has been applied by the Holy Spirit making them one in him. It is described in the New Testament as the people (*laos*) of God, as a holy nation, a royal priesthood, the body of Christ, the temple of God in which the Spirit dwells. The primary purpose of the Church's existence is to reflect in adoration the glory of God and to render to him the love which he has poured out in creation, redemption, and sanctification upon it. On earth the Church exists also to manifest God to the world that all may know and serve him also, and in this sense is a mediator appointed to lead the world to God, reflecting in its own life the one great mediator between God and man, Christ Jesus. This mediatorial function is shared by every Christian. All have the responsibility of manifesting in their daily life the love of God which is his revelation of himself, and in consequence all have a responsibility for safeguarding and applying Christian truth.

But God has also set within the Church the ministry. The apostles, or the Twelve, a nucleus called and specially prepared and commissioned by the Lord, were there first. They called others into the Church, beginning themselves the exercise of that mediatorial function which all Christians have. But those who came in did not automatically receive all the functions of the apostles. The latter had certain special responsibilities in respect of shepherding and feeding the flock, building up the temple of God, administering God's household, responsibilities which in course of time they appear to have delegated in part and eventually to have passed on to certain other Christians selected for the purpose. The apostles and the ministers associated with them exercised a peculiar authority in teaching, and in guarding the purity of teaching in the Church, and this same function was believed by subsequent generations to belong particularly to the episcopate. In the Anglican form for the consecration of bishops this view finds expression, though the form for the ordination of priests brings out the complementary point that the presbyterate is associated with the episcopate in this respect, albeit subordinate to it.[1]

[1] On the collegiate nature of the ministry see the two important articles by Dom B. Botte, "Caractère collégial du presbytérat et de l'épiscopat" in *Études sur le sacrement de l'ordre* (Lex orandi, 22, Paris, 1957), and "La Collégialité dans le Nouveau Testament et chez les Pères apostoliques" in *Le Concile et les Conciles*, ed. D. O. Rousseau (Chevetogne, 1960).

The ministry, however, does not function apart from the Church but within it. Ministers and others together constitute the people of God, and, as we have seen in the first of these lectures, in the earliest times the ministers were chosen by the *fideles* from among themselves. But they derive their authority from God, not by democratic election from the people. This authority is given to be exercised in the service of the Church and not in lordship over it, but it carries the duties of teaching, rebuking, shepherding, preserving, which, however, are all to be performed within and in association with the whole Church. Ideally the maintenance, formulation and progressive understanding of Christian truth is the work of the whole body. Nevertheless we must recognize that in this life there will be always imperfection, and that at times the ministry will fail in its duty and stray into error. When this happens the conservative, preservative function of the rest of the body becomes of peculiar importance, and as a matter of historic fact it has been the *consensus fidelium* formed over a number of years which has determined whether any particular formulation of doctrine was or was not true to the revelation given in the scriptures.

This fact of history has been well expressed by John Keble:

> The voice of the Laity, in one form or another, has always been a most essential part of the voice of the whole Church. Even in the most vital case of fundamental doctrine, the Church diffusive, in which the Laity are included, has a kind of veto, as I understand it, upon the decision of a General Council. That decision does not become Ecumenical until it has been accepted by the Holy Church throughout all the world. The Latrocinium at Ephesus is a case in point.[1]

Dr William Bright, who was very suspicious of proposals to admit lay representatives to diocesan or national synods, nevertheless recognized the same fact when he wrote in 1900:

[1] Quoted in W. Bright, *Some aspects of Primitive Church life* (London, 1898), 94 n 1, and *The Position of the Laity*, 15.

> I am not personally opposed to the House of Laymen scheme, as proposed by way of development of the existing system sanctioned by Convocation and carried into effect. The *fideles* have a clear right to say, "We cannot accept this or that new doctrinal formula"—to veto it, in short.[1]

Here Bright appears to accept two things which go somewhat beyond the general statement of principle and are very important developments of it. The first is that this lay veto can properly be exercised in a part of a divided Church. The fragmentation of Christendom presents a major difficulty in the way of the application to modern times of principles drawn from Scripture and early tradition. It is reasonable to argue that no major innovation in doctrine ought to be made by a local and regional Church on its own authority. In a divided Christendom every part of the Church ought always to be conscious of its responsibility towards its separated brethren for whatever it does.

The acceptance of some such limitation upon freedom of action does not, however, involve the conclusion that nothing at all can be done, and a local Church must sometimes make decisions about matters of faith and worship. When that happens it is reasonable that the laity of that Church should exercise in respect of those decisions the functions which we have seen to belong to the laity as a whole.

The second point which Bright appears to have assumed is that the laity can properly express their opinion through elected representatives. It should be recognized that, as will have been apparent in earlier lectures, the Church has always felt itself free to draw upon the experience of secular society in deciding upon the form that its own organs of self-expression should take. We have seen how greatly the development of the early councils was influenced by Roman civil procedure, and how in England Parliament and Convocation have been intertwined in their growth. The

[1] *Letters of William Bright*, 306; cf. *Some aspects*, 51–99.

present hierarchy of conferences leading up to the association of clergy and laity in the Church Assembly seems a natural development of this process, and it is right that we should draw upon the secular experience of the modern age, provided that the essential principles are maintained. If the clergy are to express their opinion through elected representatives as they have done in Convocation for the past six hundred years, it is difficult to see why the laity should not do so too.

That is not to say, however, that the House of Laity of the Church Assembly is a satisfactory organ for the purpose. Difficulty arises from a twofold disparity between clergy and laity. First, in the Church at large the clergy are necessarily far less numerous than the laity, and it is therefore easier to secure a fair representation of clerical opinion and responsibility in one assembly than is the case with the laity. Second, the clergy are professionals and have both the knowledge and, what is equally important, the time, to deal with difficult questions of doctrine and practice, whereas the laity are in some of these fields spare time amateurs. To say that is in no sense to disparage the importance of lay participation in the discussion, for example, of moral and social issues, but simply to recognize a fact.

It would seem, therefore, that any attempt to combine clerical and lay representatives in one assembly for all purposes is bound to be unsatisfactory, and that is to some extent the rationale of the continued existence side by side of both the Church Assembly and the convocations. The former is precluded from issuing doctrinal statements, the latter deal chiefly with what are called "spiritual" matters which require more time than the Assembly can give to them and also the quieter, more intimate discussion which is possible in a smaller body, composed of those who have the training and experience which are relevant to the matter in hand. The inescapable facts are that there is a definite amount of business to be done by the Church's representative assemblies and that the laity are able to devote less time to it than the clergy.

On the other hand it is widely recognized that the present system is open to criticism for reasons which have been given earlier in this chapter as well as for others. The laity are deprived of a voice through their elected representatives in certain important matters which concern them, there is some degree of cumbrous overlapping and waste of time, and the duality itself occasionally causes the clergy and laity to be at loggerheads through misunderstanding. But no reform yet proposed has been thought generally acceptable and it may be suggested that this is because the facts stated at the end of the last paragraph have not been faced and their implications openly recognized.

4

Once these limiting factors are stated and recognized as realities of which account must be taken, the outlines of a solution become fairly obvious. The laity must be willing for the clergy to consider certain matters or certain stages of business alone, and the opinion of the laity at something like diocesan level must be sought on at least all fundamental questions. We proceed, therefore, to suggest in more detail a scheme of this kind.

As we have seen, the Synodical Government Commission which reported in 1958 suggested that the existing House of Laity of the Church Assembly be divided provincially and each of the resultant divisions be joined as a third house to the appropriate Convocation. The first stage of our scheme is to implement this proposal by something like the legislative instruments attached to the 1958 report. The second stage is to provide (a) that the two convocations, so enlarged, may sit together as a General Synod of the Church of England which shall possess not only the present powers of the convocations but also those of the Church Assembly which should then cease to exist as a separate institution; and (b) that the bishops and clergy of the convocations shall have the power to continue to meet provincially or together as at present without the laity for certain specified purposes, which will be mentioned presently. In this way the convocations and the Assembly will be integrated in one legislative hierarchy,[1] and we can pass on to consider how they should transact their business.

First it is to be accepted that all measures and all canons must be passed by the General Synod before they become binding upon members of the Church. Next it is suggested that the procedure to be adopted in respect of them should vary according to their content. Many of the measures and most of the financial and administrative business should proceed in the General Synod in the same way as now in the Church Assembly, but measures which involve questions of doctrine and liturgy, and probably all canons, should be treated in three stages.[2] First there should be a debate on the main issues in the General Synod, then the matter should be remitted to the bishops and clergy in their provincial convocations for them to exercise their magisterial office by detailed discussion and comment, after which it should come back to the General Synod for revision and enactment. At the final stage the voting should be by houses, the form of the measure or canon being proposed by the House of Bishops who should vote first, the clergy to vote second, and the laity last so that before they exercise their right of veto they are

[1] In order to preserve the independent status of the see of York, which is a valuable bulwark against the development of a Canterbury patriarchate or papacy, it is important that in the General Synod the two archbishops should preside jointly or alternately, and that the Archbishop of Canterbury should not be the sole president of the Synod. If it were found practicable to hold meetings in the Northern province it would be reasonable for the Archbishop of York to preside when the Synod met there, and the Archbishop of Canterbury to preside in London. The position of the two archbishops in Ireland does not provide a completely parallel situation.

[2] It is assumed that there will in most cases have been a preliminary general debate leading to the setting up of a commission to draft the measure or canon, or that the matter will be brought forward by some standing committee.

aware of the considered opinion of the bishops and clergy. In order, however, to ensure a wider representation of lay opinion it should be provided, on lines something like those suggested by the 1935 Church and State Report[1] and by the procedure under the Barrier Act and Article VIII of the Declaratory Articles of the Church of Scotland,[2] that the consent of two thirds of the diocesan conferences, or of some other local assembly of bishops, clergy and laity,[3] be required for changes in the doctrinal formularies of the Church, in the constitution of the Church, and in the Ordinal and certain other sections of the Book of Common Prayer.

It is also suggested that the bishops and clergy should meet in their provincial Convocations, or together when desired, to exercise functions such as that conferred upon them by draft canon B.6 of appointing holy days to be observed provincially, and should have the right to discuss any matters of common concern and to pass resolutions about them, which might continue to be known as Acts of Convocation, provided that such resolutions should have no legal force and might be reviewed in the General Synod at the request of a majority of the House of Laity.

Some such scheme as the above has certain clear advantages. It gives the representative laity[4] a much greater degree of control of Church business than they now possess, but at the same time retains the right of the bishops and clergy to meet separately and to formulate their opinion upon

[1] *Church and State* (1936), 61.

[2] J. T. Cox, *Practice and Procedure in the Church of Scotland* (4th edn., Edinburgh, 1948), 335.

[3] See section five below.

[4] The 1935 Church and State Report has some wise words about lay representation which deserve to be remembered in any discussion of this problem (Report, 42–6). I have not felt it necessary to reopen the old issue about the franchise qualification. The Church Assembly has more than once rejected proposals to change the baptismal into a confirmation requirement, and with the present method of election and the rule that all representatives must be communicants it is doubtful whether an alteration in the franchise requirement would make any practical difference. In principle, however, I should support a requirement of confirmation.

matters which are their special province. Although it may appear complex on paper, as almost any constitution will, it is nevertheless simpler than the present dual system, while securing continuity with the historic representative assemblies of the Church and providing for the independent expression of opinion of the Northern Convocation. In these ways it meets some of the objections levelled against the proposals of the Synodical Government Commission.

It is not to be expected that such a scheme will satisfy those who put the saving of time high among their priorities. Possibly under these arrangements the sessions of the General Synod might be limited to two meetings a year, each lasting from Monday afternoon to Friday morning, and the convocations to one or two meetings a year, but as long as the Church of England is engaged in a major overhaul of its law and liturgy such work will occupy a great deal of time and it is essential that the procedure for legislation on important matters should be slow. Time for consideration and discussion is a vital element in producing a common mind, and the quiet, slow, and sometimes academic deliberations of the convocations have a valuable function to perform in respect particularly of matters of doctrine and worship.

What has been suggested undoubtedly involves a certain sacrifice of the rights of independent action now possessed by the clergy, but in doing so it provides such safeguards for the laity as to make reasonable a request that Parliament should repeal the Submission of the Clergy and such other statutes as need to be removed in order to give the Church its legislative freedom.

5

It will have been noticed that in the foregoing section it was suggested that for certain changes the consent of two thirds of the diocesan conferences "or of some other local assembly of bishops, clergy and laity" should be required. The alternative was included because it is obvious that in many parts of England the diocesan conference is the weakest link in the chain of assemblies and it is not difficult to find a number of reasons for this. In most dioceses the conference meets two or three times a year for a space of about four hours.[1] It consists of three authorities, one constituted by the diocesan bishop alone, and the other two of the Chamber of Clergy and the Chamber of Laity who may, in a large diocese, such as Oxford, amount to 650 persons. It is obviously impossible for a body of this size, meeting for so short a time at long intervals, to be a real deliberative assembly. A usual pattern for such meetings is that the morning is occupied by a presidential address and reports from standing committees, and in the afternoon there is a further address, often from a visiting speaker, about some topic that is before the Church at the time, and possibly questions or a short discussion.

The principal weakness of many conferences is that they are too big so that that ease of discussion and confidence in relationship between the members which are necessary to a deliberative assembly are extremely difficult to establish. A body of six hundred persons needs to meet frequently, or for two or three days at a time if it is to be really deliberative, and even then an easy freedom of discussion is difficult to attain, as the contrast between the large Church Assembly and the much smaller convocations shows. But, further, there is the somewhat lonely eminence occupied by the bishop. This is to some extent inherent in the nature of episcopacy,[2] but it is greatly exaggerated when the diocese is so large that personal contact between the bishop and all but a few of the laity, and even between the bishop and many of the clergy, is extremely limited.

The Doctrine Commission, which worked from 1922 to

[1] The conference is only required to meet once a year. Other meetings are at the discretion of the bishop.

[2] The problems arising from this were referred to on a number of occasions by the late Bishop of Oxford. See E. W. Kemp, *The life and letters of Kenneth Escott Kirk* (London, 1959), 89–98.

1938 under the chairmanship of Archbishop Temple, included in its report a statement about episcopacy which has more than once been quoted in conversations with representatives of non-episcopal churches.[1] The Commission said that the argument for episcopacy derives its strength from the convergence of many different considerations, and then went on:

> We may state these in summary form; but the very nature of the office depends upon the union of all these elements:
>
> 1 The Episcopate symbolizes and secures in an abiding form the apostolic mission and authority within the Church; historically the Episcopate became the organ of this mission and authority.
>
> 2 In early times the continuous successions of Bishops in tenure of the various Sees were valued because they secured the purity of apostolic teaching . . . it has remained a function of the Episcopate to guard the Church against erroneous teaching.
>
> 3 The Bishop in his official capacity represents the whole Church in and to his diocese, and his diocese in and to the Councils of the Church. He is thus a living representative of the unity and universality of the Church.
>
> 4 The Bishop in his diocese represents the Good Shepherd; the idea of pastoral care is inherent in his office. Both clergy and laity look to him as Chief Pastor, and he represents in a special degree the paternal quality of pastoral care.
>
> 5 Inasmuch as the unity of the Church is in part secured by an orderly method of making new ministers and the Bishop is the proper organ of unity and universality, he is the appropriate agent for carrying on through ordination the authority of the apostolic mission of the Church.
>
> It is, as has been said, the coalescence of all of these elements in a single person that gives to the Episcopate its peculiar importance. . . .
>
> In the Church, the household of God, the Bishop should represent in his own appointed area the principle of Fatherhood. An assemblage of persons cannot be a "father in God"; and the lack of this element is an impoverishment of the Church's spiritual life.

[1] *Doctrine in the Church of England* (London, 1938), 122f.

It is strange that attention has not been drawn to the inconsistency between this statement and the actual practice of the Church of England to-day, for it is difficult to see how this insistence that it is "the coalescence of all of these elements *in a single person*" that gives to the episcopate its peculiar importance is to be reconciled with the existence in English dioceses at the present time of forty-four suffragan [1] and twenty-five assistant bishops.[2] In four sees the diocesan finds it necessary to employ three suffragans, in seven he has two, and in only three does he manage without either suffragan or assistant. As the Early Church found by experience, it is not possible to insist rigidly on the rule of one bishop only, and circumstances will always arise which make it desirable to break the rule in a particular diocese at a particular time,[3] but the modern Anglican acceptance of suffragans as a normal part of the organization of the Church makes nonsense of the Doctrine Commission's argument for episcopacy.

It would seem then, that there is a theological as well as a practical argument for the creation of smaller dioceses than those with which we are familiar, but it must be recognized that ever since the threefold division of the diocese of Winchester in 1927 there has been somewhat of a reaction

[1] This figure includes the Bishops of Fulham and Maidstone who have special responsibilities which do not fall into the normal categories of suffragan work.

[2] This figure is somewhat misleading because of the variety of ways in which the title is used. Sometimes it is conferred on a retired bishop who is resident in the diocese, but in at least twelve cases the assistant bishop appears to be the equivalent of a suffragan elsewhere. As my biography of Dr Kirk shows, an assistant bishop may be used as a stage on the way to the establishment of a new suffragan see.

[3] Two examples come to mind. One is in the case of a bishop who has become physically unable to discharge all his duties adequately but whose presence on the bench is desirable for his wisdom and experience. In such a case the proper course would seem to be to appoint a coadjutor with right of succession. The other exception applies overseas in parts of Africa and elsewhere, where it may be desirable to have a native suffragan for a time as a stage in the transition from an English to a native episcopate. Both of these are, however, essentially temporary expedients and quite unlike the English system of suffragans.

against further development of this kind, and indeed the proposal to create a new diocese of Shrewsbury was rejected. The principal argument used against the division of large dioceses is based upon the expense involved. The bishop's stipend must be found, a house bought for him to live in, a cathedral established, and a diocesan board of finance set up. In addition two other arguments are often used. One is that the Church has not enough men of the calibre of diocesan bishops to staff more than the existing number of dioceses. The other is that in small dioceses, and particularly in those that are wholly or almost wholly urban, the bishop has not a sufficient variety of patronage to make it possible to move clergymen from the town to the country and from one type of parish to another as seems in the best interests of both them and their parishes.

Undoubtedly these arguments are weighty, but on examination the difficulties do not appear insuperable. The financial problem is in certain respects less of a difficulty now than it was as recently as ten or fifteen years ago, for the Church Commissioners now pay the stipends of suffragan bishops at a rate which needs very little added to make it reasonable for the bishop of a small diocese. The question of a cathedral is one that must be faced realistically. There is no reason at all why, in the nature of things, full-time residentiary canons and daily choral services should be regarded as a necessary part of a diocese. The essence of a cathedral is to be the bishop's church in which his chair is situate and any reasonably large parish church will serve that purpose, provided that suitable arrangements can be made about the patronage of the living.[1]

The question of a diocesan board of finance and similar organizations together with the other problem of patronage mentioned above do, however, raise a problem which must be

[1] This problem appears to have been solved with reasonable satisfaction in the case of the parish church cathedrals of the more recently created dioceses.

met in other ways. So also does the argument that the Church has not enough men of distinction to provide bishops for twice the present number of dioceses. It must however be asked what qualities are here in mind, and the answer appears to be that the English bishops are not merely local ecclesiastical persons, but also move on the national stage being all potential members of the House of Lords and must therefore be of the stature of national leaders. One cannot help feeling that in many discussions of this kind a sort of ideal bishop is set up who has rarely corresponded to any reality, someone who combines the qualities of Edward King, Hensley Henson, and William Temple. The appearance of a man such as any one of these is not common, and it is unlikely that a body of the size of the Church of England will produce more than ten or a dozen men in any one generation who are really of the calibre of national leaders. On the other hand the Church does produce many pious and able men who would be good pastoral bishops of small dioceses, men of the type of Walter Baddeley of Blackburn or Edward Wynn of Ely or some others who have served to the end of their days as suffragans.[1]

These various considerations converge to raise the question whether there is any way of meeting both the arguments for smaller dioceses and the objections which still arise. It may be suggested that a development of the ancient provincial system of the Church provides exactly that. Let as many new dioceses as seems expedient be created, and let the Church of England then be arranged in a number of regional groupings which, for convenience, we will call provinces, each with a metropolitan at its head. If, for the sake of argument, we assume that wherever there are at present in any diocese one or two suffragans or assistants there is a *prima facie* case for division, and that wherever there are three suffragans or assistants there is a *prima facie* case for the

[1] The Editor of *Crockford's Clerical Directory* for 1959–60 wrote rather hardly of the promotion of suffragans to diocesan status, but in other respects his Preface makes some valuable points.

creation of two new dioceses, we should under this plan increase the present forty-three dioceses to seventy-four, and in view of the existence of twelve assistant bishops in dioceses which have no suffragan it is probable that this number ought to be something like eighty-five. In arranging the provinces it would be desirable to take into account the study that has been made by a number of geographers and sociologists of the provincial division of England for various secular purposes. Perhaps the best known of these arrangements is that made for the organization of civil defence in the Second World War, but a number of others have been worked out, notably by the late Professor Fawcett of the University of London.[1] It would of course be necessary to relate any such scheme to the historic centres of Christianity in England, and to reach a compromise between tradition and the facts of the present day. It is not the purpose of the present writer to present any cut and dried scheme here, and there are obvious possible variants on what has been set out above. One, suggested by a friend of the author's, would be to take the twenty-four dioceses of the pre-1800 period as the provincial basis. Yet another would be to go further back still and take the eighteen dioceses of the pre-1500 period as the basis. We are inclined, however, to think that the fourteen regions of Professor Gilbert or the nine of Professor G. D. H. Cole,[2] modified where necessary to take account of ecclesiastical tradition would be the most suitable basis.

The final plan must, however, be such as will provide for the purposes for which we suggest this provincial arrangement. First that the metropolitans should be men capable of performing what may be called the "national" functions of the episcopate. They alone would sit in the House of Lords, and it might be that they alone would continue to be Crown nominees, the other bishops being chosen in some more

[1] C. B. Fawcett, *Provinces of England*, ed. W. G. East and S. W. Wooldridge (London, 1960).

[2] See pp. 250-51; also R. E. Dickinson, *City, Region and Regionalism. A Geographical Contribution to Human Ecology* (London, 1947), 281, 283.

ecclesiastical way, though that is by no means a necessary part of the scheme. Second, that some of the things which are now done at diocesan level should be done provincially. Much of the finance could be managed in this way, and also some of the patronage. The metropolitan and the other diocesans of his province would meet monthly in an episcopal synod, much as at the present time many diocesans hold a monthly staff meeting with their suffragans and archdeacons.

The principal aim of the whole operation would be to restore the diocese to something like its true theological position of being the most important complete pastoral unit of the Church. A relationship between bishop, clergy, and laity could then be envisaged [1] which is not easily established in many dioceses under the present system, and it is to be hoped that the bishops would have the opportunity really to be pastors and teachers, and not, as so many of them are now, be weighed down by the burden of committees and correspondence. Archbishop Lang wrote in 1937 "I have no time for reading books",[2] and many present-day bishops echo that sigh, but unless a man can find the time for reading, reflection, and prayer he is unlikely to be able to give his diocese that intelligent and spiritual leadership which the flock has the right to expect from its shepherd.

It may be asked what is to become of the archbishops of Canterbury and York and their convocations under this new arrangement, and we suggest that they be disturbed as little as possible. If the plan of assemblies which was adumbrated in section four of this lecture were accepted there would continue to be a definite place for the convocations. Their upper houses would be enlarged and the houses of clergy

[1] It would, for example, become possible for diocesan conferences to meet at times that are more convenient for the laity, in at least the more urbanized dioceses. It must, however, be recognized that one of the difficulties is to devise a plan which will work equally well in both urban and rural areas. In connection with all this cf. the remarks of H. Kraemer on "decentralization" in his interesting book *A Theology of the Laity* (London, 1958), 178.

[2] Kemp, *The Life and Letters of Kenneth Escott Kirk* (London, 1959), 74.

probably somewhat reduced. It is matter for discussion whether the new provincial synods, which would come into being to deal with the business of the province, should appoint to membership of convocation, or whether election should be directly from the dioceses. The convocations would become primatial instead of provincial synods, and we suggest that the diocesans of Canterbury and York should alone bear the title of archbishop. We should then also have put some significance into the title of primate which is at the moment almost completely devoid of it.

If some such scheme as the above were adopted diocesan conferences would become much more useful bodies for consultation on major issues than they are to-day. It might be that the new provincial synods could also be used for this purpose, but that would depend upon a variety of practical considerations which we have neither the space nor the necessary detailed knowledge to pursue.

6

All ecclesiastical assemblies at whatever level exist for the purpose of counsel and consent, that is to endeavour to find the will of God for his Church by bringing together the traditions, experience, and insight of different sections of the Christian community. We have pointed out a certain difference of function between clergy and laity, and we have also to recognize that they have somewhat different points of view. The clergy, who are by the nature of their calling set apart from the world and occupied with sacred things tend to look at life from the standpoint of doctrine and worship, whereas the laity who are in the midst of the world view things more from the standpoint of morals, example, and evangelism. This distinction, of course, needs qualification to make it truly applicable, and happily the development of modern theological and pastoral thought, particularly in the sphere of liturgy, is tending to remove it. But there is here a real danger that the obliteration of any distinction of outlook between clergy and laity will mean that the sect spirit has triumphed and that the sense of responsibility to the nation as a whole has been lost.[1] It must be emphasized that to be a committed Christian does not necessarily entail spending a great deal of time on Church work, and the converse is also true, that to spend a great deal of time on Church work does not necessarily mean that one is a committed Christian. We return to the fact that clergy and laity have, and ought to have, different points of view and the important consideration that they are complementary.

This aspect of the matter is destroyed by any introduction of legalism, any suggestion that it is the power of coercion alone that counts,[2] and it is to be feared that the present position of Parliament in relation to the Church encourages some to think in those terms. The legislative decisions of councils, important as they are, may not always be the things of first importance. The consideration of reports and the passing of resolutions which are not necessarily coercive laws have a valuable place because in the end moral authority is the best kind of authority in the Church. A clear example of what happens when moral authority is lacking may be seen in the history of the Public Worship Regulation Act of 1874, passed almost entirely owing to the championship and skill of Disraeli, but of which his biographers write: "subsequent experience of the scandals of imprisoned clergymen . . . has

[1] The parish communion movement has been criticized as tending to relax the discipline of the sacraments, but attention needs to be drawn also to the tendency among some clergymen of all schools of thought, to regard only those who conform to a particular pattern of liturgical observance as being the real laity.

[2] This is particularly apparent in the frequently made statement that canons ought not to include exhortation, but should be confined to directions which can be enforced in the courts, e.g. E. F. Carpenter, "Canons and Character", *Theology*, lxiii (1960), 400. Such an attitude misconceives the whole nature and purpose of canon law, and assimilates the Church's rules entirely to the enactments of a secular legislature; cf. E. W. Kemp, *An Introduction to Canon Law in the Church of England* (London, 1957), especially 75–7.

shown that he would have done better, in the interests both of the Church and of his party, to adhere to his original position, and to discourage and postpone legislation which certainly brought to the Church not peace but a sword."[1] For over sixty years the Act, though still on the statute book, has been a dead letter and it was killed by moral indignation at its consequences. It is to be feared that there are still in the Church some who think in terms of legislative victory over other churchmen who are conceived of as their opponents. Such an attitude is utterly unworthy of the Christian family, and destructive of its first principles.

Church councils are not, however, to be viewed only as bringing together the *ordo* and the *plebs*, to use the ancient terminology, but also as a communication of the traditions of the different local churches. In England this is obvious at the present provincial level. The two convocations have somewhat different traditions and outlook, as witness their attitudes to the proposals for a new rite of infant baptism, but the weaknesses which have been pointed out at the diocesan level have combined with the strength of party feeling to prevent the growth of solidarity among the representatives of each diocese. It may be hoped that one effect of a plan of diocesan reform such as has been suggested might be to make the convocations and General Synod more obviously assemblies of dioceses, in which the separate local traditions are brought together, and less like assemblies of the political kind with their party structure.

The true character of Church councils is more likely to be maintained if their religious setting is emphasized. One interpretation of Tertullian's reference to councils among the Greeks, quoted in the first lecture,[2] would suggest that as early as the second century councils took place in connection

[1] W. F. Monypenny and G. E. Buckle, *The life of Benjamin Disraeli, Earl of Beaconsfield* (New and revised edn., London, 1929), ii. 669. For a less favourable view of Disraeli's part in the passing of this Act see G. W. E. Russell, *Fifteen chapters of Autobiography* (London, n.d.), 197–200.

[2] See above, p. 5.

with an act of worship, and certainly, as we have seen, liturgical forms of more or less elaboration developed for them. It would probably be admitted by most of those who have been members of the convocations that the preaching of the word and the celebration of the sacrament give to their sessions a sacred and solemn character which the more prosaic and secular meetings of the Church Assembly do not possess. A primary purpose of any synod is to set forth the worship of God in the widest sense of that term, to order the Church and its life in such a way as may most adequately reflect his glory and manifest him to the world. It is vital, therefore, that every synod should in its meetings look towards God in worship in the narrower sense, with all its strength, so that it may rest assured that in one way or another He will lead it to correct those things which are amiss and show it those things that it must do in the service of him and of his creation.[1]

> O God, of unchangeable power and eternal light, look favourably on thy whole Church, that wonderful and sacred mystery; and, by the tranquil operation of thy perpetual Providence, carry out the work of man's salvation; and let the whole world feel and see that things which were cast down are being raised up, and things which had grown old are being made new, and all things are returning to perfection through him from whom they took their origin, even through our Lord Jesus Christ.

> Lord, we beseech thee to keep thy household the Church in continual godliness; that through thy protection it may be free from all adversities, and devoutly given to serve thee in good works, to the glory of thy Name; through Jesus Christ our Lord.

[1] Cf. K. E. Kirk. *The Vision of God* (London, 1931), 207, 444f.

APPENDIXES

APPENDIX 1

Church of Scotland Act, 1921

(11 and 12 Geo. 5)

CHAPTER 29

An ACT to declare the lawfulness of certain Articles declaratory of the Constitution of the Church of Scotland in matters spiritual prepared with the authority of the General Assembly of the Church.

(28 July 1921)

Whereas certain articles declaratory of the constitution of the Church of Scotland in matters spiritual have been prepared with the authority of the General Assembly of the Church, with a view to facilitate the union of other Churches with the Church of Scotland, which articles are set out in the Schedule to this Act, and together with any modifications of the said articles or additions thereto made in accordance therewith are hereinafter in this Act referred to as "the Declaratory Articles":

And whereas it is expedient that any doubts as to the lawfulness of the Declaratory Articles should be removed:

Be it therefore enacted by the King's most Excellent Majesty, by and with the advice and consent of the Lords Spiritual and Temporal, and Commons, in this present Parliament assembled, and by the authority of the same, as follows:

1. The Declaratory Articles are lawful articles, and the constitution of the Church of Scotland in matters spiritual is as therein set forth, and no limitation of the liberty, rights

and powers in matters spiritual therein set forth shall be derived from any statute or law affecting the Church of Scotland in matters spiritual at present in force, it being hereby declared that in all questions of construction the Declaratory Articles shall prevail, and that all such statutes and laws shall be construed in conformity therewith and in subordination thereto, and all such statutes and laws in so far as they are inconsistent with the Declaratory Articles are hereby repealed and declared to be of no effect.

2. Nothing contained in this Act or in any other Act affecting the Church of Scotland shall prejudice the recognition of any other Church in Scotland as a Christian Church protected by law in the exercise of its spiritual functions.

3. Subject to the recognition of the matters dealt with in the Declaratory Articles as matters spiritual, nothing in this Act contained shall affect or prejudice the jurisdiction of the civil courts in relation to any matter of a civil nature.

4. This Act may be cited as the Church of Scotland Act, 1921, and shall come into operation on such a date as His Majesty may fix by Order in Council after the Declaratory Articles shall have been adopted by an Act of the General Assembly of the Church of Scotland with the consent of a majority of the Presbyteries of the Church.

SCHEDULE

ARTICLES DECLARATORY OF THE CONSTITUTION OF THE CHURCH OF SCOTLAND IN MATTERS SPIRITUAL

I. The Church of Scotland is part of the Holy Catholic or Universal Church; worshipping one God, Almighty, all-wise, and all-loving, in the Trinity of the Father, the Son, and the

Holy Ghost, the same in substance, equal in power and glory; adoring the Father, infinite in Majesty, of whom are all things; confessing our Lord Jesus Christ, the Eternal Son, made very man for our salvation; glorying in His Cross and Resurrection, and owning obedience to Him as the Head over all things to His Church; trusting in the promised renewal and guidance of the Holy Spirit; proclaiming the forgiveness of sins and acceptance with God through faith in Christ, and the gift of Eternal life; and labouring for the advancement of the Kingdom of God throughout the world. The Church of Scotland adheres to the Scottish Reformation; receives the Word of God which is contained in the Scriptures of the Old and New Testaments as its supreme rule of faith and life; and avows the fundamental doctrines of the Catholic faith founded thereupon.

II. The principal subordinate standard of the Church of Scotland is the Westminster Confession of Faith approved by the General Assembly of 1647, containing the sum and substance of the Faith of the Reformed Church. Its government is Presbyterian, and is exercised through Kirk-sessions, Presbyteries, Provincial Synods, and General Assemblies. Its system and principles of worship, orders, and discipline are in accordance with "The Directory for the Public Worship of God", "The Form of Presbyterial Church Government", and "The Form of Process", as these have been or may hereafter be interpreted or modified by Acts of the General Assembly or by consuetude.

III. This Church is in historical continuity with the Church of Scotland which was reformed in 1560, whose liberties were ratified in 1592 and for whose security provision was made in the Treaty of Union of 1707. The continuity and identity of the Church of Scotland are not prejudiced by the adoption of these Articles. As a national Church representative of the Christian Faith of the Scottish people it acknowledges its distinctive call and duty to bring the ordinances of religion to the people in every parish of Scotland through a territorial ministry.

IV. This Church, as part of the Universal Church wherein the Lord Jesus Christ has appointed a government in the hands of Church office-bearers, receives from Him, its Divine King and Head, and from Him alone, the right and power subject to no civil authority to legislate, and to adjudicate finally, in all matters of doctrine, worship, government, and discipline in the Church, including the right to determine all questions concerning membership and office in the Church, the constitution and membership of its Courts, and the mode of election of its office-bearers, and to define the boundaries of the spheres of labour of its ministers and other office-bearers. Recognition by civil authority of the separate and independent government and jurisdiction of this Church in matters spiritual, in whatever manner such recognition be expressed, does not in any way affect the character of this government and jurisdiction as derived from the Divine Head of the Church alone, or give to the civil authority any right of interference with the proceedings or judgements of the Church within the sphere of its spiritual government and jurisdiction.

V. This Church has the inherent right, free from interference by civil authority, but under the safeguards for deliberate action and legislation provided by the Church itself, to frame or adopt its subordinate standards, to declare the sense in which it understands its Confession of Faith, to modify the forms of expression therein, or to formulate other doctrinal statements, and to define the relation thereto of its office-bearers and members, but always in agreement with the Word of God and the fundamental doctrines of the Christian Faith contained in the said Confession, of which agreement the Church shall be sole judge, and with due regard to liberty of opinion, in points which do not enter into the substance of the Faith.

VI. This Church acknowledges the divine appointment and authority of the civil magistrate within his own sphere, and maintains its historic testimony to the duty of the nation acting in its corporate capacity to render homage to God, to acknowledge the Lord Jesus Christ to be King over the nations, to obey His laws, to reverence His ordinances, to honour His Church, and to promote in all appropriate ways the Kingdom of God. The Church and the State owe mutual duties to each other, and acting within their respective spheres may signally promote each other's welfare. The Church and the State have the right to determine each for itself all questions concerning the extent and the continuance of their mutual relations in the discharge of these duties and the obligations arising therefrom.

VII. The Church of Scotland, believing it to be the will of Christ that His disciples should be all one in the Father and in Him, that the world may believe that the Father has sent Him, recognizes the obligation to seek and promote union with other Churches in which it finds the Word to be purely preached, the sacraments administered according to Christ's ordinance, and discipline rightly exercised; and it has the right to unite with any such Church without loss of its identity on terms which this Church finds to be consistent with these Articles.

VIII. The Church has the right to interpret these Articles, and, subject to the safeguards for deliberate action and legislation provided by the Church itself, to modify or add to them; but always consistently with the provisions of the first Article hereof, adherence to which, as interpreted by the Church, is essential to its continuity and corporate life. Any proposal for a modification of or addition to these Articles which may be approved of by the General Assembly shall, before it can be enacted by the Assembly, be transmitted by way of overture to Presbyteries in at least two immediately successive years. If the overture shall receive the approval, with or without suggested amendment, of two-thirds of the whole of the Presbyteries of the Church, the Assembly may revise the overture in the light of any suggestions by Presbyteries, and may transmit the overture when so revised to Presbyteries for their consent. If the overture as transmitted in its final form shall receive the consent of not less than two-thirds of the whole of the Presbyteries of the Church, the General Assembly may, if it deems it expedient, modify or add to these Articles in terms of the said overture. But if the overture as transmitted in its final form shall not receive the requisite consent, the same or a similar proposal shall not be again transmitted for the consent of Presbyteries until an interval of five years after the failure to obtain the requisite consent has been reported to the General Assembly.

IX. Subject to the provisions of the foregoing Articles and the powers of amendment therein contained, the Constitution of the Church of Scotland in matters spiritual is hereby anew ratified and confirmed by the Church.

APPENDIX 2

Draft Canons referred to in Lecture 8 Section 2

A.1.(1)

Of the Church of England

The Church of England, established according to the laws of this realm, under the Queen's Majesty, belongs to the true and apostolic Church of Christ; and, as our duty to the said Church of England requires, we do constitute and ordain that no member thereof shall be at liberty to maintain or hold the contrary.

A.2.(2)

Of the Thirty-nine Articles of Religion

The Thirty-nine Articles are agreeable to the Word of God and may be assented unto with a good conscience by all members of the Church of England.

A.3.(3)

Of the Book of Common Prayer

1. The doctrine contained in *The Book of Common Prayer and Administration of the Sacraments and other Rites and Ceremonies of the Church according to the Use of the Church of England* is agreeable to the Word of God.
2. The form of God's Worship contained in the said Book, forasmuch as it is not repugnant to the Word of God, may be used by all members of the Church of England with a good conscience.

A.4.(4)

Of the Form and Manner of Making, Ordaining, and Consecrating of Bishops, Priests, and Deacons

The Form and Manner of Making, Ordaining, and Consecrating of Bishops, Priests, and Deacons, annexed to the

Book of Common Prayer and commonly known as the Ordinal, is not repugnant to the Word of God; and those who are so made, ordained, or consecrated Bishops, Priests, or Deacons, according to the said Ordinal, are lawfully made, ordained, or consecrated, and ought to be accounted, both by themselves and others, to be truly Bishops, Priests, or Deacons.

A.5.(5)

Of the Doctrine of the Church of England

The doctrine of the Church of England is grounded in the Holy Scriptures and in such teachings of the ancient Fathers and Councils of the Church as are agreeable to the said Scriptures. In particular such doctrine is to be found in the Thirty-nine Articles of Religion, the Book of Common Prayer, and the Ordinal.

A.6.(6)

Of the Government of the Church of England

The government of the Church of England under the Queen's Majesty, by Archbishops, Bishops, Deans, Provosts, Archdeacons, and the rest of the clergy and of the laity that bear office in the same, is not repugnant to the Word of God.

C.1.(52)

Of Holy Orders in the Church of England

The Church of England holds and teaches that from the Apostles' times there have been these Orders in Christ's Church: Bishops, Priests, and Deacons, and no man shall be accounted or taken to be a lawful Bishop, Priest or Deacon in the Church of England, or suffered to execute any of the said offices, except he be called, tried, examined, and admitted thereunto according to the Ordinal, or has had formerly episcopal consecration or ordination in some Church whose orders are recognized and accepted by the Church of England.

MANUSCRIPTS REFERRED TO IN THE TEXT

England

CANTERBURY

Cathedral Library Christ Church Cathedral Priory Registers I and Q.

CARLISLE

Diocesan Registry Registers of Thomas Appleby and Gilbert Welton.

DURHAM

Cathedral Archives Episcopal Register of Thomas Hatfield. Prior's Register II (Large series).

EXETER

Diocesan Registry Register of John Voysey.

HEREFORD

Diocesan Registry Register of Richard Mayew.

LINCOLN

Diocesan Archives Episcopal Registers iii (Dalderby), v (Burghersh) vii (Beck), xxvi (Longland): Convocation papers Box 4.

LONDON

British Museum Cotton MSS. Faustina A.5; Vespasian E.21.

Diocesan Registry Registers of Richard Clifford and Richard Fitzjames.

Lambeth Palace Library Registers of Thomas Arundel, William Courtenay, John Kemp, John Morton, Walter Reynolds, William Whittlesey.

Public Record Office Ancient Correspondence, vols. 34 and 49. Fine Rolls, I Richard III, 2, 4, 7, and 11 Henry VII. King's Remembrancer's Memoranda Rolls, 12, 21, 28, 32 Henry VI, 18 Edward IV.

Lanthony Priory Registers (Chancery Masters Exhibits) C.115, A.3, A.11.

Parliamentary Proxies, Files 21–25.

NORWICH

Diocesan Archives Registers of Thomas Broun and James Goldwell.

SALISBURY

Diocesan Registry Registers of Robert Hallum, Thomas Langton, and Roger Martival.

WINCHESTER

Diocesan Registry Register of Richard Fox.

WORCESTER

Diocecan Archives Registers of John Alcock, Thomas Bourgchier, John Carpenter, Geronimo de Ghinucci, and Thomas Polton.

YORK

St Anthony's Hall Registers of William Booth, William Melton, Alexander Neville and John Thoresby. Sede Vacante Register.

France

AUXERRE

Archives départementales de l'Yonne, G. 1818.

PARIS

Bibliothèque nationale Baluze MSS. 5, 6 and 13.

TROYES

Archives départementales de l'Aube G. 2550.

MAPS OF ENGLAND AND WALES

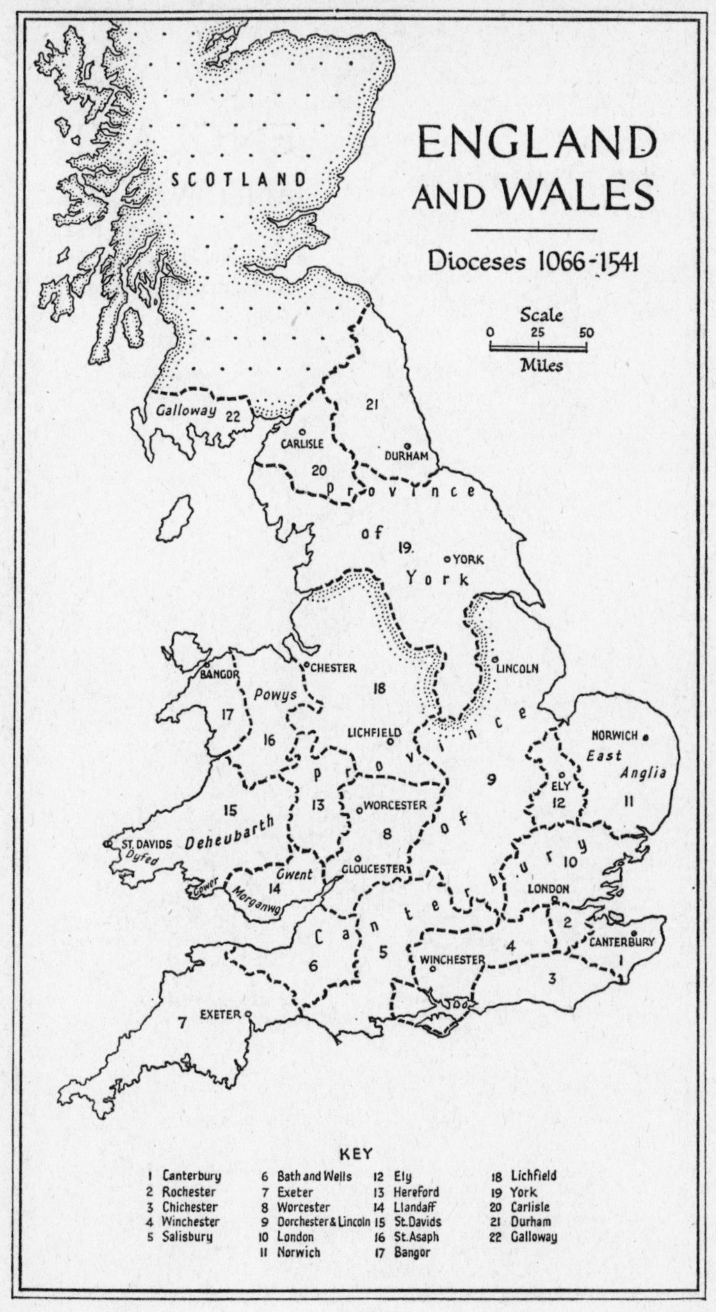
ENGLAND AND WALES
Dioceses 1066-1541
Scale
0 25 50
Miles
SCOTLAND
Galloway 22
CARLISLE
20
21
DURHAM
Province of York
19.
YORK
LINCOLN
CHESTER
18
BANGOR
Powys
17
16
LICHFIELD
NORWICH
East Anglia
11
ELY
12
9
Province of Canterbury
13
WORCESTER
8
15
ST. DAVIDS
Dyfed
Deheubarth
Gwent
14
Gower
Morganwg
GLOUCESTER
10
LONDON
2
CANTERBURY
1
4
WINCHESTER
3
5
6
EXETER
7
KEY
1 Canterbury
2 Rochester
3 Chichester
4 Winchester
5 Salisbury
6 Bath and Wells
7 Exeter
8 Worcester
9 Dorchester & Lincoln
10 London
11 Norwich
12 Ely
13 Hereford
14 Llandaff
15 St. Davids
16 St. Asaph
17 Bangor
18 Lichfield
19 York
20 Carlisle
21 Durham
22 Galloway

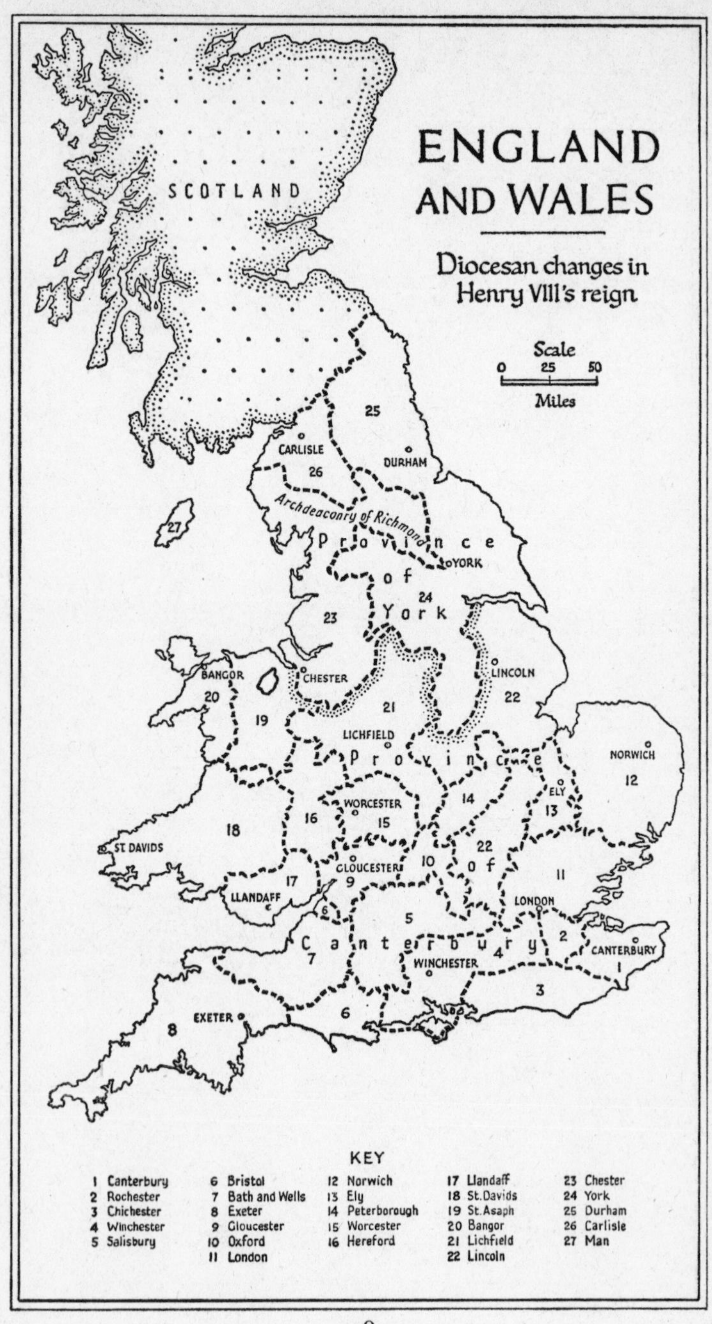
ENGLAND
AND WALES
Diocesan changes in
Henry VIII's reign
Scale
0 25 50
Miles
SCOTLAND
CARLISLE
DURHAM
Archdeaconry of Richmond
Province of York
YORK
CHESTER
BANGOR
LINCOLN
LICHFIELD
Province of Canterbury
NORWICH
ELY
WORCESTER
ST DAVIDS
GLOUCESTER
LLANDAFF
LONDON
CANTERBURY
WINCHESTER
EXETER
KEY
1 Canterbury
2 Rochester
3 Chichester
4 Winchester
5 Salisbury
6 Bristol
7 Bath and Wells
8 Exeter
9 Gloucester
10 Oxford
11 London
12 Norwich
13 Ely
14 Peterborough
15 Worcester
16 Hereford
17 Llandaff
18 St.Davids
19 St.Asaph
20 Bangor
21 Lichfield
22 Lincoln
23 Chester
24 York
25 Durham
26 Carlisle
27 Man

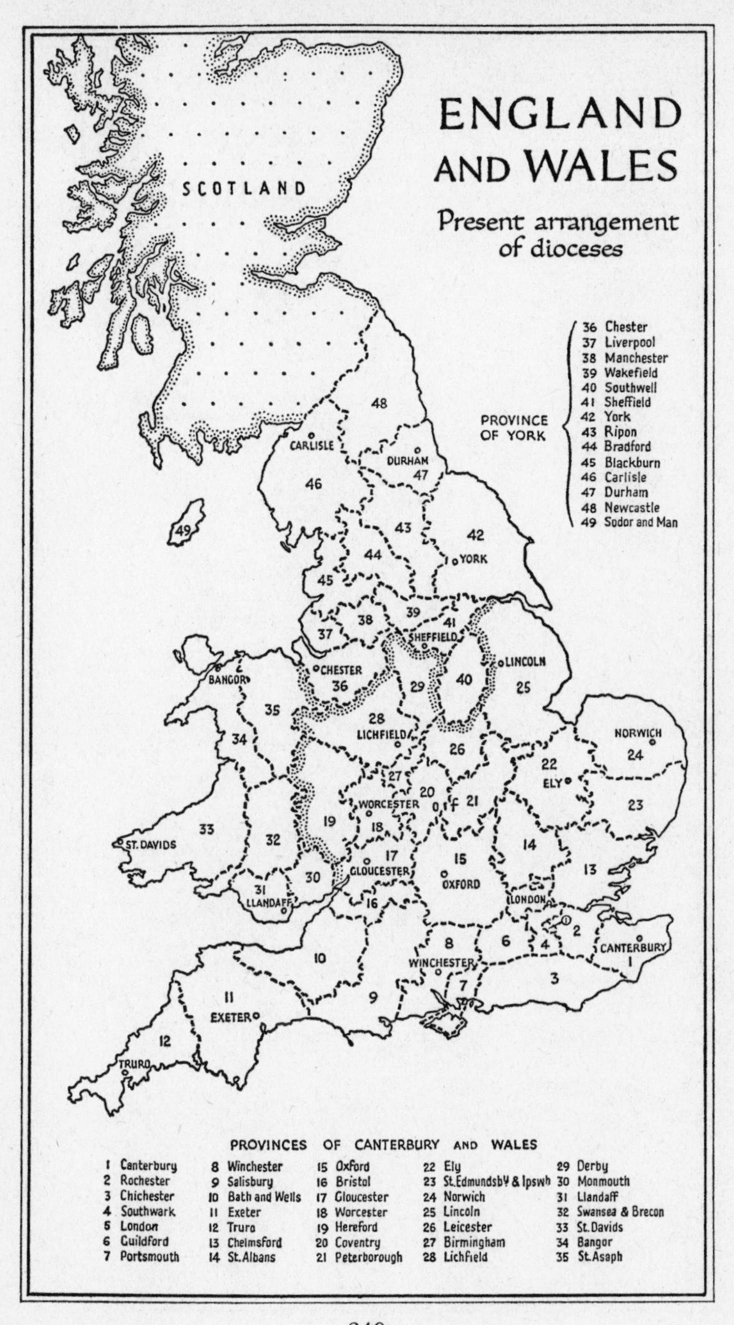
ENGLAND
AND WALES
Present arrangement
of dioceses
SCOTLAND
PROVINCE
OF YORK
36 Chester
37 Liverpool
38 Manchester
39 Wakefield
40 Southwell
41 Sheffield
42 York
43 Ripon
44 Bradford
45 Blackburn
46 Carlisle
47 Durham
48 Newcastle
49 Sodor and Man
CARLISLE
DURHAM
YORK
SHEFFIELD
CHESTER
LINCOLN
BANGOR
LICHFIELD
NORWICH
ELY
WORCESTER
ST. DAVIDS
GLOUCESTER
OXFORD
LLANDAFF
LONDON
CANTERBURY
WINCHESTER
EXETER
TRURO
PROVINCES OF CANTERBURY AND WALES
1 Canterbury
2 Rochester
3 Chichester
4 Southwark
5 London
6 Guildford
7 Portsmouth
8 Winchester
9 Salisbury
10 Bath and Wells
11 Exeter
12 Truro
13 Chelmsford
14 St. Albans
15 Oxford
16 Bristol
17 Gloucester
18 Worcester
19 Hereford
20 Coventry
21 Peterborough
22 Ely
23 St. Edmundsby & Ipswh
24 Norwich
25 Lincoln
26 Leicester
27 Birmingham
28 Lichfield
29 Derby
30 Monmouth
31 Llandaff
32 Swansea & Brecon
33 St. Davids
34 Bangor
35 St. Asaph

ENGLAND AND WALES
Provincial divisions proposed for secular purposes by E.W. Gilbert, 1941
Scale
0 25 50
Miles
SCOTLAND
NEWCASTLE
CARLISLE
Northumbria
Cumbria
Yorkshire
YORK
Lancastria
MANCHESTER
East
Midland
NOTTINGHAM
CAERNARVON
N. Wales
Midland
BIRMINGHAM
ABERYSTWYTH
NORWICH
East
Anglia
Fen
Country
CAMBRIDGE
Mid Wales
Home
OXFORD
S. Wales
CARDIFF
BRISTOL
Upper
Thames
LONDON
Severn
Counties
WINCHESTER
South West
Wessex
PLYMOUTH
ENGLISH CHANNEL

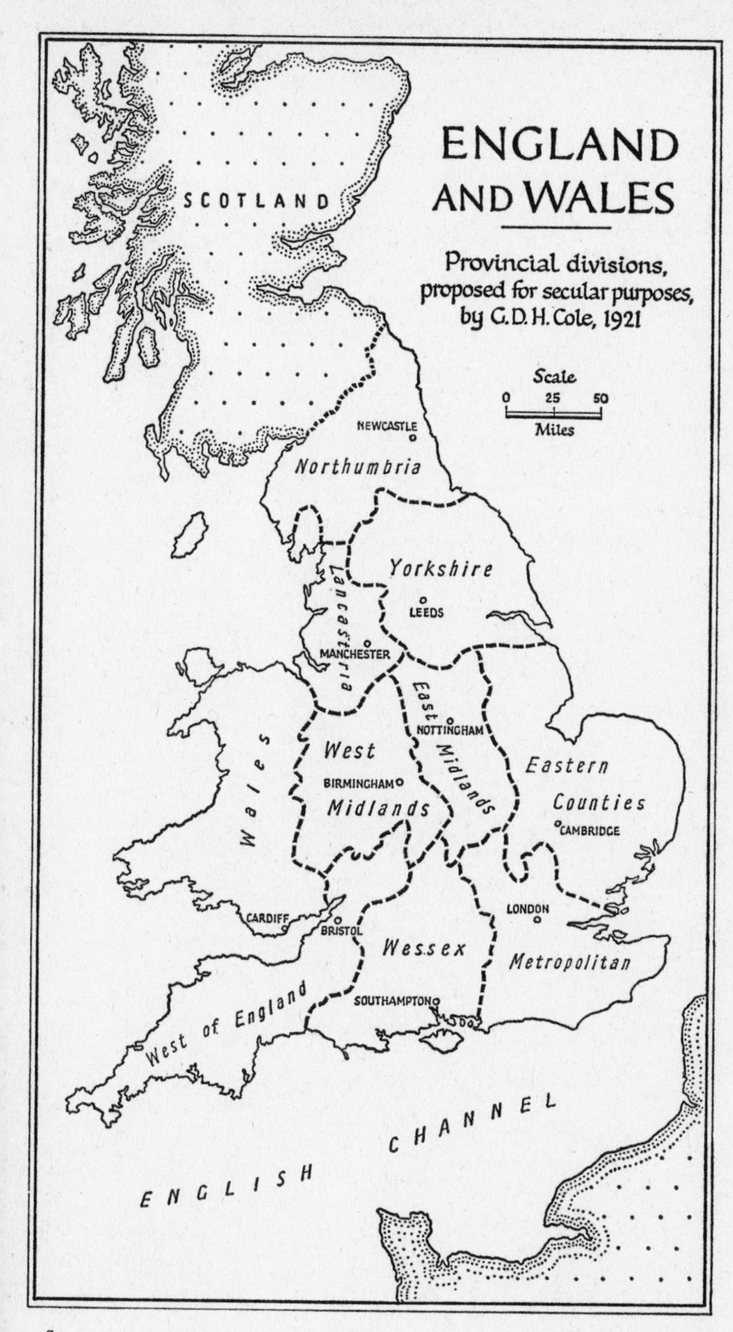
ENGLAND
AND WALES
Provincial divisions,
proposed for secular purposes,
by G.D.H. Cole, 1921
Scale
0
25
50
Miles
SCOTLAND
NEWCASTLE
Northumbria
Yorkshire
LEEDS
Lancastria
MANCHESTER
East Midlands
NOTTINGHAM
West Midlands
BIRMINGHAM
Wales
Eastern Counties
CAMBRIDGE
LONDON
Metropolitan
CARDIFF
BRISTOL
Wessex
SOUTHAMPTON
West of England
ENGLISH CHANNEL

S

INDEX

Archbishops and bishops are indexed under their personal names.